THE COMP'NY

THE STORY OF THE SURRY, SUSSEX & SOUTHAMPTON

RAILWAY AND THE SURRY LUMBER COMPANY

Compiled by
H. TEMPLE CRITTENDEN, from
September 1930 to August 1966

McCLAIN PRINTING COMPANY
PARSONS, W. VA. 26287

1 9 6 7

1415593
Introduction

The largest enterprise ever operated in Surry County, Virginia, was the Surry Lumber Company. It was the largest producer of yellow pine lumber in the East. It was among the largest railroad-logging companies in the country. It created communities, built roads, strung telephone lines, established stores and banks, sold electric power and ice, but above all, it created jobs that raised the living standard of a large number of people over a large area. It is with the railroad part of this enormous business that we are mainly concerned.

Although the Surry, Sussex & Southampton Railway claimed ownership of only a little over a fourth of the actual trackage, it operated all of it, so the story of the railroad is the story of the transportation department of the lumber company. Except for its length, the S.S.&S. was not much different from other logging railroads throughout eastern Virginia and North Carolina, but the length made the difference. It made a logging line into a railroad, but a railroad with a difference. True, the road was only 36-inch gauge and laid with 25 and 35-pound iron and steel rails, but up to the very end it had an individuality all its own.

This story has been recorded as it was told. An effort has been made to retain the atmosphere of the overall operation. There is the smell of freshly cut pine as well as the odor of hot grease and smoke. They intermingle constantly for it is impossible to separate them. The reader will mentally listen to the chime whistle of the mail train as the engine blows for the board at Dendron, but in the background is the steady, persistent whir of the saws. While mentally watching the donkeys working in the woods, the felling of trees cannot be ignored.

If the reader thinks that there are too many wrecks, a closer look will show that no two were the same. Wrecks on any logging railroad were a part of railroad logging and they make up a part of the story. The reader will also be introduced to a language that was peculiar to that railroad. It confounds the uninitiated and brings a smile to the face of the "outsider", but it too is a part of the overall picture. A passenger car was a "coe-ach", a locomotive was either a "donkey", a "jack", or "No. 2", never just an "engine" or a "locomotive", and "donkey tracks" were not made by an equus asinus quadruped. If you wanted to water a donkey in the woods, you "syphroned" the water into the tank out of a ditch or a shallow well. A "brakeman" was a "brakesman" but if he had company, they were collectively the usual "brakemen". "Woods tracks" were the little lines laid into a tract and moved as the cutting progressed. "Donkey tracks" were the lines off the woods tracks that went in today and came out tomorrow.

No attempt has been made to record all of the track in service at any given time. It is impossible for the railway was like an earthworm on a hot pavement; twisting, turning, lengthening, shortening as it reached into new stands of timber or pulled back out of cutover woods lots. So far as the railway company was concerned, the S.S.&S. consisted of only what was loosely considered to be the "main line", Scotland to Dory, surveyed and resurveyed, but always 28.1 miles, even when there was over a hundred miles of track in actual service.

The day is not too far distant when everything pertaining to "the comp'ny" will be a dim memory and that dimness will gradually fade out completely, just as some of the towns have disappeared and been forgotten. It is a certainty that the day is not too far distant when no one will remember the little railway that so efficiently served the three counties of Surry, Sussex, and Southampton.

H. Temple Crittenden
July 1966

Acknowledgement

To augment one's own knowledge of a subject is easy but it takes work. You first have to find out WHO to talk to, WHERE to go to see them if they will talk, and WHAT to ask when you do talk. You quite frequently get answers you do not expect and just as frequently you get no answers. You accept everything handed you, record both questions and answers, and the next person you talk with, you ask the same questions all over again. Sometimes you get rather confusing results, but that is research.

That reminds me of a trip made to Hopewell, Va., to talk with J. H. Conway, one of the engineers. I had gone up there to ask about the elusive 18 for I had been told that he had been one of the several engineers assigned to that engine. I had just one question and when I got nothing new in the way of information, I was lost. We talked, for I had driven all the way up there from Norfolk and I had no intention of turning right around and driving home. In some manner the "out west" cars were brought up and his face lit up like a lamp. That he DID remember them! Up to then those cars had been a rather indefinite myth but here was fact that later proved out. You never know when or where you will stumble over something.

Then there was the time I stopped on impulse, got out, squatted down farmer-fashion, and talked to an old colored man and his son, over near Magnet. I can't say even now WHY I stopped, just impulse, for no one had pointed a finger in their direction. His name? I don't know, but to him goes the credit for my knowledge of the labor train run north from Central Hill. He possibly will never know it, but he added an important item to this story.

When you look back over the 36 years that this story has been in the process of compilation and purification, and try to think of everyone who has added a little something here and there, beginning with my initial talk with Edward Rogers and A. S. Higgins while sitting around the pot-bellied stove in the general office, and ending with the final talk with Engineer "Sam" Atkinson thirty-five years later, you realize that you have done a powerful lot of asking, talking, and listening. Listening is the meat of the matter, knowing when to shut up and just listen. A lot of folks went to a lot of trouble to make this yarn possible and a goodly number of them will never see it in print.

Pictures showed up from the most unlikely sources. There are not too many in this volume for the simple reason that there are not but so many in existence. Cameras were not a dime a dozen as they are now and those that people did own back up there in the woods were pointed at something other than things that they saw every day. Possibly the largest single lot of pictures were those loaned by Miss Bertha Hart, daughter of Jim Hart, who you will meet in this story. Others came from other sources, and when that source is known, the credit line will let that person know. Some were found so long ago that I simply don't remember WHERE they came from. I am sorry, but time erases my memory as well as yours.

For the story of the Rogers family, we must thank the daughter of Edward Rogers, Miss Alice C. Rogers of Richmond, Va. When a person is mentioned in the text, generally that person had something to do with the telling of the story. Since the telling was begun, a lot of the people who added bits to it have followed the railroad into the place where all track is straight and all signals are green, but some few are still with us and maybe, if they get around to reading this, they will see that a real effort has been made to make use of what they told.

In addition to those who have been mentioned and whose names appear in the credit lines of the illustrations, I might mention such persons as Caesar Gerecke of Stony Creek, the entire Atkinson family of Dendron, Emmett Williams of Littleton, T. E. Burnett of Waverly, Joseph Seward of Elberon, C. W. Kitchen of Airfield, P. H. Whitmore of Newport News, R. L. Wellons of Franklin, and Clyde King of Smithfield. There are others, quite a few more who have added a bit here and there, and as we have been told over and over, it takes many drops of water to fill a bucket. To everyone who knowingly or unknowingly added a tiny bit of information to this story, I say "THANK YOU" and I sincerely hope that the resulting story gives each and everyone the feeling that the time spent with me was not wasted after all.

H. Temple Crittenden
Norfolk, Va.

Contents

Steele to Surry

The first problem encountered when attempting to tell a story is to find a place to begin. It has been said that the logical place to begin any yarn is at the beginning, but that is the problem. Just where is the beginning? The events which lead up to the construction of the Surry, Sussex & Southampton Railway began many years before that road was ever thought of, before a certain David Steel, or as it was later spelled, Steele, entered the lumbering picture of Surry County, Virginia. Possibly it is best to step back in Time to when Major William Allen was perfunctorily cutting timber on his plantation which fronted the James River at what is now Claremont.

It has been a known fact for many years that the Major owned more land and more slaves than did any other one person in Virginia. His holdings comprised all of Guilford District of Surry County, Jamestown Island, and a goodly portion of the land on the northern bank of the James River opposite his plantation. He owned over a thousand slaves who were used to work his Claremont Plantation at what was then known as Sloop Point, that being on the southern bank of the river, and to cut timber, crossties, and cordwood. Even so, there were times when he simply could not find enough work to keep them all fairly busy and he hit upon the idea of having a large, deep ditch dug around the entire plantation. It took some time to do it but upon its completion it became known as Allen's Ditch and was considered a permanent marker in the surveying of adjoining property. Even at this late date the ditch crops up in deeds for portions of it are still very much in evidence.

To facilitate his logging operations, an iron railed tramway was laid from his wharf at the river to the site of operations. Just how long the line was, no one knows, but it was long enough to require the use of a locomotive to haul the platform cars. It might have reached to, or possibly a little beyond, Spring Grove for it has been said that practically all of the land between there and the river was cleared. The term "iron railed" which was used to describe the railway is ambiguous, meaning simply that the wheels ran on iron rails, the form, or type, being uncertain. It is possible that the railroad was a strap-rail affair for prior to 1860 standard iron T rail was both scarce and costly. On the other hand, strap rail of a fair quality was both plentiful and cheap due to its replacement by many railroads during the period prior to the Civil War with the better T rail. Then, too, stringers for a strap-rail tramway could be had for practically nothing when cut by slave labor, which happened to be idle at the time, from Allen's own stand of timber. It is useless to surmise what type of rail was actually used other than that it was of iron.

Then came the Civil War in 1861 and the slaves were freed. There was no longer either time nor labor to work the woods lots, although the demand for both crossties and cordwood was still there, and the railroad lay dormant. Allen raised his own army and fortified Jamestown Island. Between taking potshots at occasional Federal gunboats and worrying about the enemy who was advancing up both sides of the river, the men had plenty of time to lay around, sleep, and get into fights from sheer boredom. To give them something to do, and because he was actually interested as well as desiring to be able to retrieve the solid shot used during target practice, Allen began experimenting with the effect of cannon fire on iron plates. The story goes that his experimenting had something to do with the final design of the casement of the Confederate ram "VIRGINIA" and that Allen's railroad did its part in providing the iron plates to cover it.

The truth of the yarn is that when the enemy got uncomfortably close to the plantation in 1861, and to Jamestown Island, Allen ordered all of the equipment of his railroad run off the end of the wharf into the river and the rails taken up. These were hurriedly shipped to The Tredegar Works at Richmond where they were undoubtedly piled with other rails and scrap iron. It could well be that they were rolled into iron armor plates for the "VIRGINIA" but they just as easily could have been melted down and cast into cannon or cannon balls. There is no doubt that the rails did their part in the "war effort". Just how long the equipment rusted on the river bottom is anyone's guess for history makes no further mention of it.

After the war Allen went home to Claremont, which wasn't a permanent stay, and began to pick up the pieces. Nothing could ever be like it was before for the unlimited supply of "free" labor was gone and his personal fortune had vanished. He was land-poor but that in itself represented wealth of a certain kind. The plantation was worked, although Allen was back in Richmond where he had gone to join his family, and the cutting of timber, crossties, and cordwood was gradually resumed. This was hauled by carts to Sloop Point and shipped out on schooners. It is said that he cut ties for the Prussian Government and shipped them direct to Hamburg, but it is a sure thing that he shipped more cordwood to Norfolk, Richmond, and Baltimore than he did ties to Germany. Cordwood was fuel and it was always in demand. But, so far as we are concerned, the thing to remember is that Major William Allen operated a tramway of an unknown gauge from Sloop Point to over towards Spring Grove from sometime prior to 1860 until 1861.

Working so much land, or even letting it lay idle, was expensive, there being such a thing as taxes, and money was scarce, so Allen sold bits of his plantation as the need arose. When a certain J. Frank Mancha arrived from up in Delaware in mid-1870 and expounded a scheme to make them both rich by selling off parcels of the plantation to land-hungry families from out of the state, Allen agreed to it. Accordingly, large spreads were run in the newspapers of many of the northern and mid-western cities, expounding the wonderful climate and soil of Virginia, and the availability of land at a most reasonable price. Emigrants began to arrive and the sale of land was brisk through the rest of 1870, all of 1871, and well into 1872. Among the families emigrating to that advertised Utopia was that of one David Steel, a native of New Jersey and a widower with three children, two sons and a daughter, who came south from Kent County, Delaware and settled at a point near Spring Grove. He was a timber worker, a sawmill hand, and he quite possibly worked for Allen when he first arrived in Surry County but he did not become known until after he had met and married Cornelia Warren, a widow with one daughter, on the second of June 1873. After that, with his wife apparently acting as a booster, the Steel interest began to increase.

His first step toward independent operation came in the late summer of 1873 when O. A. Sledge transferred to him his interest in a contract with Richard D. Philips and J. W. Pancost for the cutting of timber on what was called the Rudy Spring Tract in Guilford District. Under the contract, Philips furnished the money while Pancost furnished the standing timber and the mill. From Sledge, Steel acquired five oxen, three log carts, one set of wagon harness, a bogie, one bed and stead, a grindstone and fixtures, a crosscut saw, an oat cutter, and a stable and two kitchens, all for $60.80. It was Steel's part of the contract to do the actual work and to receive a third of the profit for doing it. A year and a half later he completed cutting the timber, and which was more important, he made a profit.

In the meantime, on the first of March 1874, he entered into a second contract with Pancost whereby the said Pancost furnished timber on the stump on "The Glebe" and the "White Marsh" tracts north of the stage road between Spring Grove and Surry, a sawmill which he agreed to keep in good repair, and two lighters for hauling the timber out to vessels anchored in the stream. Steel was to get a total of $800 for each 100,000 board feet of finished lumber; $500 when the tree trunks were barked on the mill yard, $200 on receipt of a bill of sale, and $100 was to be applied on his debt of $1,375, that being the amount Pancost charged him for teams, wagons, carts, and other paraphernalia necessary to do the work. Steele was definitely becoming an enterprising lumberman and it was about this time that he tacked the extra "e" onto his name, so henceforth we will do likewise. The profit realized from the two contracts furnished him with the means of acquiring both timber tracts and timber on the stump on other tracts. One tract acquired early in 1878 for $200 consisted of 100 acres of land, "except the graveyard", adjoining "the flood's", from J. A. and Milanda Pyland of Dorchester County in the "State of Merriland". Quite a bit of the timberland was owned by non-residents who were generally glad to sell it at a fairly reasonable price.

Steele now owned sufficient standing timber to warrant purchase of a mill of his own and in November 1878 he purchased from Shepherd & Co. of Richmond a second hand sawmill, boiler, and engine which had been reclaimed from L. T.

Williams, for $1,254, that being the balance due. In payment he gave two notes, one due in six months for $618, and one due in twelve months for $636. The mill was set up in the Mussel Swamp area of the county, southeast of Spring Grove, and Steele began to saw lumber. However, he had discovered that thing called "credit" and from here on out he worked it to death, playing both ends toward the middle and sometimes skating very close to financial ruin. He purchased timberland every chance he got, or timber on the stump, giving notes, when possible, in payment and depending on cash received for the sawn lumber to meet them on maturity.

Early in April of 1880 Steele purchased a second, and larger, mill. This was a new installation consisting of a 30 h.p. portable engine and a No. 2 sawmill with a 30-foot carriage, head blocks, 60-inch circular saw, and 60 feet of 4-ply rubber belting. In payment he put his mark on three notes, one due in four months for $608.82 and two due in eight and twelve months, respectively, for $608.83 each. This mill was set up on a tract of 1089¼ acres located in the fork of the Blackwater River and Cypress Swamp which he had purchased at public sale and, as usual, had given paper to cover. This particular location was known as Mussel Fork Plantation and it was here that Steele built his home.

As soon as the mill was set up, negotiations were concluded with John T. Wolverton of Philadelphia for lumber to be delivered as soon as possible after the lumber season opened in the spring of 1881, a total of 50,000 board feet to be shipped by Capt. White's schooner to Baltimore. Wolverton paid Steele $2,327.46 in advance and to secure the transaction, Steele gave him a lien on everything that he owned which was free from previous liens, including his home on Mussel Fork Plantation. Exactly a year later this contract was completed and Steele was, as usual, again in need of cash to meet pressing debts. His backlogging of standing timber was what kept him in financial straits.

Among Steele's regular customers was one R. T. Waters & Son of Baltimore. The Waters firm had been well satisfied with the prime lumber received from Steele and when he approached them relative to a loan in February of 1882, against future orders, he was advanced $11,000 covered by a six-month note for $5,000 and one for $6,000 due in twelve months. To secure the notes, a lien was given on his 100 acres at "the flood's", 49¾ acres acquired from a man named Gottleib, his interest in the Blackwater River tract, both of his mills, and the tramway being built from the mill on the Blackwater River tract to the James River as well as the proposed wharf to be erected at Sloop Point. This is the earliest reference to be found to what became known as "Steele's Rail Road", a wooden rail affair connecting the sawmill with the river and which would replace the use of wagons and teams to move the sawn lumber out of the woods. Although the tramway was under construction, it is obvious that the wharf was still in the future. Steele had paid off his entire indebtedness with the money received from R. T. Waters & Son, thereby consolidating his debts.

A month later Steele purchased from the Tanner & Delaney Engine Company of Richmond, Va., a tramway locomotive named CARRIE BROWN, after his wife, the name being a combination of an endeared form of "Cornelia" and her maiden name. Mrs. Steele was "Miss Carrie" to practically everyone who knew her. This locomotive was fitted with 8x15-inch cylinders and carried construction number 827. In payment Steele gave the usual notes, four in number, falling due at three-month intervals for a total of $2,326.15. In addition, he purchased seven platform cars and these we definitely know to have been "broad gauge". Just what was considered "broad gauge" is another matter. It is therefore safe to assume that the CARRIE BROWN was also broad gauge.

Construction of the tramway naturally ran into trouble for there were public roads to be crossed and private lands to be traversed whose owners were a bit obstinate about permitting any private individual to build a tramway across their property just because he wanted to. Steele did not expect the tramway to be a permanent installation but that made little difference when he tried to obtain a right of way. Just how he got the idea of getting a charter is impossible to say, possibly the opposition he encountered forced him to take his troubles to a lawyer. Maybe his wife suggested the incorporation of the business as self-protection for surely she could see where the promiscuous handing out of notes to cover debts was leading her husband. Whatever brought it about, papers were properly drawn up, presented to the state legislature, and on April 21, 1882, the Surry County Railroad & Lumber Company was granted a charter.

The Atlantic & Danville Railway Company was also granted a charter on the same day to build a line from some point on the James to the interior and there had been rumors that the railway company was planning to build from somewhere near Claremont Plantation, but the exact location had not been selected. Quite a bit later someone got around to wondering why the legislature had seen fit to charter two corporations to build railways through the same general area, but it so happened that the legislators were in a hurry to go home, it being an election year, and the Governor had said that they could adjourn on the 21st if they would clean up all of the business on the table. It is very doubtful if either charter was read through before being passed by a voice vote.

Anyway, Steele was now a corporation with all of the powers and privileges accorded a proposed common carrier. To fill the letter of the law, R. A. Cock, John W. Ramey, John J. Dyer, and Samuel H. Burt were named as associates but there was absolutely no doubt that David Steele was the sole owner. He then deeded his uncompleted tramway and his mills, as well as the timberland and standing timber, to the new company and continued his logging operations as a corporation. Under the charter the main emphasis was placed on the railroad for it stated that the company was to "have all the powers, rights, and franchises necessary and proper to locate, construct, and maintain a railroad, for the purpose of transporting wood, lumber, and such produce as may be brought them for transportation from Sloop Point, on James river, to Blackwater river, Muscle forks, in Surry county, Virginia, with the privilege of constructing branch roads, none of which shall exceed twenty miles in length".

It was further directed "That the said company shall have power to hold and employ such machinery and appliances as their business may require, and may purchase and hold such land and timber as may be necessary for the successful operation of said business and road.

"The capital of said company shall not be less than fifteen thousand nor more than fifty thousand dollars.

"The said company shall have power to build a wharf on James river, and for that purpose may condemn land not exceeding one acre; provided that before the rights hereby conferred shall become vested, and before the actual work of construction shall commence, at least ten thousand dollars shall have been subscribed to the stock, and twenty percentum paid thereupon: and provided further, that there shall be deposited with the treasurer of the state, under his official bond, two thousand dollars, either in money or in bonds, approved by the treasurer, to be held by such officer to the credit of the president and board of directors of said railroad company, and subject to their order when, and only after, the like amount of two thousand dollars has been expended upon said railroad, and the same certified to the treasurer of the state by the railroad commissioner, whose duty it shall be to make such examination and certificate without delay upon application."

Steele had been dickering with William Allen for some time relative to a site for a lumberyard and a wharf, and on the day after he received his charter, a written agreement between them was recorded in the court house at Surry. Steele agreed to build a wharf, construction to begin within forty days, and to lay an iron railway over a fifteen-foot right of way on the old Allen's Rail Road bed for a distance of two miles or more, the entire installation, except the iron rail, to revert to Allen after fifteen years. Thus Steele obtained a location on the river and was able to push to completion his tramway.

The gauge of Steele's tramway from his mills to Sloop Point is of little importance to us, but it is a proven fact that it was wider than thirty-six inches. It actually means nothing so far as this story is concerned but we begin to wonder when we read a short article that appeared in "The Railroad Gazette" for April 7, 1882. It is titled simply "SURRY COUNTY—" and then states "Track is being laid on this road from a point in Surry County, Virginia about three miles from the James river, southward towards the Norfolk & Western road. It is a narrow gauge line and is built on the roadbed of an old road which was in operation 25 years ago, the iron having been taken up during the war and used to roof one of the Confederate rams at Richmond." Facts, as we know them, and those stated above lack a long ways of agreeing, until we take a very careful look at them. We will find that it is nothing unusual to find the early records of railroad construction to contain only a germ of truth, something like following a huge pall of smoke to a small grass fire. At best, those early reports of the construction of the smaller railroads generally only told us that something was going on in a certain locality.

The "point . . . about three miles from the James river" would be just about at the head of Sunken Meadow Creek and quite probably where the abandoned roadbed of Allen's Rail Road ended. That would be where Steele's tramway, building towards the James River from the south, would begin making use of the old roadbed. The statement that "It is a narrow gauge line . . ." is something else again but we know for a fact that it required "broad gauge" equipment as that designation is repeated over and over again in legal documents having to do with the rolling stock. The question is, just WHAT was considered "broad gauge" and WHAT was considered "narrow gauge" in Virginia in April of 1882?

During the rest of 1882 Steele continued to buy land and standing timber, and to put out just as little hard cash as he could. The A.&D. selected the village of Claremont as their river terminal, roughly a mile and a half down the river from Allen's wharf at Sloop Point, and decided to make use of Steele's tramway as far as possible. More dickering took place between the A.&D. officials, Allen, and Steele. Allen was drawn into the bargaining because of his ownership of the right of way and his agreement with Steele. Finally, on June 28, 1883, they came to an agreement and the charter of the Surry County Railroad & Lumber Company changed ownership for $12,250.00 and other considerations. This agreed amount also covered the ties and trestles on Allen's roadbed but not the stringers and iron, Steele's tramway from the end of the old roadbed to Spring Grove, and the right of way across the so-called "Goodrich land" from Spring Grove south some four miles to Phillip's Store, later to become known as Savedge's. The "other considerations" consisted of an agreement to build an iron railroad to Phillip's Store and to haul Steele's own cars loaded with lumber over it a distance of up to six miles for 62½¢ per 1,000 board feet or from six to ten miles for 75¢. Steele would be allowed to use his own locomotive to haul not less than five loads unless it required less than that to complete the loading of a vessel. The A.&D. would pay $2,500 when Steele's Rail Road was broken, plus $5,000 in A.&D. stock, and $4,750 in the form of ten flatcars or to be applied against future transportation charges. The flats were not to cost over $250 each, to have a capacity of four or five cords, and Steele could purchase the cars himself and have them billed against the account of the A.&D. The cars could not be built by either Steele or the A.&D. but had to be purchased from a third party and were to be similar in design to those in service. Steele retained the right to construct branches as set forth in the original charter. The portion of the tramway from Spring Grove to a terminus on the James W. Andrews tract was retained by Steele. If, for any reason, the A.&D. failed to fulfill their part of the contract, the tramway would be replaced and turned back to Steele. It was further agreed that the lumber traffic to the river would not be held up over forty days from the time that the line was broken due to construction of the new railroad. The break was made on August 20, 1883.

Either the matter of gauge had been overlooked or it was taken for granted that the A.&D. would be built to a gauge compatible to that of the tramway. The agreement points to the latter being the case but the backers of the A.&D. decided to lay their track to a gauge of thirty-six inches and Steele had no alternative but to relay his line to the narrower gauge. Moving one rail in was a simple task but what really hurt was that he would require new rolling stock. Again he went to Tanner & Delaney and ordered a thirty-six-inch gauge tramway locomotive and tender at a cost of $4,200.

CORNELIA was delivered in December of 1883, a small straight-boilered 2-4-0 with wide tread wheels for operation on wood rails and a four-wheel tender. Ten new flatcars, twenty-five feet long by seven feet nine inches wide, were purchased from the Allison Manufacturing Company of Philadelphia. There being no further need for the CARRIE BROWN, she was sent to Tanner & Delaney, that firm having agreed to try to sell her. The seven broad gauge flats remained at Spring Grove on a disconnected section of track until they were eventually disposed of.

The story is that when Steele went to Richmond to order his engine, and after all details had been worked out, Delaney asked him what number he wanted assigned to the engine. Steele said, after some thought, that a number was not necessary. Delaney then pointed out that it was customary to either number or name an engine for identification purposes in case a second one was ever purchased for use on the same railroad. He then suggested that the engine be named, and, in an effort to be helpful, suggested that it be named for his wife. That was satisfactory with Steele, but there was one difficulty, he didn't remember his wife's given name. Finally it was agreed that upon his return home he would have his wife write to Tanner & Delaney and let them know the name to be painted on the cab panels. That was done, and it is safe to bet that Steele never again forgot his wife's name.

In payment for the narrow gauge engine, Steele paid so much in cash and gave the customary notes for the balance. These were four in number, falling due at three-month intervals, the first two for $742.87 each, and the second two for $742.88 each. However, a week later he was able to redeem his paper in advance, the necessary amount being borrowed from L. M. French, and that loan to be repaid with sawn lumber. The flatcars were paid for by the A.&D. as per the terms of the contract. On the 14th of January 1884, R. W. Waters & Son slapped a lien on the engine and flatcars to further protect the note for $6,000 given by Steele on February 7, 1882, and which had not been paid. On that same day the Waters firm foreclosed on the Tanner mill but allowed Steele to continue operating it. Steele was now in serious financial trouble, having finally put his mark on too much paper.

The loan of $11,000 from Waters & Son was refinanced on March 7, 1884, and Steele was forced to put up as security the CARRIE BROWN, the seven broad gauge flatcars, five log wagons, three log carts and harness, three road wagons and harness, two buggies, six oxen, four cows, a tramway locomotive and tender "purchased in 1883", his home near Spring Grove, and all lumber to be manufactured during 1884, thus practically forcing Steele to depend on the operation of the mill taken over by Waters & Son as a livelihood. In short, it forced Steele out of the lumber business as an independent. On the fifth of April Waters & Son placed a lien on a small piece of land which was unencumbered and Steele realized that unless he moved fast, Waters & Son would gather in everything that he owned. So, on April 25th he sold a large parcel of land to J. Frank Mancha for $4,589, land which had presumably been cut over as Mancha was primarily interested in farm land.

As odd as it might appear, with part of the money realized from the sale of the land, Steele continued to purchase land, one particular parcel being the mill site belonging to A. D. Goodrich. This indicates that he was determined to continue to cut timber. He possibly believed that the lien filed by Waters & Son applied only to timber cut by him as a corporation. Now he was thinking in terms of a private individual which was skating on extremely thin legal ice, too thin.

The R. T. Waters & Son outfit was now in the logging business in Surry County. Steele was out of it, in spite of his repeated efforts to recoup his losses. The Baltimore firm found him a hard man to convince. When the Tanner mill was taken over, Waters gave Steele a year in which to redeem it but with his source of income effectively plugged, there was absolutely no doubt that he would be unable to do so. In anticipation of the permanent acquisition of the mill, the "& Son" part of the firm, Frank Edwards Waters, and certain associates, chartered the Surry Lumber Company on January 3, 1885. On the 21st the Waters outfit had a clear title to the mill and on the same day consumated an agreement whereby Steele sold all of his remaining business assets to them and Richardson, Moore, Smith & Company of Snow Hill, Md., for $25,051.23 in cash and two bonds, one for $1,334.38 due in six months and one for $1,334.39 due in twelve months.

Listed among the assets transferred to R. T. Waters & Son was the CARRIE BROWN which had not been sold and was still in Richmond, the narrow gauge tramway engine and tender, ten flatcars, seven wide gauge flatcars, the tramway from

Spring Grove to the James W. Andrews tract, and all privileges under the charter remaining to Steele after its sale to the A.&D. All of Steele's employees, including himself, continued with the new firm in their same capacities. Steele had employed only colored labor, mainly because it came cheaper than white, would put up with more hardships and inconveniences, and was plentiful.

On March 21, 1885, the R. T. Waters & Son organization transferred to the Surry Lumber Company all of its holdings in Surry County for the magnificent sum of $5. These holdings consisted in addition to the equipment and tramway line, the Shepard Mill, later known as the "Little Mill", the Tanner Mill, known as the "Big Mill", 17 mules, a sorrel mare named "Daisey", three yokes of oxen, sundry log carts and wagons, numerous dwellings, sheds, and other structures, logs, saw timber and ties, and three parcels of land of 400, 49¾, and 1089½ acres, respectively. The narrow gauge flatcars were numbered 11 through 20 and were lettered simply "RETURN TO DAVID STEELE, SPRING GROVE, VA." The final fate of the "CARRIE BROWN" and the seven wide gauge flatcars is of no concern as they drop out of the picture at this point and were never used on the railway in which we are interested.

The Three "S's" Takes Form

When they bought out David Steele, R. T. Waters & Son, through the Surry Lumber Company, did not by any means gain a monopoly of the lumber or logging business in Surry County. Various individuals cut timber throughout the county, some operated small ground mills and a fewer still made use of logging railways, none of which were of any great length. One such outfit was that owned by Virginius A. Savedge at New Design, a named locality south of Carsley, between there and the Blackwater River. He obviously logged the swamp bordering the river for his railway ran from there to Gottleib's Siding on the newly constructed A.&D. For a short distance the track ran beside the county road, then through the yard of his home, and on through the woods on its way to the A.&D. As was the case with practically all of the local lumber railways, there was only one engine, a tender engine of unknown type, make, and vintage, that generally set in his yard overnight irrespective of the fact that when the engine was purchased, a shed had been built to house it.

Memory recalls yet another logging outfit which brought in their engine by road from Wakefield, the unwieldly load rolling on its own drivers while being dragged by teams of straining oxen. The name of its owner or its final destination did not leave the lasting impression that did the strange sight of its passing.

The first problem that presented itself to the new lumber company was the selection of a mill site. Use of the two Steele mills was to continue at least until the new mill was in operation. Although the charter permitted the lumber company to locate their mill anywhere within the county, an inordinate fear of malaria fever, that was thought to permeate the lowlands bordering the James River and its tributaries, dictated the selection of a site away from the river and on relatively high ground. Fortunately, such a location was already owned by the company, Steele's Mussel Fork Plantation which he had purchased from Rebecca, Nancy, and Mark Ellis, and on which

Steele lived with his family. However, there still remained a quarter interest in the original 41½ acres that was owned by the estate of a deceased brother, Robert Ellis. On July 16, 1885, this remaining interest was purchased from the three survivors, as the closest relatives, for $40, giving the lumber company a clear title to the entire plot. This acquired location was bordered on the north by Cypress Swamp, on the west by Mussel Swamp, on the east by Blackwater and Cypress Swamps, and on the south by Blackwater Swamp. During the succeeding years the location of the swamps has shifted slightly but, in general, that covers the land southeast of Main Street of the present town of Dendron, that street running northeast and southwest. Logging in the immediate area had been carried on by John Deal whose small sawmill had been located a short distance southwest of the selected mill site. Deal's sole means of transportation was a swing cart and a pair of mules. The sawn lumber was hauled out by whoever purchased it and there was only one means by which it could be done, wagons, if the dirt road was passable, otherwise the lumber remained on the mill yard until it was.

With the mill site definitely decided upon, the next move was to extend Steele's tramway to that location and begin bringing in the machinery and supplies for construction. Lumber in sufficient quantities was already to hand but a right of way had to be procured before the tramway could be extended and use made of it. To visually survey the proposed extension and to dicker for the necessary land, Steele and Richard Scott, his former woods superintendent, accompanied the newly hired Surry Lumber Company superintendent, Edward Rogers, on a trip from the end of the tramway to Mussel Fork. The only really lasting impression left by the party was created by Rogers. Apparently he had not expected to have to make the trip on horseback and came dressed in his Sunday-best. Courtesy required that smiles be suppressed but the sight of this "dude" perched on a none too respectable mount with his pants legs riding half way to his knees and trying desperately to maintain the dignity required by his position as representative of the Baltimore company left a lasting impression that brought a twinkle to the eyes of those who beheld him, as much as 75 years later.

But, the trip was made, the route decided on, and the purchase of the necessary land begun. The first transaction was completed on December 7, 1885, the land being purchased from Jacob Heffelfinger, and construction began soon after. The extension of the tramway was laid with 25-pound iron rail and by early spring of 1886 material was being hauled to Mussel Fork. It was planned to relay the strap rail of the original portion of the line with iron as renewals became necessary, not to convert it all at one time, as the tramway was of sound timber and well laid. The stringers were good, heart timber squared on three sides to about six by six inches and pegged down to heavy planks at the butt joints, the stringers then being capped with strap iron and care being taken that the joints of the iron and the stringers did not coincide. Cross members supporting the stringers at more or less regular intervals were firmly bedded, or supported over soft ground. Some of this track remained in service until around 1889 when the northern end of the original tramway was finally abandoned.

The additional labor necessary to construct and operate the new mill and to work the increased woods operations, both skilled and unskilled, both black and white, was readily available. The colored labor was strictly local, but there had been an increasing influx of "homesteaders", men with families, who were still being attracted by the broadsides published by Mancha in the various out-of-state newspapers extolling the wonderful climate and opportunities to be found beside the James, and how easy it was to become a part of the wonderful community known as Claremont Colony. Some of the immigrants did fairly well for themselves but others found that they literally had to start over, taking any job that was offered as long as it paid a wage. A number went to work for the A.&D., others took up farming, still others worked in the woods, but there were many who welcomed the chance to work for the Surry Lumber Company. These new employees lived at home, a number commuting daily from up around Spring Grove. The laying out of a camp was carried out simultaneously with the erection of the mill, but that took time.

Alpine Grant Higgins, a native of Nova Scotia, who had come south with his family from Boston, Mass., and settled over at Spring Grove, was hired as a carpenter and his first job was to superintend the erection of a sort of boarding house where the men could be domiciled during the week until individual houses could be built. After the logging camp had grown up and was incorporated, this structure was known as Hotel Dendron and was on the northwest corner of what became known as Main and Church Streets. It was nothing fancy, being a box-like three-story frame structure. This was the first structure in the town of Dendron, a town which in time came to eat, sleep, and live by the mill whistle, a typical sawmill town.

There had never been any question concerning the use of a railroad to serve the mill and to haul the finished lumber to the river. A mill the size of the one planned and as isolated as it would be would require the use of some means of mass transportation. It was realized that the continued use of the A.&D. trackage between Spring Grove and Claremont would be an inconvenience and an expense that a railroad of their own would eliminate. Another thing that was just as obvious was the fact that any railroad built would have to be constructed under the terms of a charter. The length of the proposed line to the river plus any future expansion would make it necessary to cross public roads as well as cross private property and the right of eminent domain granted common carriers would be of inesti mable value in overcoming private parties reluctant to grant a right of way for the line. It would also grant them undisputed right to cross public roads.

So, early in the year 1886 the old firm of R. T. Waters & Son and the new Surry Lumber Company jointly organized the Surry, Sussex & Southampton Railway and were granted a charter on May 26 which read, in part, "Be it enacted by the general assembly of Virginia, as follows: That George S. Richardson, Richard T. Waters, John W. Smith, John P. Moore, Marion T. Hargis, Francis E. Waters, and such other persons and corporations as may be associated with them, shall be and they are hereby constituted and declared to be a body politic and corporate, . . .". The Waters faction, as the Surry Lumber Company, was the "other persons and corporations" mentioned in the charter and was understood to be the actual owner of the proposed railroad which was to be merely a part of the overall operation.

In addition to granting the proposed railroad permission to connect with the A.&D., the charter stated that the line was "to commence at an available point on the James river, within the said County of Surry, and extend thence by such route, as it shall be by it deemed most advantageous, through the said Counties of Surry, Sussex, and Southampton, to such a point on the Nottaway river as may be by it considered most eligible, and . . . operate such lateral branches from, or extensions of its main line, not exceeding twenty miles in length, . . ., and with power, also to change the said gauge and adopt any other gauge whenever it may be advisable so to do. . . . and it shall likewise be lawful for the said company . . . to enter into an agreement with the Surry Lumber Company . . . for the privilege of using and operating a line of railroad, now operated for lumber purposes, within the said County of Surry, . . .". It was further stipulated that the company ". . . is likewise authorized and empowered to own or charter, and run such vessels, either steam, sailing or other crafts, as may be necessary to develope or accommodate its traffic." The Railway never owned or operated a vessel of any kind. Although the charter was so general as to literally give the company the run of the three counties, it was most definite in that work had to be started within one year and at least $25,000 had to be expended on the railroad in five years. This stipulation, as well as that limiting the length of branches, was applied to all railroad charters issued by the general assembly and was an attempt to discourage the organization of railroad companies for the purpose of speculation.

The directors of the new organization were Francis E. Waters, John Walter Smith, John P. Moore, and Marion T. Hargis, all of Snow Hill, Maryland. The officers were Francis E. Waters, Chairman of the Board, President, and General Manager; John Walter Smith, Vice President; John P. Moore, Secretary and Treasurer; Parker D. Dix, Assistant Secretary and Treasurer; William B. McIllwaine, Attorney on General Council; and Marion T. Hargis, Auditor. Edward Rogers, who had been a partner in the logging firm of J. E. & Edward Rogers, that had been cutting timber in Sussex County, had been hired as General Superintendent, a position that David Steele had every reason to think he would be given. Steele might not have been a business man, and that is probably why he lost out, but he was a lumberman, a good lumberman. There were originally 1,000 shares of stock with a par value of $100 per share, the largest single block being held by Waters, 331¼ shares. Rogers, the only local shareholder, owned twenty shares.

A standard narrow gauge 4-4-0 locomotive was ordered from The Baldwin Locomotive Works of Philadelphia, Pa., and in April of 1886 the new railway company began acquiring a right of way towards the James River. The point of land just east of Gray's Creek was selected as the site for a dock and a construction permit was granted by the local court in May, but there was a restriction inserted which made it mandatory that any structure erected be at least eighty feet to the east of the dock used by the Frederick Gottleib "bogie track".

Gottleib was a German lumberman who owned and operated a small sawmill near the present village of Elberon and operated a wooden-rail tramway running from there to the James River. His motive power consisted of two grey mules that were worked in tandem. This tramway passed through Surry at about a point where the building that housed Edwards' General Store now stands, a tenth of a mile east of the court house, and it is natural to suppose that merchandise was occasionally conveyed, as a favor, of course, to and from the river. However, by the time that the construction of Surry Lumber Company's railroad, as it was generally referred to, had reached Elberon, the tramway had fallen into disuse and the railway company was able to take over the right of way where it proved advantageous, particularly between Surry and the river. Gottleib had not ceased his logging operations but had moved his mill to a point northwest of Mussel Fork and was shipping his lumber out over the A.&D. from his own siding. His wharf had been allowed to deteriorate until it was practically unusable. It had never been anything but a place, or a structure, where barges could be tied up.

The construction of the company's wharf was let to the Elizabeth Improvement Company and work was begun as soon as the equipment could be assembled. It was ready for use before the first of 1887, cost $10,000, and was said to be the best of its kind on the entire river. Scotland Wharf, as it was named, immediately became a regular landing for the steamboats maintaining a more or less regular scheduled service between Norfolk and Richmond, or Petersburg.

For a time the Baldwin No. 2 and Steele's CORNELIA, which had been numbered "1", were the only locomotives in service. The small tender of the No. 1 was discarded, the tank part removed from the four-wheel frame and mounted on a flatcar. This was then used as a tender which made it possible to operate longer between stops to "wood up". Although definite information concerning the appearance of the engine is too vague and unreliable to accept, it is a known fact that she would not operate satisfactorily on the light iron rails due to the wide tread and deep flanges of her wheels. Her use, after the arrival of No. 2, was restricted as far as possible to the hauling of logs from the woods to the mill at Mussel Fork. When being used for this service, she could be run at a slow speed and at least part of her work would be over wooden rails for which she had been built. It has been suggested that the flanges were eventually turned down in an effort to make her more suitable for operation on iron rails but that is strictly supposition, there being absolutely no proof that it was done. During the entire time that she was used by the Surry Lumber Company, the engine was referred to as "John Tucker's engine" for John Tucker, a colored man, was her engineer and had been ever since she was delivered to Steele by the builder. Certainly he was more familiar with the idiosyncrasies of that particular locomotive than anyone else.

The line was completed to Scotland Wharf by the early fall of 1886, the wye being put in during November. The lumber company acted as prime contractor and sublet work to local individuals or had it done by daily hire, whichever proved the most economical. Alpine Higgins constructed all of the wooden culverts, bridges, and trestles, and continued on with the company for a number of years as a carpenter and maintenance man.

No outstanding geographical obstacles had to be overcome in the construction of the track to the river as the terrain was of a rolling nature, except right at the river. The right of way was prepared by throwing up dirt from shallow parallel ditches on each side of the survey. The oak ties were put in place and the 25-pound iron rails spiked down. The track followed the contour of the land, no effort being made to ease any of the short but sharp grades encountered as the line neared the river. The longest trestle was just north of Mussel Fork, across the running water in Cypress Swamp and that wasn't over fifty feet in length. Wooden culverts took care of the drainage ditches and bottoms. The only excavating done was that necessary to get the track past the side of a hill. At the river it was necessary to get the the track down a rather steep bluff to the dock. This was done by means of a switchback and even here as little manual labor was expended as possible.

The track approached the river at a right angle, following the Gottleib tramway, but swung sharp to the west at the top of the bluff, leaving the tramway, and dead-ended after traveling a short distance. After allowing room for a train of about ten cars to clear the switch, actually 620 feet, a track took off and started down the bluff, the grade being quite sharp and dug out on a long curve towards the river. While headed down and still curving, the track passed under a highway bridge, then straightened out about a hundred feet above high water mark and ran straight out onto the wharf. The wye was actually an extension of the east end of the main line of track along the top of the bluff. This line cut across the old tramway line which was still in place. In fact, parts of the line had to be dismantled when the track north from Elberon was built. This tramway cut straight down to the river, making use of a shallow gully to ease the grade and short sections could be found for a number of years after the iron railroad was in use.

While the railroad to the river was under construction, the company had continued to make use of the connection with the A.&D. but once the river was reached and the wharf completed, the connection at Spring Grove was broken, although it is more than probable that the switch was left in for sometime thereafter, simply not used as there was no reason to make use of the line to Claremont.

Although the Surry Lumber Company had procured a charter for its railroad and legally it was a common carrier subject to a certain amount of control by the state's corporation commission, the owners had no intention of letting anything interfere with the primary purpose for which the line was being built, that of serving the Mussel Fork mill. The construction of the railroad did not receive the publicity generally accorded such an enterprise for the simple reason that the necessary funds for constructing and equipping the line were already available. There was no problem so far as finances were concerned. The first bit of news that filtered down the river as far as Norfolk was actually no news for it consisted of a filler piece in one of the daily papers stating that the "Luray Lumber Company is building a railroad from the James river to Jerusalem". The substitution of "Luray" for "Surry" is not surprising for the penmanship of the reporters back in those days quite frequently left much to be desired. Even today letters addressed to Surry turn up in the Luray post office, and vice versa.

It is quite true that the company had its eye on Jerusalem for on March 29, 1888, it was reported that the S.S.S.&S. had completed its survey to that town and that would be the terminus of the road. Tracts of timber were being bought in Southampton County, of which Jerusalem, better known by now as Courtland, was the county seat, but the lumber company had no intention of cutting timber down there in the immediate future. The chances of a railroad following the survey were slim, indeed.

A scheduled passenger service had not been included in the company's plans when it obtained the charter but being a common carrier, the company was literally shoved into it by the demands, and complaints, of the local inhabitants. This very reluctant service was provided by the operation of a mixed train on an approximate schedule, the entire roster of passenger equipment consisting of a second hand combination car. Where it came from is anyone's guess. The company obtained the contract to haul the mail almost as soon as the so-called "mail train" began to make regular trips but only pouch mail was handled. At first, all of the mail came in from the river, being brought up from Norfolk and down from Petersburg and Richmond on such riverboats as the "ARIEL", and later on the "POCAHONTAS", "MOBJACK", and "SMITHFIELD". Back in those days the James was a highway into the interior and the traffic on it was heavy enough to say that the river was crowded. The majority of the heavy freight was handled by schooners and barges while the package freight, mail, and passengers were taken care of by the steamboats.

The opening of the line between Mussel Fork and the river was a gala affair in which everyone along the route participated. The train consisted of No. 2 and several flats with seats placed thereon. The rate of speed was relatively low and a stop was made at several points along the line until there was a goodly number of passengers on board, the ladies sitting primly erect, clutching their raised parasols with one hand and the seat with the other. It appears that the trip was made prior to the purchase of the combination car but it was made without incident, although sparks might have caused a few uneasy moments. Between Mussel Fork and the river there were four designated stops: Sexton, Elberon, Moorings, and Surry, the latter referred to generally as "the Court House". The only regular stop was Surry and it was the only one that could boast of a station of any size. Smaller station buildings were erected at the other stops, which were designated as flag stops, and a siding was put in on the west side of the main line at each one. At Surry the main siding was between the main line and the station, thus making it possible to place freight cars beside the raised freight platform.

The building of the A.&D. and the S.S.&S. seems to have set off a rash of proposed railroads in the area. Rumor had it that on the 15th of March, in 1887, the company was going to start extending its line from Mussel Fork on south to Wakefield to connect with the Norfolk & Western and by the first of July trains would be running through to that point. Undoubtedly a connection with the N.&W. would have had its advantages but the real "port of entry", and departure, so far as the company was concerned, was Scotland Wharf. Construction towards Wakefield was eventually begun but not according to the schedule set up by the rumor for there was sufficient standing timber still available on the tracts formerly owned by Steele. A little later on, in December 1888, to be exact, a railroad company was organized to build from Surry to Smithfield and meetings were held along the proposed route to raise the necessary funds. A meeting was held at Surry on December 11 but these fund-raising gatherings were far from successful and the entire scheme folded. In fact, that was the final result of all such attempts.

In a short time it became evident that motive power suitable for use in the woods on light, temporary track was necessary and a small nine-ton 0-4-2 saddle-tank logging locomotive was ordered from the Baldwin Works during the early part of 1888. She was delivered in the spring of that year, carried the road number "3", and was the first of the famous "donkeys". To haul loads to the river, a 2-6-0 tender engine, numbered "4", was also ordered from Baldwin and was delivered around the last of '88 or very early in '89, the boiler test date being in October of '88. After the delivery of No. 4, No. 2 spent most of her time on the mail train but at times worked the woods run. The "Steele engine" was relegated to the position of spare locomotive, with no regrets.

The first fatal accident occurred on July 6, 1888, when David Steele, who had been working as a woods boss, was killed instantly by a locomotive. There are four versions of the accident, mainly because no one actually saw how it happened. It seems that the CORNELIA was not fitted with a regular cow-catcher but only with a footboard across the front end and everyone who was present at the time agreed that Steele had been riding this footboard as they shifted cars in the woods, jumping on and off as necessary, and that he fell, stepped, or jumped in front of the moving engine and was run over, being killed instantly, but they do not agree as to how or why the accident happened.

The crew was working over between Slabtown and Spring Grove, that we know, and one story has it that they were working on a section of track still laid with strap rail, that an end of one of the straps came loose and snaked up. Steele put his foot down on it to hold it in place until the engine could roll upon it but, in some manner, his foot became caught under the strap and he was pulled off the footboard and fell between the rails in front of the moving engine. The second version is that he lost his balance, fell off the footboard, and the engine caught him before he could roll clear. The third version is that he jumped for the footboard as the engine came up to him, missed his grab and fell between the rails. The fourth version, which many who knew him personally believed and which had a wide circulation, was that he deliberately stepped in front of the moving engine. That is hard to believe for certainly there are easier and less messy ways of entering the next world. In view of the conflicting opinions, it was officially stated that he was simply "Killed by locomotive", and with that statement there is no argument.

To make minor repairs to the mill machinery and the railroad equipment, the company set up a small machine shop in a lean-to with Alvin S. Higgins in charge. All heavy work had to be let to an outside firm, most of it going to the Petersburg Iron Works, operated by the Titus Brothers, who either sent mechanics to Mussel Fork or had the work sent to Petersburg. When a locomotive was sent in for a periodic overhaul and only general repairs were necessary, Titus Brothers would send out two men, brothers, one of which was a boilermaker and the other a general mechanic, who remained on hand until no longer needed.

Alvin S. Higgins was the son of Alpine Higgins and, like his father, was a native of Nova Scotia. He attended school in Boston and was considered unusually capable and popular. He went to work for the company in 1886, at the age of fifteen, and during that same year married Lucy V. Matthews. He eventually worked his way up to the position of Master Mechanic, Purchasing Agent, and Architect, at least those were his official titles, and he was responsible for the drawing of the plans for all of the later mills and most of the company-owned structures erected at Mussel Fork and elsewhere. One of his many hobbies was music and he organized and played in the town band which held regular concerts during the summer months in the bandstand before the hotel. Alvin also had his faults that occasionally got him into trouble with some of the married and single men, and there were occasions when he showed up after an absence, quite battered. And, he liked his strong liquor.

Although logging was still being done up in Mussel Swamp, between the mill and Spring Grove, the standing timber on the tracts taken over from Steele was being rapidly depleted and a gang had been sent into the woods south of Mussel Fork. This new tract had been purchased from the Shaw Timber & Land Company. Consequently, a grading gang was pointed in the general direction of Wakefield and told to start preparing a grade. A trestle was built across the Blackwater River and rails began to follow hard on the heels of the grading gang. Logging crews were right behind the track gang and logs were being hauled out before the echoes of the spike mauls had died.

By June of 1889 the track had reached a point two miles south of Wakefield, having crossed the Norfolk & Western at grade, and timber was being cut in Sussex County as well as in Surry. Only six miles of track of the former Mussel Fork-Spring Grove line remained in service. All of the wooden tramway track was out of service, except for a small amount of woods track. Both of Steele's former mills had been shut down and all timber cut to the northwest of the Mussel Fork mill was railed there for processing. The supply of logs was such that the mill was kept running at full capacity and the demand was such that every boardfoot of lumber coming off the saw carriage was sold by the time it was stacked. At times, as many as seven large three and four-masted schooners lay at the wharf, and in the stream, waiting to be loaded with either lumber or cordwood for Baltimore, New York, Boston, and Portland. The demand for cordwood had not decreased noticeably as yet and the demand equalled that for sawn lumber. The company continued to cater to both demands, turning standing timber unfit for lumber into cordwood.

For a time after 1889 very little was done towards lengthening the main line south of Wakefield. Regular service was maintained between there and the river, the engine being turned at Wakefield on a short wye jammed in between the main line north of the N.&W. crossing and Wildcat Swamp, its length being restricted by the proximity of the swamp. The line beyond Wakefield was operated strictly as a logging line although the operation of trains over it gradually fell into a more or less scheduled pattern.

Trains were running on the new railroad and forest products were being shipped steadily out from the wharf at Scotland but this activity went unnoticed outside of the immediate area. Information that filtered out was either history or indefinite. As late as April 28th of 1890 a short article appeared in a Virginia paper stating that a large lumber village had been built by a Baltimore firm between Wakefield and Surry. The mill employed around 400 men and the village contained stores and a hotel as well as other structures. As an afterthought, mention was made of the fact that the company was building their own railroad to the river at a new landing called Scotland. Obviously the lumber village had not been named. One thing is for sure and that is that the people who lived along the railroad and had begun to depend on it, took the little narrow gauge to their collective hearts. When spoken of, it was always "our railroad".

So far as is known, the first real trouble that the company, as a whole, encountered was the freeze of January 1893. Subsequent cold spells tied up operations but this one of 1893 was the first one that really gave the company a taste of what could happen during a winter. First, it got cold, which was nothing unusual, but it remained cold, day after day, and that was unusual. The mercury never once climbed up above the freezing mark. The river began to congeal, the ice creeping a bit further out from the shore each day. Soon the river was a solid sheet of ice and as it thickened, traffic slowed down and then stopped.

On the night of the 15th it snowed. It really snowed, and the next morning it was decided not to attempt to reach the river or Wakefield. The cold continued but on the 17th it was decided that some sort of service would have to be started. The engine crew got through to the river with surprisingly little trouble but when they rolled out on the wharf all they could see, both up and down stream, was a smooth expanse of snow covered ice. This couldn't last forever, but on the 18th it snowed again. It has been said that in all, thirty-six inches of snow fell. This second fall was not too bad so again the engine crew broke through to the wharf. On the 21st someone took the trouble to walk out on the ice a ways and measure the depth of the snow and the ice; eighteen inches of the white stuff on top of eight inches of ice.

The weather in Tidewater Virginia is as fickle as a young girl with too many beaus. A couple of nights later the wind suddenly went around into the south, the mercury began to rise, and the snow to melt rather rapidly. It took a bit longer for the ice to break up and still longer before the steamboats and barges began to pass up and down the river again. Six years later it happened again.

By 1894 the track had crossed Lightwood Swamp just below Airfield Pond dam and in so doing crossed over into Southampton County. As the main line inched south, woods tracks radiated off it like twigs off a branch. Just who owned these twigs, the railway company or the lumber company, apparently didn't matter. That problem would have to be settled later.

For several years after the trains began to run, the company owned only two boxcars which is indicative of the amount of freight, other than forest products, that was handled. The company certainly did not go out looking for business but under the terms of the charter they could not turn any away. Let us say that they simply did not encourage the use of their railroad by the general public. Into the two boxcars went such items as furniture, ice, dry goods, meat, sugar, liquor, flour, and anything else that had to be protected from pilferage and the weather. The vast majority of large consignments of freight were transported on flats. If rain threatened, the consignment remained under cover until the weather cleared. Actually, this was no great inconvenience to anyone for back in those days a merchant thought nothing of waiting a week for delivery of merchandise ordered from Petersburg. Then, too, most of the freight arrived in less than carload lots and it traveled via the mail train, being loaded and unloaded while the train waited, and there was always one of the boxcars in the train. During the late summer and early fall a certain amount of farm products, such as peanuts and potatoes, were hauled and flats were invariably used for that traffic. It wasn't until later, much later, that the seasonal farm traffic reached the point where cars had to be parceled out.

There were, of course, ten flat cars to start with, the former Steele flats, but by the end of June 1889 six additional such cars were purchased. During fiscal 1890 five more were procured, and in fiscal 1895 an additional nine showed up. The original two boxcars continued to be the total number of such cars in service until '94 when one more was obtained. Surely, by this time log cars were beginning to make their appearance but if so, they were considered to be the property of the Surry Lumber Company and no record was kept of their number, nor when their use was first introduced.

Eventually the timber over towards Spring Grove was exhausted, and the removal of the rest of that line began, the rails to be used over and over again until they were literally worn out. Slabtown, an extremely roudy settlement that had sprung up around the "Big Mill", was left to be reclaimed by the woods, such businesses as could be easily moved going elsewhere while others remained until they died a natural death. A saloon was one of the businesses that chose to remain. In either late 1892 or early '93 the dismantling crew reached the trestle over the upper end of Cypress Creek, a rather swampy area at that particular point. The structure was carefully taken down, bent by bent, for erection at another location. On a Saturday night, while the structure was still in the process of being dismantled, a man came down from Slabtown, drunk to the point of oblivion but still able to stagger along. He was subconsciously walking the grade as he had done for many previous Saturday nights. When he came to where the trestle had been he kept right on going, trying to walk the non-existent ties. The next morning he was found by two small boys, face down in the mud, dead.

Slabtown obviously got its name from the fact that slabs were split there. These were made from four-foot sections of selected straight-grained cypress logs, were a half inch thick, four feet long, and of various widths. Their manufacture was strictly a manual operation from the skinning of the logs to the splitting of the balks. The company engaged in their manufacture for only a short time for the ordinary wood shingle was already replacing slabs as roofing material. When Slabtown was finally completely abandoned, there were places where the cypress bark was knee-deep.

The inevitable finally happened in 1894. The mill burned. It caught fire during the night and by the time the employees had been assembled and organized into bucket brigades, it was beyond saving. Their attention was then turned to the stacks of sawn lumber and those they were able to save. The logs that were piled near the mill were scorched but not damaged to the extent that they were a total loss. The stored lumber kept the company in business until a new mill could be erected. As soon as possible, the company began to cast around for a complete sawmill to be used until the burned one could be rebuilt. A mill consisting of band and gang saws was found at Jones Bay, purchased, dismantled, moved to Mussel Fork and set up before the debris from the fire was cleared away. Although the company was again sawing lumber, the financial loss had been considerable and certain temporary economies had to be instituted. Edward Rogers, the general superintendent, offered to work a year without pay but the offer was declined, with thanks.

As soon as the Jones Bay mill was in production, the original site was cleared and another mill erected there. The Jones Bay mill was called "A Mill" while the new mill was "B Mill". This was actually the beginning of the enormous spread that kept the narrow gauge in business for many years to come.

Early Operation

The passage of the "Jim Crow" Law by the Virginia Legislature made it necessary that a new combination car be procured to make possible the required separation of races. Consequently a three-compartment car was ordered from Barney & Smith and delivered in 1895. Immediately upon delivery, the original combination car was disposed of. This new car was the only piece of passenger equipment ever owned by the company which was equipped with hot water heat, the heater being in the larger of the two passenger compartments. The circulating water pipe ran around the sides of the car, on the floor, in a continuous loop. There was an expansion tank on the roof. When the system was in use, it was the duty of the conductor to see that the tank always had water in it to ensure the system being charged. Each night he had to climb up on the roof to fill it before going home.

The car was divided into a small smoking compartment at one end, a baggage compartment in approximately the center, and a larger passenger compartment at the other end. When in use as the sole piece of passenger equipment on the mail train, the smoking compartment was used for the colored passengers. After 1900, however, when a straight coach was purchased, the car was occasionally "turned around" when the traffic was heavy, the smoking compartment catching the overflow from the coach and the passenger compartment being used for the colored passengers. It might be stated, too, that this car was the only "new" piece of passenger equipment ever owned by the company.

Eventually the track reached Boston, 28.1 miles from the river, and the company set up a logging camp there, this being the center of logging operations in Southampton County for some time. Actually, it should be said that the company set up a logging camp on a location 28.1 miles from the river and named it Boston, for there was nothing there prior to the construction of the camp and only a dwelling and an abandoned store after the company left. Trains ran fairly regularly between Boston and Mussel Fork but no common carrier service was offered south of Wakefield. The farmers around White's Crossing, which later became known as Manry, got together and circulated a petition asking that a station be erected there and regular service be extended to that point. The petition was forwarded to the railway company and promptly shelved upon receipt, no answer being given one way or the other.

After a reasonable length of time, another petition was circulated asking that the service be extended to Boston. Certain of the names appeared on both petitions for the idea was to get train service south of Wakefield. It made very little difference whether the trains turned at White's Crossing or Boston, just so long as they ran to one place or the other. This time the petition was forwarded to the Public Utilities Commission, where it was filed in March of 1896. A letter was sent along explaining about the first petition and asking that the second petition be given favorable attention. A copy of the letter was sent to the company with a request that it be acted on favorably. The company promptly climbed on its high horse and wrote the commission stating that it disliked very much being pressured into something which would be unprofitable to it and that common carrier service between Boston and Wakefield would most certainly not show a profit.

That blast didn't set too well with the Commissioner who directed that the company find out just what the people wanted, then do something about it. The company, finding that they had talked themselves into a corner, tried crawfishing by pointing out that some of the signatures appeared on both petitions and until the petitioners could make up their minds as to what they wanted, there was nothing it could do. Back from the Commissioner came a letter stating that the company had a charter as a common carrier and it was up to it to start acting as such if it wanted to retain that charter. He further stated that the commission couldn't see what difference it made whether service was terminated at White's Crossing or Boston as long as trains had to run through to Boston for turning, which was so as the company had put in a wye at that point. Eventually the company gave in and agreed to make Boston a regular stop with a station building, and White's Crossing a flag stop without one. So, two runs a day began hauling passengers and freight south to Boston. The company was correct in its contention that the service would not be profitable, and it never was, so far as common carrier traffic was concerned.

That bit of unpleasantness took place in 1896, the same year that Mussel Fork grew up and became a town. The new corporation was called "Dendron", the name being derived from the Greek meaning "tree", and was a most appropriate selection to say the least. Arthur Rogers was its first mayor. The town council had its first meeting on April 17 and was made up of A. S. Higgins, J. E. Rogers, J. A. Deering, R. H. Faison, T. D. Parker, and J. D. Hart, thus leaving no doubt that the town was owned and run by the Surry Lumber Company. It was a mill town, a one-industry town, but a town with a difference, as one of the officials pointed out, for there was no "wrong side of the tracks". Everyone in town was either directly or indirectly connected with the lumber company, even those who worked for the railroad. This statement was a rather facetious remark brought about by the fact that during that particular period in the history of the company, the mills were to the east of the tracks and the town to the west. Everyone literally lived on the west side of the tracks. Later on conditions changed but in '96 that official was quite correct in his statement. **1415593**

It had poured rain all night and daybreak found Cypress Swamp, just north of Dendron, as we will now refer to Mussel Fork, brim full and running over, the water covering the railroad trestle and some of the fill. The chocolate-colored flood moved lazily along the edges but out where the trestle spanned the usually placid little stream, it moved at a steady trot. The flood was not something unusual nor was the current exceptionally swift, nor was the water higher than usual under the circumstances. Cypress Swamp was simply staging another of its flash floods and when Chevallie brought the early morning train down from Dendron and started out over the fill, he did so with only the usual amount of caution. There were twin disturbances of the water which indicated that the rails were in place and there was no roil to indicate a washout. Everything appeared perfectly safe, just exceedingly wet, but when the engine reached a point about a hundred feet from the submerged trestle, she slowly began to tilt to the left, and she didn't show any signs of stopping that tilting. Along her left side the water began to boil violently as the whole fill on that side seemed to slide out from under the track. Getting stopped was no problem at all, and the engineer and his fireman went out of the right gangway with all possible speed. The engine slowly lay over in the water with a gentle splash and much hissing, the leading truck becoming detached as she went. She finally came to rest with her wheels and running gear in the air and the boiler and cab practically submerged.

Cap'm Palmer was taking up tickets at the time and as the combine came to a bucking halt he did some fast footwork and grabbing to prevent being thrown to the floor. The first of the two flats of cordwood between the engine and the combine went into the washout that immediately formed where the fill had collapsed, but the second contented itself with simply jumping the track. No one was hurt, although the engine crew got a thorough but not very clean soaking. As soon as Palmer had tied down the passenger car and made sure that it would not be washed away, and that none of the passengers were hurt, he walked back up to Dendron and reported the accident. An engine was sent down immediately to haul the car back to the depot while the dispatcher put up a notice canceling all runs until further notice. By 1889 the company had strung some twenty miles of wire and all dispatching was done by telephone.

The water dropped almost as quickly as it had risen and it wasn't long before a wrecking crew was wading around in the mud and water, putting chains around the boiler and rigging hauling tackle to a large tree on the opposite side of the track from where the engine lay. Rogers, the superintendent, knew his business and soon everything was ready. The block and tackle was hooked to the chains and to the tree, and the hauling line made fast to the front coupling socket of the heaviest engine available. The men stood clear, Rogers signaled the engineer who started his engine slowly up the grade towards Dendron, taking the slack out of the gear. As soon as the gear was taut the engineer fed a little more steam to the cylinders, the exhausts became more labored and wider apart while the gear began to hum with the strain. The tree began to slowly lean and consternation was expressed that it would snap off, or some of the gear give way, before the engine could be broken free of the mud, but Rogers refused to ease off. More and more strain was exerted, with everyone holding their breath and backing away from the straining tackle. Suddenly the engine broke free with a sucking noise, like pulling a boot out of a mud hole, and everyone let go with a relieved sigh.

After setting the locomotive on her feet, the real job of re-railing her began. First, it was necessary to jack her up and the track built under her, then she was carefully lowered onto the rails. The main rods were taken down before she was moved to prevent possible scoring of the piston rod bushings and cylinder walls. Only after that was done and she was firmly on the temporary track was she hauled up on solid ground and on to Dendron. Once in the shop she was completely dismantled and thoroughly cleaned. Mud had worked its way into every conceivable part and into some parts which defied explanation. However, the job was soon completed and the little olive-green, brass-bound eight-wheeler was back hauling the mail train. Of course, the fill was back in service much sooner than was No. 2, and while she was laid up her place was indifferently filled by No. 1.

There were five of the Rogers brothers who came from England in 1873 and settled at "ELCOMBE" in Lunenburg County, Virginia with their father. Ernest and Edward operated a small plant near their home where the manufacture of dogwood and persimmon shuttle cocks was undertaken for a short time, and then moved to a location in Dinwiddie County, about six miles from Petersburg, Virginia. There they set up a sawmill for the primary purpose of furnishing lumber for the construction of an insane asylum. That completed, the mill was moved to a point near Stony Creek, not too far from Petersburg. When they had cut out there, they moved again, this time to a nearby location which came to be known as Loco, and there the two brothers operated as J. E. & Edward Rogers. Both men married local girls from near Loco and eventually were considered members of the community, which, in itself, was quite an accomplishment. Edward was, of course, the first to work for the Surry Lumber Company, being hired as general superintendent of the entire operation by the Baltimore officials in, it is said, 1887 but more likely the year before for we have already found him checking the route for the logging line from Steele's mill to Mussel Fork in '86. Prior to the hiring of Edward, all business had been handled direct by the Baltimore office. Ernest then brought Philip into the Loco operation and he went to Dendron as mill superintendent, replacing Joe Roberson at the time of his death. A short time later Philip was brought in to survey and estimate standing timber.

In 1898 Mr. West, the first logging superintendent, died and Philip was promoted to that position. Arthur, the fourth brother, remained on the farm in Lunenburg County with his father until the place was sold in 1891. He then entered the mercantile business in Petersburg as a partner in the firm of Barham & Rogers. The partnership lasted only a short time and from there he went to West Virginia. Upon the death of Mr. Eldred, the company's first bookkeeper, Edward offered Arthur that position and it was accepted. Although it appears that the Dendron part of the Surry Lumber Company threatened to become a family affair, the head office never found cause to complain. Each one of the brothers knew his job thoroughly and they functioned perfectly as a team.

Procurement of additional equipment was dictated strictly by the requirements of the mills. Common carrier traffic was light to begin with and remained so. As has been said, the S.S.&S. was strictly a one-industry road. The original No. 1, the former CORNELIA, was, of course, a logging tramway locomotive; small, with low drivers, slow, and none too powerful, being fitted with either nine by fourteen or nine by sixteen inch cylinders. She was not built for heavy work or fast running and when out on the main line she was like a farm horse on a race track, not that the main line was exactly a race track. She had been used to haul the construction train until No. 2 arrived around August or September of 1886, and then she had been put back into the woods.

No. 2 was a 16½-ton standard design narrow gauge 4-4-0, not unlike many others of the same design turned out by Baldwin for general service. She was just as much at home in the woods as she was out on the main line and was an excellent all-purpose engine, as long as she wasn't overloaded. She had ten by sixteen-inch cylinders, 43-inch drivers, and was designed to burn either wood or soft coal. There were no brakes other than hand brakes on the rear tender truck, but in March of 1895 driver brakes were installed and possibly at the same time brakes were installed on both tender trucks, the beams being outside of the trucks and attached to the underside of the tender frame. This made it possible to drop the trucks without completely dismantling the brake rigging, or so it was claimed. Both engine and tender were painted the standard Baldwin olive-green, which came very close to being black, and were striped and lettered in gold. The boiler jacket was planish steel bound with polished brass. Other than the planish steel boiler jacket, this was the color scheme applied to all of the early engines, including the woods engines, although it didn't take them long to come out in a dull black dress, sans all striping and lettering, other than the engine number in chrome yellow and later, in white.

Although No. 3 was ordered in October 1887, she was not delivered until February of the following year, and, as was previously stated, was the first of a number of more or less identical woods engines of an 0-4-2 saddle-tank design constructed as simply as possible. There was no gauge glass, only two try cocks, and no brakes. The two safety valves were set to pop simultaneously at 120 pounds pressure. She had eight by twelve-inch cylinders, thirty-inch drivers, and was designed to burn wood exclusively. The weight was given as nine tons, give or take a few pounds, and although the engine was built to operate on extremely light, rough track with grades up to 5 percent and to require the very minimum of upkeep, it was both rugged and dependable. It has been said that the only two things required to keep it running was a trickle of water dripping from the bottom try cock and a fire in the firebox.

The basic design of No. 3 was so satisfactory that three additional woods engines were built from the same set of plans. In fact, a fifth engine was built in 1892, but for the Standard Kiln Dried Lumber Company, their BRUNSWICK. The No. 5 was delivered in October 1889 and had three improvements over the first of the series. The tread of the truck wheels was increased from three to 3¾ inches, the number of try cocks was increased from two to the usual three, and the connections for the injector feed lines were moved to the bottom of the legs of the tank where strainers were installed, thus making it easy for the engine crew to clear the suction lines in case they became clogged, which happened quite frequently. In each case the alteration was brought about by operating experience.

The third woods engine, No. 7, arrived two years later, in September 1891, and again certain detail changes were evident. The boiler pressure was kicked up to 130 pounds, asbestos boiler lagging was used, the feedwater syphon valve on the steam dome was a permanent fixture, and metallic packing was used for the piston rods. There was not enough cash readily available to pay for this engine and it was delivered with Baldwin property plates affixed.

In July of the next year, 1892, No. 9, the fourth woods engine, was delivered and except for the absence of property plates, she was an exact duplicate of No. 7. By this time most of the bugs caused by the rough operating conditions had been ironed out and the lumber company was well pleased with the service rendered by the saddle-tanks. From the day the first one went into the woods until the day that the last one came out, the little engines were called "donkeys" because of their power and toughness, which was out of all proportions to their small size, and it was a name used by everyone from the top brass to the lowest mule skinner. Judging by the number of these 0-4-2 saddle-tanks built by Baldwin, it was a design that was extremely popular with logging companies in most of the southeastern states.

Two months after No. 3 was delivered, No. 4 was ordered. Soon after the mills were in full production, a demand for heavier power made itself felt and No. 4 was the result. This engine was the first of two practically identical twelve by eighteen-inch moguls with 37-inch drivers. She arrived from the Baldwin plant around early October of 1888, and was, of course, the largest engine on the line. This engine came fitted with steam brakes and weighed approximately twenty tons, of which 16½ tons were on the drivers. In September of 1891, No.

6, the second of the duet, was received. The tender of both engines was fitted with hand brakes, but that of No. 6 was also fitted with steam brakes.

When Ernest and Philip Rogers joined the company in the winter of 1894-95, they brought with them the locomotive they had been using on their logging tramway at Loco. This engine was a seven by fourteen-inch 0-4-2 saddle-tank, slightly larger than the woods engines already in service, was built by the Richmond Locomotive & Machine Works, Richmond, Virginia in 1891, and was a peculiar contraption in that the cab was completely enclosed, without doors. Entrance was gained by crawling up over the rear coupler and through a sort of tunnel under the bunker and through the rear wall of the cab. Immediately upon arrival at Dendron she was put in the car shop and a door cut in each side of the cab, the tunnel being blanked off but not removed. The summer following her arrival, a rather serious fault became painfully evident. There was insufficient lagging between the boiler and the saddle-tank. The feedwater would become so hot that it would flash into steam when hit by live steam in the mixing chamber of the injector, this causing the injector to fail. Although an attempt was made to remedy this condition by the installation of additional lagging, it was never completely overcome.

When built, the engine had been assigned road number "1" and she retained that number when she came to the Surry Lumber Company, replacing the "Steele engine", which was dismantled. All of the parts of the scrapped engine were disposed of except the boiler, that being used to replace a smaller boiler used to generate steam for the pump supplying feedwater to the mill boilers. When the first mill was erected, a small stream running into the Blackwater River was dammed and a pond formed. A small structure was erected to house a boiler and a steam pump from which a pipeline was laid to the storage tanks from which the water was fed to the boilers. Due to the increased size of the mill installation, the installed pumping facilities had proven inadequate, so when the Tanner & Delaney boiler became available, it was used to replace the smaller one. The replacement was quite small, as boilers go, but it was capable of generating more steam at a higher pressure than could the old one.

As the haul from the woods to the mills increased in length, longer trains became necessary to ensure a constant supply of logs, and longer trains required heavier power. The moguls could not handle the increased tonnage. A fourteen by eighteen-inch 2-8-0 with thirty-seven-inch drivers was ordered from Baldwin and was received around September of 1896. This was No. 8, the first of the so-called "jacks", and it replaced No. 4, that engine being given the job of working the mill yard. The heavier engine was a complete success and in May 1898 a second jack, No. 10, arrived, but, due to increased business, the second mogul was retained in main line service.

By now it should be apparent that the tank engines were given the odd numbers and the tender engines received the even numbers. At first glance it would appear that it was a case of woods engines and main line engines but in later years engines carrying even numbers worked in the woods as well as out on the main line.

The first effort to turn the "8" on the Dendron wye ended in disaster for the legs were on too sharp an arc and the center drivers dropped on the ties. It was necessary to completely rebuild the wye, easing the lead-in arcs and spreading the main line switches. The original wye had been put in to turn the engines working the Slabtown line, the tail pointing toward Wakefield, so when the line was extended to the south, they simply built off the tail of the wye.

J. F. Whitley, the engineer running No. 4, had an argument with Wyatt Parsons, one of the colored brakemen, over who was supposed to throw the switches when turning the engine. There were harsh words on both sides but Parsons threw the necessary switches and started walking back to the engine, which had been backed into the tail of the wye and was waiting for him. On his way he acquired a coupling pin and as he passed the cab he heaved it at Whitley. It connected, striking the engineer beside the head and breaking his jaw. Suddenly realizing what he had done, Parsons left town forthwith and made his way to Wakefield, where he lived. After considerable time he came back to Dendron, was arrested, and served time for his action. When it came to its employees, the company had a long memory.

All engines burned wood, although the second jack came fitted to burn coal. Good pine cordwood was both plentiful and cheap. Standing timber that was either too small or unfit for lumber was cut and split into cordwood, and a certain portion of that was set aside for engine fuel. This portion was cut to the proper lengths and stacked beside the track where it remained to dry out and season for as long as possible before being used. Green pine was sure trouble when used as fuel for even the freest of steamers. It would cause the tubes to soot up in short order, and the turpentine caused the soot to cake and harden until it was almost impossible to break it loose with the slice bar.

There was a distinct art to firing with wood, and throwing balks through the fire door was not the way to do it. The donkeys were fired with a single tier of twenty-four-inch sticks; the 4-4-0, the moguls, and the No. 1 from over at Loco used thirty-six-inch sticks in a single tier; but the jacks used twenty-four-inch sticks in three tiers. They were real hogs when it came to fuel. If wood was poorly placed on the grates, a suddenly opened throttle would slam it up against the tube sheet, reducing the draft to practically nil, and unless the throttle was closed and the fireman did some fast work with his hook, he soon had a bad case of low steam on his hands.

Although the company had expected malaria fever to cause a certan amount of sickness, there were only a few cases. However, in the summer of 1895 cholera morbus and its little brother, cholera infantum, broke out and spread rapidly throughout the area. During the hot summer months there were numerous deaths but the malady seemed to die out with the advent of cold weather. During the following summer they took an increasing toll of the population, but then, just as it had the previous year, the first frost seemed to kill the germs and the sickness gradually disappeared. There were scattered cases, but the two related gastric disorders seemed to have run their course.

David Steele had left a son who was also named David. When old enough, he had gone to work for the railway part of the company, worked his way up to the right side of the cab and was eventually assigned No. 2 as his regular engine. He had grown into a man of unusual strength, had married, and was raising a family. He lived in a company house at Dendron and, like most of the other employees, augmented his wage by raising chickens and tending a garden. One Saturday night in mid-July of 1896 he heard a commotion in his back yard, the chickens were squawking and making every effort to escape from the run. Steele picked up a lamp and went out to see what was causing all of the fuss. There was a dog in amongst the chickens, charging back and forth, either after the chickens or trying to get out of the run. A closer inspection disclosed that the dog had apparently gone mad. How he got in was of no importance at the moment but it was imperative that he be disposed of as quickly as possible.

Steele set the lamp down on the steps, moved in, and when the dog charged, grabbed him and literally tore his head off. In the scuffle, Steele was bitten on the face and he was under no illusion as to what had to be done, and quickly. He immediately went to Rogers' home and obtained permission to take No. 2 for a hurried trip to Wakefield where he could receive treatment by a doctor, there being none in Dendron at the time. Steele then routed out Archie Atkinson, his fireman, and between them they soon had sufficient steam blown up to start the engine rolling. As the pressure built up, the speed increased until No. 2 was rocketing towards Wakefield like a runaway comet, the stack showering the sky with live cinders and sparks.

The doctor was seen, the wound treated, and Steele returned home at a more sedate pace. Monday morning he was back at work, apparently none the worse for his experience, and he continued to work for some time. Then, one day he did not report to take out his engine. He sent word that he wasn't feeling too well, and from that day on he felt progressively worse. Steele died on September 27, 1896, from hydrophobia, and he died horribly, as hydrophobia victims tend to do. J. F. Whitley took his place running No. 2 while Archie Atkinson continued to fire.

A rather steep grade north of Wakefield, but south of Anderson's Crossing, was known as Bull Hill as long as anyone can remember and it is only reasonable to assume that there was a reason for it being so called. Persistent questioning finally turned up one man who claimed that he remembered the event which gave the grade its name. If the story is true, and, mind you, it can be just a tale, it must have happened in the middle 1890's.

Anyway, there was this farmer who owned a full grown, pedigreed bull, a huge beast that considered himself master of everything that moved and who ignored no challenge, imagined or otherwise, to do battle in defense of his lordship. To him, the panting, snorting locomotives were so many upstarts who dared to challenge his right to wear the crown and when a train hove into sight, fighting the grade, he promptly went through the fence as though it wasn't there and took a spraddle-legged stance in the middle of the track, pawing and snorting, all set to do battle with his tail up and his head down. The engine crew would blow the whistle, ring the bell, blow the cylinders, yell, cuss, throw things, and raise all the racket they could, but they eventually had to stop the train to keep from hitting the animal. As soon as all of the noise had ceased, the bull would consider the battle won and could be driven back into the pasture. A brakesman with a hefty length of cordwood from the tender, or a brake club, had to stand by while the train dropped back and made another try for the hill. Naturally the bull would come charging again but the swinging club and considerable nerve would hold him in check until the engine had passed. The brakesman would swing up on the last car, thumb his nose at the critter, call him a few choice names and the train would be on its way. As the noise of the train was diminished by distance and the mechanical interloper was obviously in rapid retreat, the bull would quiet down, until the next time. There were times, though, when the bull won and the train was stopped a second time. So far as the crews were concerned, having to make a second, or a third, run for the hill was a nuisance, a blasted nuisance, particularly in wet weather. So far as the farmer was concerned, having to constantly repair the fence was also a nuisance. So, the bull spent more and more time in the barn but every time he was let out to graze, he kept an eye cocked towards the railroad.

Finally, one engineer had all that he could take and made up his mind to do something about it. Whatever was done, had to be done very discreetly for to damage a valuable bull, and deliberately, was to expose the company to a lawsuit and the guilty party to instant dismissal. The engineer figured out just exactly what was to be done and got his crew down behind the tender, so to speak. The headend brakesman was to ride the front sill of the first car and when the engineer bunched the slack, he was to pull the pin, let out a yell to let the engineer know that the pin was out, and stick with the cars as they rolled back down the grade and as far as possible up the opposite one. The other brakemen were to do nothing until the cars ran out of momentum on the far side of the bottom and then they were to tie them down, tight, and hold them there. Thus the cars would be in position to allow the reassembled train to make a run for the grade again. So far as they were concerned, the front link had broken, and there was a broken link provided to prove it. The engineer figured that the fewer who were in on the deal and actually knew what happened, the safer his job was.

With everything set, the train started up Bull Hill, the engine roaring and pounding, working a little harder and making a little more noise than usual. The engineer didn't ease off but let her struggle and silently thought that it would be just his luck for this to be the day that the bull was either in the barn or over on the far side of the hill. Suddenly, there he came, tearing down the hill, through the fence, and into the middle of the track. The engineer's face lit up like a headlight as he let the engine continue to pound up the grade until it was almost on top of the bull. He then shut off, shot a little steam into the engine brake cylinder, just enough to cause the engine to momentarily pause, taking the slack out of the first coupling. The brakesman pulled the pin. The engineer was looking back to be sure that everything went as planned, the brakesman shook the pin at him, the engineer yanked open the throttle, the engine jumped ahead as though someone had stuck a burr under her tail. The surprised bull suddenly found himself airborne to land well clear of the track, slightly hurt and thoroughly shook up, but far from dead. The engineer shut off and drifted back to where his train was waiting for him, a satisfied grin on his face.

From then on the pugnacious, but apparently wiser, bull confined his bellowing and pawing to the far side of the fence. When questioned about the bull's sudden reluctance to challenge the trains and his injuries, the farmer commented that he had undoubtedly hurt himself bustin' through the fence and due to his age he probably wasn't up to much runnin' and pawin' any more. Anyway, everyone was very happy over the change, except the bull.

Some years later Bull Hill witnessed another "derailment", but this time of a legitimate nature, when No. 12 hit a sun kink. Sidney Barker saw the kink as his train headed down the hill but he couldn't get stopped in time and ended up with the engine and one or two cars on the ground. Fortunately, no one was hurt.

West Hope

The supply of standing timber that was considered suitable for cutting into prime lumber was being exhausted at an exceedingly rapid rate and the company had leased and purchased additional timber tracts to the west of Dory, the name by which Boston was now known. When a post office was put there, the department said that the name had to be changed as there was one Boston already in Virginia, so Dory it became. Some of these tracts had been held for some time and for several reasons it was imperative that the timber be removed as soon as possible. Eventually, a total of eleven stands were purchased outright inside of the bow of the Nottoway River in Sussex County, and ten stands northwest of the bow in Prince George and Sussex Counties, the majority of which was in Prince George. In addition to these 21 stands, a huge amount of timber was owned between Dory and Assamoosick Swamp, and a smaller amount between the swamp and the Nottoway River. The timber stands north and northwest of the bow in the river, as well as those immediately inside the bow were purchased as reserves, and frankly, to keep them from falling into the hands of the small, independent loggers.

To reach the timber tracts west of Dory, it was necessary to build a branch line capable of carrying the heaviest equipment and it was during the fall of 1897 that construction was started on what was eventually known as the West Hope Branch. This was to be the main stem from which branches would radiate into the areas to be cut over, and from them would run temporary woods tracks, donkey tracks, into the individual stands. However, there was the restriction of a twenty-mile maximum branch imposed by the charter, and the proposed main branch would certainly exceed that in length.

After construction was actually started, the company's lawyer went to Richmond to see what could legally be done to remove the obstruction and on January 22, 1898, an amendment to Section 4 of the original act was approved. This amendment permitted the railway company to lay any length of track on branch lines over a right of way owned by the Surry Lumber

Company, or any second party, so long as such track was not used for common carrier service. However, it was permissible to operate such trains as were required to support the logging operations, such as those required for the transportation of men and supplies into the woods.

By late 1898 the line was as near completed as any logging line ever was and ran west from Dory, down to and across Assamoosick Swamp, climbed up the far bank and ran through the woods to the lowlands bordering the Nottoway River. The track then crossed the river, just north of the original highway crossing known as Peters' Bridge, swung in a long, ragged arc to the north, passing south and west of Sussex Court House, and terminated on the south side of the Stony Creek-Sussex Court House road. From this main branch innumerable woods tracks eventually radiated in every direction, being put in and taken out as the need arose.

Billy West, the Surry Lumber Company's woods foreman, was given the job of superintending the locating, clearing, and construction of the right of way while a Mr. Richard Scott laid the track under a contract with the railway company. However, before the work was completed, West died quite suddenly while out superintending construction just south of the court house. When he collapsed, he was immediately taken to a local farm house, a doctor summoned, but he died in a very few minutes, apparently from a heart attack. Bob Brown was promoted and it fell his lot to complete the right of way. The main logging camp, located where the railroad terminated at the highway, was laid out and partially completed by West before he died, and when completed by Brown, the company considered it only fitting that it be named for the dead superintendent, so West IIope it became, the name being derived from the fact that it was thought that it was "West's hope" to complete the camp, by a certain date.

Although the entire main branch was not to be of a permanent nature, the procurement of a right of way over privately owned land still had to be made occasionally and there arose the problem of procuring the right of way as cheaply as possible. According to the amendment to the charter, the procurement of the necessary land was a problem for the Surry Lumber Company but no one paid too much attention to who did the dickering. In some cases the land was loaned while in others the owners saw a chance to get their hands on a little hard money and held out for a cash settlement.

One particularly determined owner was a farmer named Parker, known locally as "Doc" Parker, and he owned quite a large amount of land so located that the company could not very well build around it, if they wanted to get out certain stands of timber. Parker wanted rail service and was most emphatic, no rail service, no right of way, but there was the "no common carrier service" clause of both the charter and the amendment. However, there was nothing to prevent giving free service. After a bit of dickering, it was agreed that the company would erect a station convenient to Parker's holdings and free service would be provided as long as the track was in use, free between there and Dory.

Brown was given the job of erecting the promised station and he not only superintended the construction of the eighteen by thirty-foot station and platform, but also erected a commissary and several dwellings for the housing of certain company personnel. When the job was completed, he backed off, surveyed the place as a whole, and remarked, "It is a real chubby little place", so Chub it was named and Chub it remained until it ceased to exist. The village was very much alive two days a week, the two days on which the "free train" made a round trip between there and Dory. The run was actually an extension of the regular morning Scotland Wharf-Dory trip, being made during the time the train would usually lay over at Dory. Except for the wye, the layout at Chub was of no real value to the company. On the other hand, West Hope was strictly a logging camp and consisted of a large blacksmith's repair shop, a commissary, numerous dwellings, a stable, and a run for the mules used in the woods. The shop was located between the legs of the wye used to turn the engines and had a siding leading to it. The leg of the wye running west terminated behind the commissary.

At the time that the right of way was being constructed between Chub and the bridge over the Nottoway River, permission was asked and granted to change the location of the county road so that the trestle could be started further back from the main span. The road was relocated, a crossing put in, and the trestle built, the structure being about seven feet high where it crossed over the old road. One dark night a man came charging down the road on horseback and missed the new turn-off to the left. He gave it no thought until a stringer suddenly caught him in the chest and sent him sailing over the rear end of his mount. There was no doubt that he was hurt and there was also no doubt that the company, or someone, should have erected a barricade across the old road. He brought suit and for a spell it looked as though the company was going to have to mortgage its last spike to settle the claim, but the lawyers got together eventually and settled out of court.

The new West Hope branch crossed the narrow gauge Clare-mont Branch of the Southern Railway, the former Atlantic & Danville extension of Steele's railroad from Spring Grove, between Lumberton and Yale at a point called Griffin Station. This grade crossing was protected by a hefty pole across the logging line on both sides of the Southern. The idea was to force all trains using the S.S.&S. track to come to a full stop before crossing the Claremont line, a broken pole being prima facie evidence that someone had failed to obey the rule. The fireman, or a brakesman, would raise the poles, the train would cross over and a brakesman near the rear would drop off, lower them and snap the locks, then run and climb on again. The poles had to be raised and lowered by someone in the train crew, not by an outsider wishing to be helpful. The switch locks ensured that.

One morning "Sprat" Barker was taking Philip Rogers into the woods on a motor car. It is most probable that there was a heavy ground fog at the time for at times it gets as thick as split pea soup in there on a fall morning, or that their attention was elsewhere. Either way, they didn't see the poles in time to get stopped. The one on the near side of the track wiped them off the car as slick as a whistle. Neither man was hurt, to speak of, other than bruises.

Quite a lot of logging had been done south of West Hope when it was found that time was running out on some of the leased holdings over in Prince George County, to the north. To reach these holdings, the company extended the main branch a total distance of about nine and a half miles, the extra trackage being an extension of the eastern leg of the wye at West Hope. From there the line ran north approximately five and a half miles to the Nottoway River which was crossed, for the second time, by means of a combination truss bridge and trestle, known as Peeples' Bridge, climbed over a ridge, dropped down and crossed Jones' Hole Swamp on a structure known as Zigler's Trestle. This trestle was named for a farmer who owned and worked a few acres of ground nearby, which also explains the naming of Peeples' Bridge.

From Zigler's Trestle the track climbed a fairly long grade towards the Jerusalem Plank Road where a small logging camp, named Straw Hill, was erected. The name was the obvious outgrowth of the construction of the camp on top of a hill in a straw field. The track then ran a degree or two east of north more or less parallel of the Plank Road, and down across a depression known as Cherry Orchard Bottom, through which a small stream ran to Jones' Hole Swamp. As the track climbed out of the depression, it swung an additional degree to the east, crossed the road at a sharp angle, and terminated about a mile and a half from the road crossing. For all intents and purposes, this was the end of the main branch but it was actually continued on around to the west and up over a hill to what was known as Judge Timothy Reeves' farm, the main house standing on the hill to the left, going in. At this point a stub siding was installed and to this siding the jacks brought the empties and picked up the loads, the empties being left standing on the so-called main line.

To get the empties ahead of the engine, the entire train was turned on the Straw Hill wye and the empties shoved to the Reeves farm where the donkeys took over, although the heavier engines frequently eased in over the light track to a trestle at the bottom of the hill west of the farm to take water by means of a syphon installed for watering the donkeys. However, they went in light and at a slow walk. When bringing the loads out of the woods, the donkeys always shoved them back into the stub siding.

From Judge Reeves' farm the donkey tracks ran west down across the trestle to a point near Nine Mile Bridge on the Plank Road. This particular bridge crossed Warwick Swamp and was so named because it was considered to be nine miles from Petersburg, "so close you could smell the ham fryin'", as one of the engineers expressed it. Up until some time ago there was evidence that the line crossed the road and followed the south bank of the swamp for a short distance to the west.

Time has altered nearly all of the landmarks in that particular area. Nine Mile Bridge is no more and unless you know exactly where to look, it is practically impossible to see any trace of of even the main line into the area. Few people living along Route 35 know it as the Jerusalem Plank Road and fewer still who live on Route 637 between 640 and 35 remember that it is the old railroad grade. In Prince George County no one remembers there ever having been a large scale logging activity in the area. A Virginia Department of Conservation & Development plaque concerning the history of Prince George County on Route 35 marks the site, approximately and unwittingly, of Straw Hill. Cherry Orchard Bottom is a slight depression in the same road a short distance to the northwest. The site of Nine Mile Bridge is passed some eight miles south of Petersburg on U. S. Route 301 with no indications that a railroad ever operated within miles of it although someone experienced in such matters can tell that the area has been logged over some time in the distant past. In fact, the present high speed route south no longer crosses the swamp at the former site of the bridge but the old route can still be used. This is definitely more scenic and if one has in mind the comp'ny's activities, certainly more nostalgic.

The settlement at Straw Hill consisted of a mule run and a tar paper shack to house the feed and the stableman. Around and about were other temporary shacks to house a few loggers and drivers, but the settlement's chief claim to a very minor fame was the fact that it straddled the county line between Prince George and Sussex Counties. Back in those days a county line was much more important than it is today.

The tail track of the wye ran down the south side of the Plank Road, to the east, about two and a quarter miles to Belcher's Pond, which isn't there now, then crossed over to the north side of the road, crossed the Cabin Point road, and ended two miles from the point where it crossed to the north side. From this point donkey tracks radiated into the woods to the north and

SURRY LUMBER COMPANY
MANUFACTURERS
KILN DRIED NORTH CAROLINA PINE
DENDRON, VIRGINIA

BALTIMORE, MARYLAND

This picture was used as a letterhead for the Surry Lumber Company stationery and as a large advertising picture to be hung on walls of large offices. The engraver took unlimited liberties when it came to showing the trains, but the layout of the mills is shown quite accurately.

The original No. 2 on a string of the ex-Steele flat cars.
Taken at Surry in 1888.—C. R. Rees

Francis Edwards Waters, president of the railway company and last president of the Surry Lumber Company.

The first of the donkeys, No. 3. That man leaning up against the cab is Herbert Gilliam, who just happened to be there. He was an engineer. The man leaning on the running board and with the oil can is Bob Wellon, the donkey's "driver".

The Mogul No. 4 back in her woodburning
days.—Richard Cole

Engine No. 4 brings a string of loads into the Dendron
yard.—Miss Bertha Hart

No. 2 in Cypress Swamp. Supposedly the first serious accident the company ever had, certainly the first caused by high water.—Miss Bertha
Hart.

Mr. Edward Rogers, General Superintendent of the Surry Lumber Company and the S.S.&S. Railway from 1886 to 1930. The picture was taken in 1888.—Miss Alice C. Rogers

Alvin S. Higgins, master mechanic, purchasing agent, and architect for both the railway and the lumber company. The picture was taken in 1886 when he was 15 years of age, getting married, and already working for the company.

A cordwood train in the Dendron yard headed for the river in 1888. The buildings along the line from the far left to the center are the company commissary, the station, and the office building.—C. R. Rees

The company wharf at Scotland.—Joseph Seward

Engine No. 5 on the pay train at Sedley.—C. B. Owen

The first of the jacks, No. 8, on a log train waiting
for orders.—Miss Bertha Hart

SURRY SUSSEX & SOUTHAMPTON RAILWAY.

F. E. WATERS, President,   Baltimore, Md.
PARKER D. DIX, Vice-President and Treasurer,   ″
M. T. HARGIS, Auditor.   Snow Hill, Md.
J. W. MORRIS, Secretary,   Baltimore, Md.
EDWARD ROGERS, General Superintendent,   Dendron, Va.
J. C. CAUSEY, Assistant Superintendent,   Sedley, Va.
WALTER H. ROGERS, Traffic Mgr. and Claim Agt., Dendron, Va.

No. 3	No. 1	Mls.	March, 1927.	No. 2	No. 4	
			LEAVE] [ARRIVE	... .		
†9 55 A M		0	......Dory......			
10 05 ″		2.0	...... Manry	9 38 A M		
11 15 ″		8.2	....Wakefield....	9 20 ″		
11 45 A M	†6 00 A M	14.8	.....Dendron.....	8 30 ″	3 00 P M	
12 03 P M	6 18 ″	17.0	.....Elberon......	8 08 ″	2 50 ″	
12 12 ″	6 28 ″	19.2	.....Moorings.....	8 00 ″	2 37 ″	
12 25 ″	6 40 ″	22.3	.......Surry.......	7 48 ″	2 25 ″	
1 00 P M	7 00 A M	28.1	....Scotland	†7 25 A M	†2 00 P M	
			ARRIVE] [LEAVE			

† Daily, except Sunday.   STANDARD—*Eastern time.*

Connections.—At Wakefield—With Norfolk & Western Ry. At Scotland—With James River steamers.

This is the way the trains were supposed to run but the only accurate departure time was that of No. 1 from Dendron.

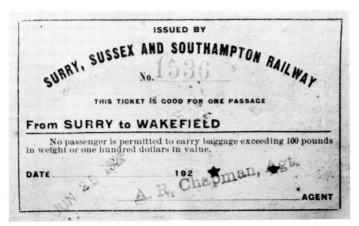

It took one of these, or cash, to get from here to there. The tickets came in books and both the ticket and the stub had to be filled out and signed before the conductor would accept it.

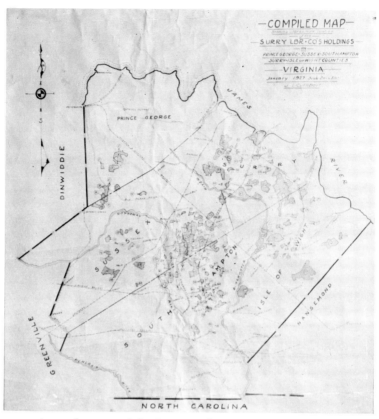

A complete map of the Surry Lumber Company's holdings in
the five counties touched by the railway.

No. 9 and her crew pose for her
picture.—Miss Bertha Hart

P. T. Roach, Superintendent of Logging at West Hope, and
his "transportation".—R. L. Edwards

The woods bosses working out of West Hope line up before going in for
the day's work. You either rode a horse or walked.—M. H. Ferrell

The Surry Lumber Company foremen pose for their picture at West Hope. Standing, left to right, George Muriel, Frank Wilkerson, Edgar West, William Field, Arthur Rollison (engineer), and George Hoggard. Seated, left to right, Peter Roach (in charge), Ed Tom Tench, Willie F. Lewis, Sr., Hugh Taylor, and ———— Harrell. The wide-brimmed hats turned up in front were the style in the woods.—H. E. Ellsworth

The Surry Lumber Company's commissary at West Hope. That is R. L. Edwards, the agent, in the door. A branch of the railway ran behind the store for ease of unloading supplies.—R. L. Edwards

The second of the jacks, the 10, and the first to be delivered fitted for burning coal. The man in the gangway is Floyd Hargrave, the fireman. Archie Atkinson, engineer, leans out of the window. Then we have a man named Parker who was the regular brakesman, and finally Ed Bland, one of the assigned brakemen. Later on Parker fell off a car and got himself hurt.—Mrs. Archie Atkinson

Engine No. 6 is shown working the "new" mill yard at Dendron in 1914.

A picture taken by the Berkley Machine Works of possibly the first of the so-called 600's. It was a crude contraption, to say the least.—Mrs. P. P. Causey

Transporting granite for the Confederate monument up Main Street at Surry, over temporary track from the station to the courthouse square, a tenth of a mile. July 1910.—Joseph Seward

Logs and more logs. The railroad depended on logs as much
as did the lumber company.—Mrs. R. L. Edwards

Possibly one of the largest logs ever cut by the lumber company. The
fact that someone saw fit to photograph it indicates that.

The Second No. 2 on a passenger train entering Wakefield, Va. Note that the engine is still a Vauclain compound. The picture was obviously taken soon after the engine was put in service.

Engine No. 2 of the Mail Train waits for the transfer of passengers and freight to be completed with the steamer *Pocahontas*, down from Richmond, before backing in on the train and leaving for Wakefield, Va., on what was generally known as the "noon train".

northeast but this operation was of a minor nature. The entire main branch was approximately twenty-seven miles in length and was the only trackage west of Dory that was considered to be at least semi-permanent. The entire line as far as Reeves' farm was ballasted, or sanded, as it was called, and kept in a reasonably good condition.

Ballast came from the so-called gravel pit at Chub, located on the south side of the track, just west of the station. A switch led in to temporary trackage which was shifted as the sand was dug out, for it was strictly sand rather than gravel. Flatcars would be shoved out on the track in the pit for loading and as soon as the men had completed that task they would climb on and the cars would be hauled up the line to the point where the ballasting was to be done.

In 1899 "Sam" Atkinson was sent up to Chub with No. 2 to work the ballast train but after he had picked up his loads at Chub and started up the grade west of the river bridge, he found that the little eight-wheeler was just too light for the work for she couldn't even get her train up out of the bottom. He then dropped back to Chub and called Dendron, explaining the trouble. He was told to bring in his engine and pick up No. 4, which he did, and after that there was no more trouble, at least so far as making the grades was concerned.

Sanding the track, as it was called, was a constant procedure for sand washed badly. When the branch was first built, the track was laid on the bare ground and the ballasting had to be done after the line was in use. The flatcars used in the ballast train had a hole cut through the decking midway of their length. When a car was to be loaded, the hole was covered with a steel plate and the sand piled over it. Upon reaching the point where sanding was to begin, the plate was fished up from under the sand, four men would grab hold of as many shovels and get set to start shoveling, two at the leading edge of the hole through the deck and two at the front end of the car. As the train moved slowly forward, the four men shoveled the sand down between the rails, piling it up over the ties. As soon as all of the sand forward of the hole had been unloaded, the two men working over the forward coupling would move back to the rear of the hole and the other two men began tossing sand over the rear coupling, between the cars. Each car was relieved of its load in the same manner until the whole train had been unloaded.

When unloading the sand, no attempt was made to spread it, just to get it down between the rails. Spreading it was something else. The trailing truck of the last car was naturally the last one to be relieved of its burden, so, a tie, or a small log, was laid across the track in front of the leading pair of wheels of that truck. As the train moved slowly ahead, the wheels shoved the tie in front of them, leveling off the sand to the tops of the rails. Of course, once in a while a tie would jam at a rail joint and the leading pair of wheels would climb over it, but that made little difference as long as it tore loose and slid along the rails in front of the rear pair. Sure, ever so often the pair of wheels would climb over the tie and fail to drop back on the rails, but a derailed flatcar was nothing to get unhappy about. A small log gave the least trouble, so far as jamming was concerned, but it also had a tendency to roll up over the pile of sand and so didn't work so well. Ties were therefore used when one was available and the man in charge generally saw to it that one was.

This method of sanding the track was not confined to the West Hope Branch but was employed over the entire system. After the track was sanded for the first time, it was generally leveled, square-nosed shovels being used to drive the sand down under the ties. The only thing that recommended the use of sand was the fact that it was both free and plentiful. Woods tracks got no sanding and only enough leveling to make fairly sure that the wheels would stay on the rails.

If a piece of swampy ground was to be crossed, small pine trees were felled and the entire trunk, or sections about ten to twelve feet in length, would be used in place of regular ties, thus distributing the weight of a train over more surface. If a small stream was to be crossed by a temporary track, two, or more, tree trunks would be used as stringers and the ties laid on them. Occasionally, such temporary trestles, or bridges, had to be supported by cribbing to prevent them from sagging too much, or even breaking in two, under the weight of a train, but this was not a general practice. Woods tracks which were expected to be in use for less than a year, and most were, received no attention after being laid unless they reached a point where they would no longer support a donkey.

When it had become necessary to transfer the logging activities from south of West Hope to up in Prince George County, the area abandoned had not been completely cut over. In a way this was advantageous as it actually increased the yield per acre by allowing the younger trees to mature before the loggers worked back to them. You might say that the company unintentionally practiced the modern method of tree farming, something that was completely unthought of at that time, certainly by the Surry Lumber Company.

A goodly number of the donkey tracks beyond Straw Hill went into some of the most impossible places imaginable. Getting in was comparatively easy for the grade was generally descending, dropping down into swamps or lowlands, but getting out was the problem. There were times when getting out a single load was a real production. If the load was too heavy, or the grade a little too steep, or the rails a little greasy, the donkey driver would make one or two tries but if he couldn't see that he was getting anywhere, he would lean on his whistle cord and the other donkeys working the tract would come running. Then, all coupled together, they would grab hold of the loads and grunt and strain, and blow all the leaves and squirrels off the overhead branches, but the loads would eventually come creaking and groaning up out of the woods.

Those donkey tracks were slapped down on the bare ground with no thought of grade, unless the ties slid down the hill when dropped in place. Any place where a tie would stay wasn't too steep for a donkey to climb, or so was the rule-of-thumb when laying such track. A story is told of a line built off the main branch some years later just west of the Chub trestle and which ran from here to there in a more or less straight line. When the job was done, a donkey was turned in the gate and started up over the line to see if it was more or less laid to gauge and to see if there were any dangerously soft spots in the line. The donkey did all right until she reached a grade over which the track had been built, and there she stuck. The track gang had had no trouble building the track, so why couldn't the en-

gine get over the hill? Even with a running start, and running
light, she just couldn't get up over the hump. In disgust
the track gang dismantled that particular section and relaid it,
around the hill.

It must have been a beautiful sight to see when the donkeys
teamed up and came blasting up out of the woods with six or
eight loads. Ever so often they would haul the loads all the way
to West Hope when it was time to knock off, and it was then that
they really put on a show. It is doubtful if anyone ever really
appreciated the experience of driving a donkey down a grade
as fast as he dared go to insure making the opposing grade, but
the noise and motion of two or three of those little engines charging up a steep grade would make glad the heart of any retired
railroad man. So far as we know, the longest such train was
handled by the 3, 5, and 7, and consisted of eighteen loads, the
run terminating at West Hope where the loads were turned over
to a jack for the rest of the run to Dendron. How many times
they scared teams half to death as they came blasting up
through Cherry Orchard Bottom, we will never know, but the
mental picture of such a train is something to remember, particularly when each engine dug in its toes as the slack ran out
and added its beat of power to the symphony of steam.

Those little nine-tonners were light on their feet and their
ability to drag heavy tonnage up steep grades was limited, but
they were capable of doing surprisingly well when driven by
an experienced hand. They were fairly fast although speed
was the last thing Baldwin had in mind when the engines were
designed. When in service, none of the engineers were fool
enough to try racing over woods tracks, but they didn't drag
their feet, either. When an engineer got overly cautious on a
piece of light and particularly rough track, and didn't make the
time it was thought he should, the woods boss would loudly and
profanely remind him that those wheels were round and that
he was being paid to roll them.

Running out on the main line, or the main branch line, was
a different story. Some of the drivers liked to let their donkeys
have their head, to "sort of blow the soot out of the stack", and
some boasted that a donkey could do a mile a minute with ease.
It is extremely doubtful if any of them ever actually worked

their engine up to such speed but the fact that they were built close to the ground and that the noise of the exhaust quickly reached a roar because of the low drivers, gave the impression of speed when actually it did not exist. All of the donkeys had one bad fault and that was their tendency to hunt rather violently at speed. When the front end began to snap from side to side, you had to shut off and slow down, right then, or she was apt to jump the track and take off through the bushes like a scared rabbit.

During a conversation with Emmett Williams, who ran No. 3 until he quit the company late in 1903, a comment was made that it appeared that his engine was a jinx for she seemed to be always in trouble. He bristled indignantly and said, "Oh, I don't know about that!" and lapsed into an indignant silence. Possibly that particular donkey wasn't involved in any more accidents than any of the others, it just seemed so, for she was the oldest of the lot and had more time to get into trouble. The little woods engines operated under the most unbelievably adverse conditions and hence were prone to get into trouble frequently. Such little things as derailments were so commonplace they were completely ignored. A day in the woods during which one did not occur was something to talk about, the frequency being proven by the Baldwin Reorder Book which shows a constant flow of orders for cylinder cocks, and the fact that the donkeys ran without cylinder jackets. It just wasn't worth the expense and trouble to keep replacing them.

Willie Elmore was one of those human squirrels called brakemen, who scampered over the loaded log cars to set the brakes when the engineer called for them. When everything was running as it should, the brakemen scattered along the train had little, if anything, to do and generally rode perched on top of a load of logs. Riding on the ends of the cars between the loads was downright dangerous for if the engineer suddenly bunched the slack for some reason, the loads could shift and anyone caught down there would be crushed.

Willie was riding a load some 22 cars back from the engine while J. J. Inghram, with No. 8, was batting the breeze that cold morning in March of 1900. The train came swaying and bouncing down the line towards the last sharp curve before entering the tangent leading to the wye at Dory. As the cars entered the curve, the jouncing and centrifugal force dislodged the top log on the car in front of the one on which Willie was riding. The log rolled off the top of the load to the outside of the curve, nosing down as it fell. When the end hit the ground, it whipped around, picking Willie off his perch like a hawk scooping a sparrow off a branch, and apparently killing him instantly. It was the custom as a train entered a curve for the fireman to lean out of the gangway and watch the cars to make sure that they were all still coupled together and on the track, so he saw what took place. The train was brought to a stop as quickly as possible and the entire crew ran back to do what they could but Willie was beyond human help. Thus that particular bend in the track became known as Elmore's Curve.

Between Dory and Straw Hill there were five trestles over seventy-five feet in length. The first one west of Dory was over Assamoosick Swamp, was 202 feet long, and was at Mile Post 19, or four miles west of Dory. All mileage was computed from Dendron which means that you had to be quite definite in stating that you were either north or south of Dendron when reporting in. The second structure was a combination trestle and bridge 3,119 feet long which carried the track over the lowlands to the east of the stream and over the Nottoway River, eight miles west of Dory. This crossing was generally referred to as Nottoway Trestle although it occasionally took the name of the highway bridge, Peters' Bridge. The bridge was a wooden truss and spanned the channel down which the water normally flowed, while the trestle spanned the lowlands that were subject to frequent flooding although they were planted in corn year after year.

The third trestle was across Hunting Quarter Branch, fifteen miles west of Dory and about three-quarters of a mile north of the Double-barreled Road Crossing. This trestle, which actually carried the track over a swamp in which there was practically no running water, was 161 feet long. The fourth structure, called Peeples' Bridge, was twenty-three miles from Dory and also spanned the Nottoway. Like Nottoway Trestle, Peeples' Bridge was a combination truss bridge and trestle but only 599 feet long and differed from the structure at the first crossing in that the bridge and trestle were separated by a short dirt fill at the north end of the bridge. Neither truss bridge was over 250 feet long.

The final trestle was 25½ miles from Dory and was over Jones' Hole Swamp which, as we have already stated, fed into Belcher's Pond and eventually into the river near Freeman's Bridge. This was a comparatively short trestle, only 97 feet in length, and known as Zigler's Trestle.

Irrespective of the stories that one hears about burned bridges and the wrecks that were caused by them, the company had very little trouble with fire damaging such structures. Nottoway Trestle caught once from hot coals dropped by a passing engine but the watchman extinguished the blaze with water from barrels placed along the structure for that purpose before any real damage was done. Even so, the structure was closed to traffic until carpenters could be brought out from Dendron and the burned timbers replaced.

Levi Whitney was watchman and pumpman at Nottoway Trestle for a time but he had an aggravating habit of getting dead drunk and letting the tank run dry. The crews would revert to the former method of watering up there and drop a syphon hose into the river, but Levi finally staged the granddaddy of all drunks, which was too much. Gus Ellis came through with his train, found the tank dry, and Levi ossified. It wasn't the first time that Gus had found the tank empty but this time he decided to do something about it. For some time he tried to wake Levi but all he was able to get out of him was a few grunts and snorts. Gus gave up but he made up his mind that Levi was going to be taught a lesson he wouldn't forget. When he reached West Hope he reported, in a rather excited voice, that he had found Levi dead, omitting the drunk part. Naturally, the top brass and the law descended on the Nottoway pump house from all directions. When it was found that Levi was merely staging one of his periodic drunks, everyone was mad at everyone else, but Levi was yanked off the job and eventually ended up at Central Hill on the branch by that name, which, in later years was built east from Surry. When the brass finally got around to asking Gus why he had reported Levi dead when he was only drunk again, Gus replied that he had tried to find signs of life in him but couldn't, so he thought he must be dead.

John Turner took Levi's place, but he, too, had the habit of hitting the jug and during one of his jags he got his overalls caught in the exposed pump gears. He was in a fair way of getting himself chewed up when pure fright sobered him and he thought of dropping his knife in the gears as he couldn't reach the controls of the gasoline engine which drove the pump. There was a powerful lot of crunching but the idea worked and he got free, but it put the pump out of service for several days.

Both the tank and the pump house were built out on the trestle, the pump drawing its water through a long pipe from the river and it was the only tank on the branch although there was a syphon at Assamoosick Swamp as well as one at Nine Mile Bridge. All of the engines were fitted with steam syphons and hose for filling their tanks at any place where fairly clean water was available, so tanks were not too important.

Ev'ryday Railroadin'

The year 1899 is remembered as the year of the big snow, or the year of the big freeze, depending entirely on who is doing the remembering. Irrespective of anything else, it was a downright severe winter, on a par with that of early '93. In mid-January a mass of polar air swept down from the nor'west and tumbled the mercury well below the freezing mark, and held it there. The sap in the trees froze solid, making it impossible to log for the trunks of the trees were as hard as marble and the saws made no impression on them. During the nights it sounded as though a hunting party was out in the woods taking potshots at shadows for as the sap in the trees froze, it expanded, and the trunks would burst with a loud report. During the day other noises covered that issuing from the woods but they continued, day and night. The mills closed as the log supply diminished. The train crews were pulled out of service as the supply of logs already cut in the woods was exhausted, and although the mail train continued to run, it had the road to itself. Oldsters began to talk of it being the hardest cold snap they had ever experienced.

By Saturday morning, the 11th of February, the cold had moderated slightly and the sky had turned grey. By noon it was snowing. When the mail train tied up for the day the ground was white and snow was accumulating in the bottoms. All that night, all day Sunday, all Sunday night, and all day Monday and Monday night it snowed steadily and hard. Monday not a wheel turned. Tuesday morning the snow showed signs of letting up and it appeared that the worst was over, but a wind had begun to blow and the snow to drift, piling up in deep drifts wherever some obstruction caused the wind to drop it. Cuts and ditches had disappeared along the right of way except in protected places and only occasionally were the rails left exposed where the wind had swept the snow before it. It was realized that the first crew out would most certainly run into trouble but just how bad it was going to be, no one actually knew.

No. 2 was made ready to take out the regular mail run but on this particular day it was to consist of the eight-wheeler and the coach, nothing more. Willie Doyle was the engineer, Richard Cole was firing, Frank Eppes was braking, and Cap'm W. L. Gladden was the conductor. The train left Dendron on time and made out fairly well until it entered a small cut in Scotland Field, just before reaching the switchback down the bluff to the river, and there it stuck tight, the snow reaching right up to the running boards of the engine. It was later ascertained that the snow averaged two feet on the level and that No. 2 had stuck in about five feet of the fluffy white stuff.

After making several attempts to back free of the cut, Doyle gave up and Cap'm Gladden plowed his way down to the wharf from where he called Dendron for help. By some odd fact, the 'phone line was still in service. Rogers must have surmised that the mail train would run into trouble for he had stuck close to the 'phone and as soon as the call came through, he ordered No. 8 made ready for the run north to assist No. 2. While steam was being blown up, two by ten-inch boards were bolted to the cowcatcher, forming a crude snow plow. When the engine was ready, Rogers told John Inghram to take her out as it was his regular engine and he could possibly get more out of her than anyone else when the going got rough. Most of the idle crews had gathered at the shop on the chance that there would be some sort of employment for them. If they didn't work, they didn't get paid and the long period of enforced idleness had already cut heavily into their next pay envelope. Rogers put them all to work loading shovels, picks, and wrecking tackle onto a deck car which was tacked on behind the engine. Rogers and as many men as possible jammed themselves into the cab and the train left town at about 10 a.m.

They made very good time as far as Surry. When No. 2 had passed over the street crossing at the north end of the station, it had swept it clean of snow, exposing the collected water underneath, which promptly froze. As more water ran downhill under the snow from up the street, it in turn froze when it reached the exposed crossing, gradually building up the ice until it completely covered the rails. When No. 8 rode up on the ice she swerved and headed for the ditch, which was filled to the top with snow, but Inghram managed to get stopped with only the engine and tender off the rails. Rogers was the first one off but he chose the wrong side and when he dropped down off the engine step he went into the ditch, the engine being that close to it. He went right down up to his arm pits, his long overcoat billowing out on top of the snow. Only his ego suffered injury, fortunately, but the rest of the men went out of the opposite gangway.

A few attempts were made to rerail the engine and tender but she refused to ease back over the ice and Inghram didn't dare take too many chances due to the fact that she was too close to the ditch and any jockeying might cause her to slide into it. The men stood around wondering what to do. It was impossible to bring out a third engine for Rogers had brought all of the available men with him and there was no one left at Dendron who he felt could be trusted with a locomotive under the prevailing conditions.

In the meantime, No. 2 was running low on water. None of the crew had any idea when the relief train would arrive but it was felt that some effort should be made to keep a little water in the tank. Enough buckets were rounded up here and there to supply each member of the crew with one or two and they began carrying water across Scotland Field from a spring owned by John Brown, a farmer. It was slow, disheartening work, but there wasn't enough pressure left to blow steam back into the tank and melt any snow that might be shoveled in. To conserve fuel the fire had been allowed to get low, thus reducing the temperature of the boiler water below the evaporation point.

Conditions at Surry remained stagnant until around noon when John Sam Gale came down the road, driving his string of sixteen mules, all hitched together to form a single team, from his logging operation over on Swann's Point. The crossing was blocked so he pulled up to see what was going on. After looking over the situation and being told why the engine couldn't be moved under its own power, he allowed that his team could haul the train back up over the crossing and Rogers was perfectly willing to let him prove it. The two men knew each other personally, so the idea of any sort of payment for services to be rendered was considered ridiculous. The team was hitched to the rear coupler of the deck car, Sam Gale began to talk to his team as though they were so many men and had to be told exactly what was expected of them, and then he walked ahead of them slowly. The harness tightened and the team began to pull. The train began to move. Only then did Inghram dare feed a little steam to the cylinders. Back over the crossing they went and once clear of the ice, rerailing the equipment was no problem at all. The team went on its way and the men got busy chopping out the ice. When the crossing had been cleared, the train ran on down to the stalled mail train, where it arrived about mid-afternoon. They hadn't been able to get away from the court house until about 2 p.m.

The mail train engine was in a bad way for not only had the water-carrying been none too successful, but the fuel was running low. No. 8 was run down behind the passenger car and coupled to it. After considerable snorting and pawing, the mail train was hauled free and the men went to work shoveling most of the snow out of the cut while the crew of No. 2 began blowing up steam with the remaining fuel and water. As soon as there was a small head of steam, and with the help of No. 8, the mail train was shoved to the wye and turned. After considerable juggling both trains were made into one with No. 8 leading, and a start made for home. By the time No. 8 was ready to roll, No. 2 was practically dead, the fuel and water being exhausted.

The wind was blowing a gale and although it had stopped snowing, the dry snow was drifting rapidly and it was found that all of the cuts had drifted full again after the relief train had come through. In some cases new drifts had been built across the track. Progress was slow but steady until the cut through Moody's Field was reached, about a mile north of the Surry station, and there the train stuck fast. Inghram did his best to break free but the weight of the train had jammed the engine into the snow-filled cut like a cork into a bottle. Liberal use of sand in an effort to gain traction did nothing but cause the spinning drivers to grind dishes in the railheads. These depressions were very much in evidence until the light iron was replaced by heavier steel some time later. After several fruitless attempts to break free, and finding that the drifting snow was rapidly making conditions worse, the men again went to work with the shovels, concentrating on getting the snow away from around the running gear and clearing the track behind the train so that it could be backed out of the cut. Finally it was possible to back clear and the men began to cut into the choked cut, not trying to remove all of the snow but enough to let the train ram through. The engine was cut off the train and went to work on the drift. After several attempts it broke through, they put the train back together, the men wearily climbed into the coach, and the run was continued on to Surry.

By the time the train had reached the court house, the sun had set, the sky being practically clear, and the wind had dropped considerably but it was still very cold. This time Inghram stopped just clear of the crossing to be sure that it hadn't iced up again. It had, but was soon chopped clear of ice and the train continued on its way. Between Surry and Dendron the wind had erased all indications of the train having passed that way earlier in the day but no real trouble was experienced, the improvised snow plow taking care of the drifts quite nicely, and they were able to reach Dendron by dark.

The thought of having to do all of that digging over again the next morning because of the wind and the drifting snow wasn't at all pleasant but the wind continued to drop and the amount of driftage during the night was negligible. Clearing the line south of Dendron required a certain amount of work but after being broken out by the improvised snow plow, the mail train was able to get through without any trouble and from the 15th on regular service was maintained as far as Wakefield. Although the main line was back in service and the mail train was running, it was still some time before it was possible to start cutting timber again because of the cold.

About June of the same year, 1899, the mail train jumped the track in Judkin's Bottom, just north of the point where No. 8 stalled coming back to Surry, and everything ended up on the ground. It happened about noon and the wreck was blamed on a broken rail. They were stepping right along when it happened, running for the opposing grade which was short but steep, so there was no chance of getting stopped. The engine went off into a convenient field and the freight cars jackstrawed behind her. The passenger car ended up leaning against a large tree like a tired mule and although everyone was pretty well shook up, no one was badly hurt, or even hurt.

There is a tale of a derailment in which one of the boxcars that turned over contained several cases of bottled-in-bond whiskey. It was inevitable that some of the bottles were broken but when they got around to tallying the collected bottle necks against the empty sections of the wooden cases, there were not enough necks to go around. No matter how carefully they searched, not another one could be found. It was a situation that arose at nearly every wreck in which bottled spirits were involved, this inexplicable loss of bottle necks.

Although we talk of wrecks and near-wrecks, it must not be thought for one instant that life on the "Three S's" consisted of one hazardous experience after another. Nothing could be further from the truth. All roads had wrecks, and the worse the wreck the more indelibly it is impressed on the minds of the men. That is what they remember, year after year. No one ever remembers the clear, spring-like days when everything was running as it should, and yet, that is exactly the way it was most of the time, out on the main line. We have to ignore the woods branches for they were more a part of the logging operation than of the actual railroad. The S.S.&S. was no better, or no worse than a hundred other narrow gauge lines throughout the East. It was built to haul logs and lumber and that is exactly what it did, six days a week. It was a rough line, the light rail soon being bent by the loads to conform to the configuration of the right-of-way. The sand ballast looked nice when first put in place but that which remained after the first really hard rain was soon mixed with the soil. The constant up and down movement of the ties under the passing weight of the wheels left the track as springy as a mattress. Sidings, of course, were only a place to temporarily leave equipment, except at Dendron where they were constantly in use, and it made little difference how rough they were, as long as an engine could ease a load in and get out without being derailed. When the line was originally built, stub switches with ground throws were installed throughout. Target stands were not installed as they were considered to be a hazard to personnel, but by 1900 practically all of the stub switches had disappeared and standard switch points with target stands had been installed. In the mill yard, they stuck to ground throws, though.

Glebe Switch was put in around 1898 and was located just south of Surry. The line from it swung to the west in a long arc, crossed the road to Dendron at a ninety-degree angle and continued straight into the woods, crossing the old stage road, now Route 10, between Spring Grove and Surry at about a forty-five-degree angle a mile and a half from the point where the Dendron road cut off the stage road. This branch terminated some four or five miles further along in the general direction of Claremont and the far end of this line switched back and forth in the woods like the tail of a fly-bitten mule. Both lumber-logs and cordwood came out of there.

Between Moorings and Elberon, two branches ran to the west, the first one runing in a more or less northerly direction, crossed Pigeonroost Swamp, shortened locally to Pigeon Swamp, and ran parallel to the stage road for a considerable distance. Like the line from Glebe Switch, the upper part of the line was moved about and eventually crossed the road approximately five miles from the Spring Grove-Dendron fork. It terminated much nearer Claremont than did the line from Glebe Switch.

The second of the two lines cut off the main line a short distance south of the first and ran practically straight into the woods. This line went in during the early 1890's and was used to bring out cordwood exclusively, being known as the Poplar Spring Branch, the name being taken from a large, cool spring near the upper end of the line. It was during the time that this line was in service that the Surry Lumber Company's two-master HESTER WATERS sailed regularly between Scotland Wharf and Baltimore, hauling cordwood and lumber. South of Elberon was a branch to the east, put in to haul out timber belonging to a man named Spratley and, like the Poplar Spring line, was a comparatively short spur.

South of Dendron, just across the Blackwater River trestle, there was a line running to the southeast known as Pond's Spur. A short distance from the main line switch the spur split, the track to the right terminating in a gravel pit within sight of the main line, in fact, right beside it, and the one to the left bearing off into the woods for about a mile. In all cases, the switch points of the branches faced north, making it necessary for all trains working north from Dendron to back in. And, just to keep the matter of ballast straight, the gravel in that pit was nothing more than coarse sand, just like that out of the Chub pit.

This backing in was partially the cause of a rather serious incident at Glebe Switch in 1901. Sam Atkinson was to shove a string of empty deck cars into the branch and Eddie Height, a brakesman, dropped off to open the gate as the train ran past the switch, preparatory to backing in. The last car cleared, the brakesman threw the lever over and waved the engineer to come on back. As the trucks of the first car cleared the points, Eddie swung the lever over again, turning the second car down the main line. Suddenly, things began to happen. Eddie backed away from the switch in alarm, stumbled, fell flat in a hole left when dirt was removed to level the switch stand, just as a car reared up, spun over, and slammed down on top of him, exactly like swatting a fly.

The fireman had been looking back at the time, watching Eddie and the cars. When he saw the flats begin to go everywhere except up the branch, he let out a yell and Sam started getting stopped as quickly as possible, so, when the flats went wild and the car slapped down on top of Eddie, the engine was practically standing still. Sam and his fireman dropped off and ran back to see what they could do for the brakesman but felt sure that he was far removed from any human help. While they were looking over the wreckage which covered Eddie's "body", Sam remarked, "Well, it sure looks like they got Eddie", but out from under the mess came an answer, "I'm all right, Mister Atkinson", and he was. When they got him out from under the pile of wreckage he was several shades lighter and shaking, but unhurt. Eddie never could explain why he threw that switch but it has happened before and will undoubtedly happen again, as long as switches are manually operated.

At the height of the logging activity up on the West Hope branch, an average of four trains a day of twenty-five to thirty loads were brought down to the mill. In the early morning, the first train up through Cherry Orchard Bottom was usually the labor train, hauled by one of the woods engines, and then the donkeys running light. There were generally three, one on the labor train and two light, and right behind them came a jack hauling a string of empty log cars. This engine would drop its string of cars, pick up such loads as had been left over from the night before and set around until its tonnage could be filled out. Then, back to Dendron. The last train of logs arrived at Dendron in the late afternoon or early evening. In the early evening the labor train would bring the men out of the woods and after it was clear, the donkeys would file out. These would run only as far as the camp serving the area at the time. Actually, there was no hard and fast rule as to what was to be the first in and the last out. They ran as convenient and as necessary to get the men and donkeys in the woods at a certain time, to get them out at the end of the day, to keep the loaders supplied with empty log cars, and the mill supplied with logs. The most important of these, was of course, to keep the mills supplied and that governed the operations in the woods.

Sam Atkinson's brother, Archie, was bringing No. 1, the Loco engine, back to Dendron from Surry, running tank first, or bunker first, it being a saddle-tank, when just after crossing the Sexton trestle they met a load of logs running free after getting away up at the mill. That was a right sharp grade leading down to the trestle and the load was running right along. There wasn't time to do anything but shut off and dive out of the gangway before the load of logs piled into the rear end, completely wrecking the bunker and cab. Neither of the men were badly hurt, mainly scratched up, but the donkey was a mess.

It had been raining hard all of that day in February 1903, pouring in torrents. It wasn't too cold, certainly not down to freezing, but there was a promise of cold to come as the wind was whipping around into the nor'west. The rain continued on through the night but by the early morning of the second day a watery sun was trying to break through the overcast. The wind was still blowing and it was getting colder, but still above freezing. The labor train left West Hope for the woods at the usual time for rain never stopped them from cutting timber, and when they crossed Peeples' Bridge it was noticed that the river was piling debris against the bents. The accumulation was beginning to put quite a strain on the structure. On reaching Straw Hill, the engineer called Dendron and reported the accumulation and the rising water. Rogers quickly got together a crew, armed them with long poles, and loaded them on the first thing going south to Dory. Before leaving he called Chub and told Emmett Williams, the engineer on No. 3, to meet them with his engine for the run to the bridge.

Williams picked up Rogers and his gang, ran to within a quarter of a mile of the threatened bridge and left his engine setting on the main line. The men continued on by means of a pump car as water was beginning to seep between the ties on the approach to the bridge and it was doubtful if the fill would support the donkey. During the rest of the morning the men poled debris between the bents while the water continued to slowly rise. The seepage turned into a steady rush of water and the track disappeared beneath the surface. No one paid too much attention to it but around noon the force of the water suddenly flipped over the track, turning it over like a picket fence, swept out the dirt fill, and took out the telephone line. Poles were hurriedly dropped as the men scrambled for safety. Some were poor swimmers and those who could helped those who could not. One man who showed some reluctance to trust himself to the flood was approached by another who offered to help him, but to his surprise the uncertain one pulled his watch out of his pocket and handed it to him as he said, "Never mind me, just see that my watch doesn't get wet." The watch was duely transported to high ground while the owner managed to flounder across the deep portion of the washout as best he could. People do funny things under stress.

Although the men in the woods realized that something was wrong, they continued to cut timber until it was time to return to camp. The fact that the telephone had gone out was nothing new for the thing was always doing that, and the fact that nothing had come up from West Hope could easily be explained by a derailment. The fact that they had lost all contact with their main camp was nothing to get upset about.

By the time the labor train was ready to leave, it was beginning to get dark and the headlight was lit. The swamp under Zigler's Trestle was full and the men began to wonder about the river. When the train pitched over the rise and headed down towards Peeples' Bridge, the engineer shut off, put his valve gear in reverse and let the pressure hold her. He wanted to be very sure that he could get stopped if there suddenly appeared nothing but water in front of him. They eased out over the trestle which felt a little soft but not too bad. It was still above water although the water was so close to the ties it looked as though the whole structure was floating. The little island between the trestle and the bridge was still there but just then the headlight reached across the truss bridge and showed nothing at the far end but rushing water. The rails curved sharply downstream and disappeared beneath the surface. The train was stopped immediately with the cars standing on the trestle and the engine partly on the short fill between trestle and bridge, and partly on the bridge. The first idea was to back off the structure and get back to solid ground but that part of the trestle over which they had come suddenly collapsed and down the river it went.

For a time the weight of the cars held down the remaining bents of the trestle but gradually the pressure on them increased to the point where they began to lean and it was evident that they, too, would soon break free. Although the donkey was safe setting as it was, it never dawned on anyone to move the entire train out on the truss where it would have been safe. They were in a ticklish position and any movement appeared to be too dangerous to try. The idea of going into that cold, rushing water wasn't at all appealing but as it looked as though the entire structure would go out at any moment, and as the trestle under the cars had begun to settle and slew around, the logical thing to do seemed to be to get free as quickly as possible. One brave, or thoroughly frightened, soul went overboard. That was all it required to start a mass exodus. Everyone joined the birds, or the fish, as the case may be, and got free before the boxcar and the flat, which comprised the entire train, broke loose from the engine and disappeared with the rest of the trestle, leaving the donkey perched out in the middle of the rushing flood. The fact that it was dark and nothing could be seen did nothing to quiet the nerves of the engine crew and there was no assurance that the engine would stay where she was, so they took to the water with the rest of the men.

There were several unintentional heroics that evening for a number of the men couldn't swim a stroke. Willie King, a burly individual, hit the water without giving the fact that he could not swim a second thought and was in a fair way of being drowned when P. T. Roach, the camp superintendent at West Hope, and a man half his size, saw his predicament and hauled him ashore. The wonder is that when noses were counted, every man was found to be safe. When Roach went into the water, he was wearing his slicker, and when he crawled up the bank, he was still wearing it. The steadily increasing cold quickly froze it stiff. When he managed to reach his home at West Hope, he stood it up on the porch and the next morning it was still standing there, still frozen stiff.

The river dropped back to nearly normal as quickly as it had risen, that being the nature of rivers in that section, and the next day the company had a crew dumping fill into the washout. In the meantime carpenters were busy assembling new bents, cutting stringers, and preparing to replace the trestle. The truss bridge was quickly made accessible and the stranded donkey hauled out of the way. Then the real work began. At the time the trestle was constructed, foundation piling was driven to support the bents and naturally these piles remained in place, the flood having swept away the bents set on top of them. To replace a trestle it was only necessary to erect new bents on the old piling which had been cut off just above the ground, brace the bents, put in stringers, lay the ties and rails, and it was ready for service. So, three days after the washaway, the donkey stranded up in the woods was sent home, others took its place, and logging continued as before. You might say that it was all part of the day's work.

Personnel

Although men off other railroads occasionally wandered into Dendron looking for work, they quickly found that running trains on the Three S's wasn't exactly like running them on the larger roads, and soon wandered on again. If they remained they had to learn all over again for there was something to it other than pulling a throttle or hitting the fire door with a stick of wood. Railroading by the seat of their pants, the company telephone, and just plain common sense was a lot different from operating by a set of hard and fast rules. There was no rule book on the narrow gauge and only one general rule. If in doubt, wait.

Some of the men literally grew up with the railroad and the method of operation came naturally to them. They had begun at the beginning when everyone knew where the trains were at any time of the day, or where they were supposed to be. As more trains were added, they simply learned a little more, and thought nothing of it. If you lost track of something, there were the telephones scattered along the line. Call Dendron and ask. However, if there was no telephone handy, you took a chance and smoked through until you found one. But, of course, there was that one general rule. If in doubt, wait.

Waiting wasn't always convenient, though; that waiting for something that might never arrive. Maybe the opposing train was waiting for you. Maybe, but you took a chance. Except in case of a major accident, it was up to the crew to get their train over the road, and such things as derailments, broken rails, or minor mechanical failures were not considered to be major accidents.

The mill hands worked by the mill whistle but the men on the railroad worked as necessary to keep the saws humming. The first crew left Dendron in the very early morning, long before the mill hands were up, but they were home while the mills were still busy. Working on the railroad had its compensations as well as its dangers. The line was undoubtedly as safe as any logging line in the East, which isn't saying much at best. Many of the men really enjoyed working on the railroad, the freedom from rules, the being on their own, while others worked on it because it was a way of making a living. Irrespective of why they were there, there is no doubt that they were real railroaders in every sense of the word. Never sell the logging railroader short for he was a breed found nowhere else.

The earliest representatives of the Surry Lumber Company to be seen in Surry County, as has already been mentioned, was Edward Rogers and his two companions who rode through the area between Spring Grove and Mussel Fork over the proposed route of the extension of Steele's tramway. The untimely death of Steele has already been recounted. Richard Scott was made superintendent in charge of getting out cordwood and as late as 1895 he resided with Jesse Hobson, a section foreman. There were two of the Scotts, John and Richard, and both quit the company and went to work for the Camp brothers who were rapidly building a small logging outfit into what became known as the Camp Manufacturing Company at Franklin, Virginia.

Hobson was stone deaf but when out on the job, his men would look after him and keep him out of danger as far as possible. At one time a train of cordwood was coming up while Hobson was standing with his back to it. Just as the engine got within a short distance of the track crew, Hobson stepped up on the track, directly in front of the engine. One of the men made a grab for him and hauled him clear as the engineer practically swallowed his chew of tobacco in his effort to get stopped. A deaf section foreman was too much like asking for trouble so Rogers found another job for him.

The Rogers brothers ran the show and Edward Rogers ran the Rogers brothers. Mister Ed lived across the street from the station in the house with the bay window on the left side, as distinctive a dwelling as Edward was a man, the distinction being literally the bay window. He was as near "the law" in Dendron as it was possible for anyone to be, but he received his orders from the mythical beings in Baltimore. These gods had a habit of showing up now and then, and when they did everyone in town knew of it in short order. News got around, fast. They were always to be expected during the hunting season when they would arrive with friends, men of importance, both politically and in the lumber business, for the Waters family had their fingers in many pies up in Maryland. The first indication of an impending visit would be a telephone call and an inquiry as to the availability of game. Finally a date would be set, if the hunting promised to be good. On arrival of the visiting party, it was up to Rogers to furnish transportation to the desired location, and back, and guides. At Christmas there was always a "request" for Christmas trees, holly, and mistletoe, and occasionally there was the matter of locally cured hams to be sent to certain Maryland addresses. It was good "business", or so it was considered. However, as long as there was a steady flow of lumber headed north, the Rogers brothers were left alone to run the Dendron end of the business as they thought best and it can be truthfully said that they held up their end, with the help of a better than average lot of employees, both black and white.

It seems that at least one member of every fairly large family living in the three counties originally logged over by the Surry Lumber Company worked for either the railroad or the lumber company at one time or another. All six brothers of the Atkinson family tried it, some for a short period and others for a longer time. The oldest of the lot was Charles L., who went to work in the machine shop around 1892. After about a year he was promoted to fireman but quit after receiving his promotion. It seems that the company had a rule that if you were late reporting for work, you were fined a dollar and still had to put in the day on the job. Charlie was late showing up to get his engine hot on about the second day firing, and as he was still getting only eighty cents a day, he couldn't see working over a day for nothing. He didn't even stop by his engine but went right straight to the office and quit.

The second in line was Archer. He went to work at about the same time as did his elder brother, and was in engine service practically all of his working life. His first job firing was on No. 2, the mail train engine, from which he graduated to running the second No. 1. From that he moved over to No. 6, and finally to No. 10 which he ran until the mills closed down and both he and the engine were pulled out of service. Robert L. was a short timer and worked with Alpine Higgins on the bridge gang. The fourth, Edward Thomas, known for some vague reason as "Sam", began as a car cleaner, worked his way up and through the machine shop to engine service, and ended up as conductor on the mail train. Jesse, known as "Dinks", was foreman of the locomotive shop and assisted Mr. Jim Hart. The youngest, John, worked in the machine shop.

It appears that the most colorful of the six was Edward, who has been and will be from here on out, referred to simply as "Sam". It is extremely doubtful if even now, 1965, he would answer to his given name. His wife even calls him "Sam", and certainly mail addressed to him in that manner reaches him with only the usual delay. He was born on the 26th of June 1875 in Surry County, to the northwest of the present town of Dendron. His father was J. T. Atkinson, a farmer in Surry County, and his mother was Martha Ann West of Sussex County. From age six Sam was subjected to the coming and going of log trains up around Slabtown and after 1886 the shrill whistle of the log train engine blowing for the road crossing north of his home was as much a part of his everyday life as was taking care of the livestock. He dimly remembers David Steele and his two mills but Steele's CORNELIA was just a logging engine to his young mind. He saw his older brothers go off to work on the new railroad at Mussel Fork and at age 20 he followed them, his first job being to keep the new Barney & Smith combination car clean and to look after the mail sacks. Not only was he now actually working on the railroad but he was also a regular boarder in the home of his brother Archer.

That went on from September 1895 to the following April when he was relieved of the mail sack chore and went to firing extra, but the cleaning job was still his. Something like a year later he was moved over into the shop where he did odd jobs when he wasn't firing. Eventually he began firing regularly for his brother and now that he had a steady job, he felt safe to dive into the sea of matrimony on the 29th of November 1899. "Mrs. Sam" was the former Della Gay Wilcox, daughter of Sarah C. Ramey and Magnus S. Wilcox, and she was really asking for it when she coupled up with Sam. Thereafter they settled down in a house on Liberty Street in Dendron and have been there ever since.

The life of a railroad man on a logging railroad at the turn of the century was far from pleasant and that of his wife paralleled that of the husband. A regular fireman had to be ready to leave Dendron at 5:30 in the morning, which meant that he had to be up by 3:00 and be on hand at least an hour before leaving time to be sure that his engine was hot and greased, and that the tender was filled to its capacity with water and wood. In the winter he would frequently be up and out of the house by 2:30 for it took longer to blow up steam when there was a frost on the ground. The hostler kept a fire on the grates but it did little more than keep the water in the boiler from freezing. The ritual of leaving home in the wee hours was always the same, summer and winter; get up, get dressed, stoke the kitchen stove and see that it was drawing properly, and leave the house with as little noise as possible. Just before it was time to leave Dendron, breakfast and lunch would be brought by some member of the family and handed up in a tin lunch bucket with a container for coffee set into its top. Keeping the coffee hot was no problem for there was always the boiler head on which to heat it. Breakfast generally consisted of strips of salted side meat, the ancestor of what is now generally referred to as "breakfast bacon", eggs, and large, thick biscuits. The side meat and the eggs were cooked in either a long handled skillet or a carefully scrubbed coal shovel over the fire when the engine wasn't working too hard.

It took some doing but road firemen got quite proficient at cooking in this manner and under normal conditions, no engine crew ever went hungry if there was a farm nearby where fresh food could be purchased. So, somewhere along the route, breakfast was served, engine style. Lunch came out of the same tin bucket, carefully packed separately from the food to be prepared for breakfast, and it was strictly the product of the wife's ingenuity. There would possibly be fried chicken, or ham, in generous portions, or if it was cold weather, maybe some fresh pork or beef. Always there were biscuits, or crackling bread, or corn bread, and coffee which had been carefully saved from breakfast. The mainstay of the present-day lunch, sandwiches, did not exist, for loaf bread, as it was called, was strictly a delicacy and most people preferred to eat it while still warm. It's good that way, too.

When Sam left early in the morning, he made his two trips and was home fairly early in the afternoon but when he was second out, which was every other week, he would be out until late in the day for logs he brought in had to hold the mills during the next morning until the crew that was first out could get back. A whistle was blown at 5 a. m., warning everyone that in exactly sixty minutes they were to be on hand to begin the day's work. At exactly 6 a. m., the deep-toned mill whistle let go with a long bellow and the belts in the mills began to whip and slap, and the saws to whir. They continued to whip and slap, and the saws to whir, until 5:45 p. m., six days a week except for 45 minutes for lunch. Prior to the construction of the "big mill", which literally doubled production of the plant, engines 4 and 6 made two trips a day each, but when production was doubled and the jacks were brought in, it took six trips a day to keep the saws supplied, two trips from each camp. Three crews made two trips a day, one long and one short haul. The first crew out, just as the mail train started north, was generally through for the day by 3 p. m., but the last crew out was lucky to be home by the time the family went to bed. There was one compensation, though, they could sleep late, at least until 5 a. m. After three crews went to work on the main line hauling logs, by rotation, one crew had to get out early only one week in three, which wasn't considered too bad.

Sam got married and began to raise a family on eighty cents a day, but eighty cents bought something back in those days. While firing he gradually became familiar with the art of throttle jerking and spelled his brother now and then. His next step was to be appointed extra engineer and thus he gained more and more experience. When the 14 arrived in 1902, she became "Sam Atkinson's engine" and remained so until 1925 when Sam became conductor on the mail train due to the sudden death of W. L. Gladden, the former conductor. From then on he trundled up and down between Scotland Wharf and Dory until the last train ran on the 28th of August 1930, a Saturday. Sam had his share of incidents while out on the road, as did everyone else, but he stoutly maintained that he had only one serious wreck. Just what he considered "serious" is a matter of opinion.

A. W. Faison, known to everyone as Whurley Faison, was the next man to be hired after Sam. He was "brung up" over at Cyprus Church, near Dendron, and was one of four brothers;

Jett, Charlie, Hubert, and finally Whurley. There was also a sister. Their father, Ellic Faison, was a farmer and prior to going to work for the company Whurley helped around the farm. A dislike for farming and the promise of a steady wage for what appeared to be easy work, were the reasons for the move.

Whurley gradually worked his way up the ladder to eventually become engineer on the mail train during the time that Sam was conductor, but Whurley's penchant for hard liquor was a nuisance at times. One day when coming up from the river, Whurley whistled for a station stop and brought his train to a neat halt at the road crossing in Judkin's Bottom, thinking that he was at Surry. He had made previous unscheduled station stops but none quite as rank as this one and Sam figured that it was time to do something about it. If Whurley kept it up, sooner or later the brass at Dendron would find out about it, if they didn't already know but were being lenient, and be forced to fire Whurley. Sam had a real heart to heart talk with Whurley's brother who worked in the mill and for a time Whurley did pretty well, but he never did "reform". He ran the engine on the mail train until the road closed down.

Back there in 1895 David Steele was running No. 2, which was some time before Faison got the job, Quincy Hancock had No. 3, Joe Whitley had No. 4, Charlie Wrenn had No. 5, John Robbins had No. 6, Leroy Lain was running No. 7, and Henry Kitchen had No. 9. Linwood Hunley was the extra engineer. Each was paid $1.50 a day, as was the conductor on the mail train. The fireman got 96¢ a day, and a day for any of the train crews was from the time they left wherever they spent the night until they got back for the next night. Colored brakemen and the shop help received 80¢ a day, and their day was from 6 a. m. to 5:45 p. m., six days a week. A log train was in the charge of the engineer, there being no conductor on anything other than the mail train. The number of brakemen carried on the trains hauling logs depended on the length of the train. An average train of 25 loads carried three. The length of the trains increased to that number of loads when the jacks were brought in and the moguls went into yard service.

The men were first paid once a month, around the 15th, and the money was taken to them if they were not working out of

Dendron. Later on the company got around to paying off twice a month, but during the time the pay was handed out monthly, the practice was to pay in full just before Christmas and not again until six weeks later, in February. One week's wages were always held back to insure against an employee walking off the job while owing an account at one of the commissaries or with company property, such as a switch key. The fact is that at first switch keys were issued all brakemen without a deposit, they simply signed for them, but the number lost and had to be replaced forced the company to require a dollar deposit on all keys. That, for some strange reason, practically eliminated their loss.

During January the company books were closed so that the yearly report could be compiled. A man by the name of Eldridge was the first regular bookkeeper and he also acted as local treasurer and paymaster, traveling to Baltimore for the money and bringing it back to Dendron via the Norfolk & Western from Norfolk. There was no bank in Dendron at that time and it was necessary for the money to lay in the company's iron safe for at least one night. Certain employees armed with shotguns stood guard in the room with the safe each night that the money was on hand. Unfortunately, for our story, nothing ever happened.

Not only did Eldridge make up the pay roll, but he paid each man personally, traveling from camp to camp until the last man had received his money, and it is said that he knew each man by name and the name of each member of his family. Nearly every pay envelope contained one or more canceled chits from the nearest commissary and sometimes there was very little actual cash. Other than the feel of having it, cash money was of little use in the woods but that didn't detract from the excitement of pay day.

R. Emmett Williams was born and raised on his father's farm at Littleton, Virginia, a village consisting now of two dwellings and a general store, which contains the post office, on the old Jerusalem Plank Road in Sussex County. The building of the West Hope Branch to the south of Littleton offered Emmett an escape from farm life, and he felt that engine service was what he was cut out for. He lost no time getting a job as fireman of a donkey and he spent about a year feeding pine balks into the little firebox before he moved over on the right side. He really liked his work, irrespective of the long hours and personal danger involved.

In the meantime he got married and his wife Maude had no use for Emmett's vocation, claiming that one day he would be brought home on a board. She was a farmer's daughter and was a firm believer in farming as the only way to make a living. She argued with Emmett, long and volubly, but he could see no danger in what he was doing, certainly no more than in anything else. Maude refused to be placated and hammered away constantly.

During the week Emmett was allowed to keep his engine, which was usually No. 3, at Chub overnight, where he lived in a company house. One night he was coming home from up towards Straw Hill when his headlight went out. That was nothing unusual nor was the fact that it could not be relit anything to be alarmed over. All of the engineers had experienced the same thing a number of times and rather than run with a blind eye they would take out the oil lamp and set a lantern up between the reflector and the front glass. At best, the old oil headlights were of little use so far as illumination was concerned and although this substitute gave even less light, Williams expressed it nicely when he said, "You couldn't see anything with it but anybody could see you."

After Emmett had put a lantern in his headlight, he climbed back in the cab and started for Chub again, but he ran rather slowly for there was no telling what you might meet on the track, anything from a fog ghost to a very substantial cow. The donkey eased on down to and across the truss bridge over the Nottoway and as she swung around the curve on the trestle over the lowlands, there suddenly appeared between the rails in the very dim light something that looked like a tow sack of grain. It was too late to stop and when the donkey went over the obstruction, Williams commented more or less to himself that whatever it was felt powerful solid and as soon as they reached solid ground he stopped the donkey. He, and two or three others who were riding with him to Chub, dropped off and walked back out on the trestle to take a look at that tow sack.

They found the body of a colored man who had made it a practice to walk home across the railroad bridge, using it as a short
cut, after getting "well oiled" over at Chub. On this particular
night it must have appeared to him that the structure had been
lengthened since the last time he was over it, or he had over-
estimated his ability to negotiate it. In either case he had laid
down to rest for a spell, and went to sleep. The donkey had
made that temporary rest a very permanent one. A man was
left with the body while the engine was run on to Chub from
where the main office and the sheriff were notified. The
amount of caterwauling and predicting of dire events done by
Maude when she was told of the accident can be easily imagined.

Emmett had a brother named Samuel who occasionally fired
for him and together they did a good job with the donkey, but
Samuel wasn't as much in love with his job as was Emmett.
Samuel stoked the firebox strictly for what he got every pay
day, nothing more. On this particular afternoon in October of
1903, they were working in the woods beyond Cherry Orchard
Bottom and had picked up a string of loads to bring out to
where a jack waited to haul them to Dendron. Some of that
temporary track was unbelievably rough and the habit of fas-
tening two rails together with only one bolt per rail didn't insure the ends staying in line. No. 3 was due to have her drivers
turned the next day for the flanges were considered to be dangerously sharp. Considering all things as they were then, that
means that they were in a pretty sad shape. As the engine
groaned and strained to get its load out, it suddenly hit a rail
end that was out of line and before anyone could unload,
pitched over on its left side, pinning Samuel in the smashed
cab.

The rest of the crew extricated Samuel as quickly as possible
but he was in such pain and apparently was so badly hurt that
they didn't dare move him. One leg was horribly crushed. Dr.
Slade, a company doctor, was hurriedly brought up from Sussex Court House while other men rounded up Dr. Prince and
Dr. Daniels. It was a case of surely one of the three doctors
could be found but it so happened that all three were available.
The injured man was placed in a boxcar and his injuries in-
vestigated.

The three doctors were all for taking off the leg right then and there, in the boxcar, but brother Emmett thought otherwise. After some argument, the three doctors and Mr. Philip Rogers, the logging boss who was then living in a large, new home at Straw Hill, climbed into the boxcar and Sam Atkinson dropped the car down to Chub as gently as the track permitted, he and his jack having been waiting for a train to be made up. On arrival, the injured man was carried to his brother's house and had his leg removed, the kitchen table being used as an operating table. The operation was a success but the ordeal was too much for Maude and she intensified her campaign to get her husband to quit the railroad. The accident had unnerved Emmett, too, for it was something else again to have something like that happen to your own brother. Maybe Maude had reasons for her dislike of railroading, certainly of the type of railroading practiced in the woods. One day soon after the accident Emmett talked with Sam about how much he actually enjoyed railroading and how dead set his wife was against it, and how determined she was to get him to quit and go farming.

Emmett was arguing with himself as much as anything else. Sam listened and finally said, "If I liked railroadin' as much as you say you do, I wouldn't let no one run me off." Williams shook his head in resignation as he commented, "You just don't know my Maude." So, Williams quit the company and went back to farming but still close enough to the West Hope line to hear the whistles and still closer to a spur running north from the main branch. He didn't like farming any more than Maude liked railroading, but Maude was happy, and what was more important, quiet.

He hadn't been at it too long when a summer thunder squall caught him out in the field plowing. Emmett took cover under a tree, leaving the mule and plow standing in the rain. He had just made himself comfortable when a bolt of lightning split the plow down the center and killed the mule. Suddenly, Williams lost what little interest he had in farming and in placating Maude, and ignoring the pouring rain, took off across the field for home. He tramped in, dripping wet, and informed Maude, "You talk about railroadin' bein' dang'rous; I never come so close to gettin' kilt before!" For once Maude could think of no argument and in a few days Emmett went off and got himself a job firing on the Norfolk & Western but eventually came back to the old home place at Littleton. Farming might have been too dangerous but when he came back he did a little of it. He concentrated, though, on running a small sawmill, and lost a couple of fingers at it.

Thaddeus Powell, known simply as Thad, was one of the many colored brakemen who sometimes took more chances than they should have. As a result of this chance taking, Thad was possibly one of a very few who got squeezed between two cars while making a coupling, and lived to tell about it. It was just common sense not to step between cars from the inside of a curve when making a coupling for sometimes the clearance at the inside ends of the buffer beams was only an inch or two. He made his mistake at Wakefield Siding when an engine was backing in to pick up some cars that were right at the clearance post of the siding. Unthinkingly he stepped in from the inside of the lead-in to set the pin and before he knew it, he was caught. Although he screamed from fright and pain, he was badly crushed before the engine could be stopped and eased away from him, but he lived, in almost continuous pain, which lessened as time went on. He never was right again but he returned to work and was put on the bridge gang under Alpine Higgins, and when Higgins quit, he continued under Wyatt Slade.

It so happened that Wyatt had to go to Scotland Wharf to do a little repair work and he took Thad along on the motor section car. The job was completed and they started for home but they had gone only a short distance when the motor car had other ideas. The motor quit and refused to start again. It was getting on late in the afternoon so Wyatt and Thad set the scooter off the track and started walking. Why Wyatt didn't phone in from Surry, no one will ever know, but he didn't and they kept walking. In the meantime, Dendron began to wonder what had happened to them and after a while the wonder grew into worry. A crew was called in and an engine sent out to see what was wrong. Sure enough, the crew met the two men around Elberon, still walking the ties, headed for home. Thad used to say that he would do anything other than walk from Scotland Wharf to Dendron again.

Muncie Parsons was also a brakesman but he was a brakes-man among brakemen. He broke for John Inghram and Hugh Barrett on the 6 and 8, and he was strictly a head end man. His seat was always on the lid of the tender tank, if the engine was bringing in a string of empties, or on top of the first load if a train of loads was headed out of the woods. His specialty was replacing broken bent links on the fly, something no other brakesman could be induced to try for a slip could easily prove downright fatal. There was no question as to what had happened when the bent link between the tender and the train let go for the engine would leap ahead and begin to run away from the train. When that happened the engineer would let her run so as to stay out of the way of the cars, and it was then that Muncie would go into his act. He would crawl down to the bumper beam and pull the pin to free the broken link, which would drop down between the rails to be picked up by a track gang. In the meantime the fireman had crawled back over the tender to pass signals and as soon as the half of the broken link was free, he would signal the engineer to slow down, thus letting the train run up on the engine. When the cars were within reach of the tender, more signals were passed and the engine speeded up slightly to pace the loads. Muncie would reach over and free the other half of the broken link. The fireman would pass down a new link, Muncie would insert it into the coupler, drop that pin and then guide it into the other coupler as the engine was slowed a bit more. The pin was dropped in place, Muncie would wave his hand at the fireman and the fireman would wave to the engineer, and away they would go. It sounds simple, but it was neither simple nor safe, and it took plenty of nerve. Bent links generally broke when the engine took up the slack at the bottom of a grade, so they couldn't waste any time changing links or the cars would be hauled to a standstill by the grade. The idea was to change links before the cars halted for once that happened, the chances were that you had to double the hill. The way things were done on the S.S.&S. would give a modern safety engineer ulcers.

During the entire time that the mail train was in operation, only three men held down the position of conductor; a man named Palmer, W. L. Gladden, and Sam Atkinson. Practically nothing is known of Palmer other than he came south from Bal-

timore when the company began operations and he left in 1895.
No one remembers him too well. His place was taken by Gladden, son of W. L. Gladden, who ran the Dendron commissary
and hotel. To differentiate between father and son, the father
was known as Bill Gladden and the son as Willie. Willie was
one of four brothers and helped around the store, one of his
duties being to carry the company mail to the general office.
Back in the early days R. T. Waters made fairly frequent trips
to Dendron and he took a liking to Willie, considering him to
be a "right bright young man" and it is safe to say that Willie
"made up" to the old man for, after all, he was practically the
owner of the entire outfit even if his son did run it. So, when
Palmer left and the position of conductor became available,
Waters put in a good word for Willie with Rogers. That was
literally an order in kid gloves so Willie got the job.

Among other things, Willie was a fairly good musician, his
instrument being the cornet, the music of which Waters was
quite fond. When the town band was organized, he naturally
played in it. Willie was also rather proud of his appearance and
when out on his run was always neat and businesslike.

Originally, the Gladden family had been "imported" from
up around Salisbury, Maryland, and as each member died, he
was shipped back north, the immediate family moving back to
their former home where they could be near relatives. Willie
was no exception, and when he died in 1925 he, too, was shipped
north.

Possibly Clarence Owen was what would have been called a
typical commissary manager except for the fact that he made
it the hard way, so to speak. Like practically all of the operating personnel, Owen was raised on a farm, being born up near
Stony Creek in 1885. In August of 1906 he applied for a job with
the company and Philip Rogers sent him to Vicksville
as a clerk in the company store. At that time Richard Owen,
Clarence's double first cousin, was superintendent of the Vicksville camp. Come Christmas, Clarence went home for the holiday and when returning to Vicksville, he naturally came over
to West Hope and rode a log train to Dory and a string of empties down to Vicksville.

Nat Turner was running the Vicksville commissary at that
time and when Clarence walked in, Nat came close to walking
out. It so happened that a man in the store at West Hope had
come down with smallpox and Clarence was known to
have stopped off there. It was nothing personal, but Nat would
appreciate it if Clarence would return home for a while, long
enough to be sure that he hadn't picked it up. Clarence wasn't
exactly in love with that clerking job and had been thinking of
returning to the farm. This definitely decided him and he
headed for home. When he got off the train at Dory, who
should be standing there waiting to board the train for Dendron
but Philip Rogers and the first thing he asked was why he was
going home. Clarence explained about Turner's fear of smallpox, his request that he stay home for a while, and his own decision to return to farming. Rogers was a bit put out for, as he
put it, he had a case of the pox in his back yard and it wasn't
anything to get all excited about, but Clarence went on back to
the farm.

In February a man to clerk in the West Hope store
under Herbert Owen was badly needed and Rogers thought of
Clarence. A letter was sent off asking that he come over and
talk, which he did. Rogers out-talked him, so Clarence stayed
on as clerk. Around 1910 Roy Edwards replaced Herbert Owen
but Clarence stuck with it. When the store was moved to Surry,
he went with it. Finally, his big day arrived, late in 1912, when
he was sent back to Vicksville to take over the store in which
he had begun his company career, and in 1920 when the Sedley
store was opened, he moved there, being manager of both
stores until the company went out of business.

Once in a while one of the drifters that showed up at Dendron
would decide to work a while before moving on. The prize of
the lot was a tramp named Halpen who showed up around 1898,
having walked the ties from Wakefield, possibly through plain
curiosity as to where the light, tight track led. He asked Higgins for work, saying that he was a painter by trade. Such an
artisan was needed at that time so Higgins stuck a paint brush
in his hand, handed him a bucket of paint, and he went to work.
He actually was a painter. Halpen, and he was always known
only by that name during his short stay, painted the combination car, the boxcars, the flatcars, the log cars, and anything

else that needed it, but his masterpiece was the mail train engine, No. 2. She had begun to show rust spots and obviously could stand a little attention, so she was pointed out to him and he went to work on her.

When the engine finally rolled out of the shop she was wonderful to behold and it is a sure thing that none of the others ever got such a paint job. Glossy black on running gear, smoke box, cab, and tender, bright red axle ends, but he sort of tapered off when he got to the lettering. The name of the road spelled out as it was when the engine arrived from the builder was too much for him so Higgins agreed to the road's initials in large ornate letters on the tank of the tender and the engine number on the cab panels rather than the road's initials. However, Halpen did himself proud when it came to the places he found to put the engine number. That was in bright red and it ended up on each side of the headlight, the sand box, each cab panel under the window, on each side of the tank collar, and on the back of the tank. She was the most numbered engine on the road until she began to get dirty and then the red and black tended to blend when viewed at a distance, not that anyone ever mistook her for another engine, numbers or no numbers.

That was the high point of Halpen's career with the S.S.&S., and it was shortly thereafter that he told Higgins that he felt out of place, being a standard gauge tramp on a narrow gauge railroad. He drew his pay and left as he had arrived, walking the ties, back towards Wakefield. He had done all of his painting within a period of about three months but contrary to what might have been expected, he earned his pay while in Dendron.

When the engine went back on her regular run, her crew was as proud as Punch of her and Willie Doyle, the engineer dickered with Eugene Younglove for a painting of her. Younglove was postmaster, lumber checker, and amateur artist at Scotland Wharf. The engine appealed to him almost as much as it did to the crew and he agreed to do her "portrait" for $25. It was done, in time, but Doyle couldn't see it being worth what he had agreed to pay and there were words over it. Younglove was no engineman and he didn't see the same things that Doyle did when looking at an engine, which was to be expected. The artist had taken liberties, too many liberties, and had left off certain vital parts, according to Doyle, and he balked at handing over the money. Younglove kept the painting for a while but finally gave it to the fireman, possibly to spite Doyle as much as anything else, and so far as we know, it is the only one of Younglove's many paintings that has survived to this day. Sam Atkinson eventually ended up with it and it hangs in his dining room at Dendron.

Willie Doyle had come over from Fergusson's Wharf around 1896 when his uncle went broke trying to log out String-of-Logs Pocoson. We will stumble over Fergusson again when we get down to around Central Hill but right now suffice it to say that he was Doyle's uncle by marriage. Doyle had replaced Steele on No. 2 but he didn't last too long because of poor health. He ended up with yellow jaundice and went back to live with his sister at Fergusson's Wharf.

One thing that can be said for Willie is that he went to a lot of trouble to escape that dollar fine that was imposed if he was late leaving Dendron on time when beginning the day's runs. Prior to the time the company hired a hostler to keep the engines hot all night, getting up steam in the morning took time. On a winter morning it took longer, and sometimes the fireman didn't allow enough time to thaw out a frozen hose or injector line. He was then in trouble and without help, the engine crew saved the company a good part of their day's wages by being assessed that dollar a head. It wasn't a case of just getting up steam enough to leave town at 5:30, but it fell the lot of the mail train crew to blow the 5 a. m. "waking up" whistle for there was no one to do it at the mill. Sometimes it took considerable doing and it was against this five o'clock deadline that the crew worked. We won't say that Doyle should get all of the credit for the very ingenious method devised to insure the blowing of the whistle on time, but he surely must have had a hand in it.

It must be remembered that it takes a lot longer to get up enough steam to work the blower than it does to put the needle on the mark after the blower has cut it. The problem is to get enough steam to start a draft. Some railroads used a compressed air hose, others a blower, but the S.S.&S. never got around to such niceties and depended solely on a natural draft and time for the first phase of raising steam. Doyle always left his train fully made up over night, standing in the yard, so that in the morning all he had to do was get up steam, drop down to the tank and take on water, move on a bit further to the station, and when the time came to leave town, leave. Generally he was at the station when it came time to blow the five-o'clock whistle. But, let's say that on this particular morning they had been held up by a frozen hose between the tender and the engine. To thaw that took time. You couldn't very well build a fire under it, although it has been done, so when it came time to drop down to the tank, there was no steam, not even enough to work the blower, and it was getting uncomfortably close to five o'clock. It was always possible to raise steam on a donkey a lot faster than on the passenger engine and by this time at least one of them was alive. It was used to shove the train out of the yard and down to the water tank. As soon as they had begun to move, Doyle had hauled the valve gear into full reverse and opened the throttle, wide. The pistons thus began to function as air pumps and to fill the boiler with air. The blower would gurgle a time or two and begin to work. Air or steam made no difference to it. If the crew was lucky, by the time the tank was full and it was time to wake up the town, there was enough steam to blow the whistle. If there wasn't, the donkey took care of that chore and the engine crew continued to struggle with the fire. The extra half hour made all the difference in the world. It didn't make any difference how sluggish that 5:30 departure was, just so long as they left town on time, the dollar was safe.

It has already been stated that Joe Whitley's brakesman eventually went to jail for laying that coupling pin up against the side of his head, he undoubtedly had provocation for Joe was not the easiest man in the world to get along with. In fact, he and the company sort of parted company by mutual consent. You can't say that he was out and out fired but it was working around to that. It began when he balked at doing his two-day stint on the log train run during a Christmas holiday. Each engine crew got a week's holiday but each of the three road crews had to work two days during that week to keep the mill in logs. Whitley claimed that he was due a week off and working two days of it wouldn't give him a week. He and Jim Hart had some rather harsh words about it but he simply refused to do his part of the running. That didn't exactly set well with the other two crews who had to split his time between them. After that was over, other little unpleasantries centered around him until he figured that he would be better off elsewhere and he went to work for the Camp brothers.

Jack Rollison ran the company's first skidder, a crude affair used to snake logs up out of low places where it was too swampy to work a team. Then, when Causey came to work for the company as superintendent in later years and brought in improved skidders, he had Jim Owen hired to look after them. Owen did things in a big way, particularly when it came to eating and raising a family. Possibly one had something to do with the other, but he never bothered to buy a ham or a side of salt meat, but would pick out the largest hog available and purchase the whole thing. Admittedly, it took a lot of grub to keep him, his wife, and nine kids satisfied.

One day he happened to go into the commissary when the manager was opening a barrel of apples. Owen admired the apples and 'lowed that he could eat a peck, cores and all, right by himself, at one sitting. The manager saw a good deal coming up so told him that if he could, he would give him the peck of apples but if he couldn't he would have to pay for the entire peck. Owen said that was reasonable enough. A peck of apples was put in a basket, Owen perched himself on the counter, and the eating began. It wasn't too long before it was obvious that the manager was going to be out the price of a peck of apples but he had begun to worry about Owen. No one could eat that many apples and not have gastric trouble. He finally said that he would admit that Owen could eat a peck of apples and he needn't finish the whole lot. Owen claimed that a bargain was a bargain and he would finish them off but he would leave off eating the cores, if it was all right with him. He did. That Owen was one eatin' man.

Before we move on to other things, we should take a look at the man who kept the engines running, J. D. Hart, known as Jim Hart. His father was the Norfork & Western agent at Wakefield and Jim supposedly worked for that road at one time but when he came with the Surry Lumber Company he left the remains of a blacksmith's and wheelwright shop behind at Wakefield. He had been doing pretty well there but on April 7, 1887, his establishment burned with a loss of around $2,000, only a part of which was covered by insurance. It was claimed that the plant was deliberately set afire but it was never proven for no one could think of anyone mad enough at Hart to do such a thing.

He was married to Miss Ada Bishop, and had three daughters by her, all of which he also left at Wakefield. He went back there over Sundays, riding a rail tricycle each way, but during the week he lived in a tiny one-room house, just he and his bottle. He brought enough food from home to last him most of the week and when that ran out he did his own cooking. Later on he started boarding with the widow Steele and it was then that his wife decided it was time to move to Dendron.

When Hart first came to Dendron he fired a little, then ran a little, but his knowledge of steam engines caused Rogers to put him in charge of the engine shop when it was set up. He was a pretty good machinist and set all of the valves, after a man came down from the Baldwin plant and taught him how. He was not very tall, red headed with a red mustache, weighed around 140 pounds, and had a tendency to turn red like a parboiled lobster in hot weather. He was easy going and went out of his way to stay out of trouble. He was not above getting pleasantly drunk but when his family moved in, his wife put a stop to his apparently only pleasure. She had a brother who leaned on the bottle a little too heavily which "turned her against strong drink", as Jim expressed it. It wasn't long before she had him regularly attending the local Baptist church and he became a model citizen. That, and his tendency to sidestep trouble and take the easy way out, caused him to live one of the most sedate lives of anyone in town. One can't help but wonder if it didn't get downright tiring at times.

These have been only a few of the interesting personalities to be found along the line. Others will crop up from time to time. These at whom we have taken a look are certainly no more colorful than those not mentioned but they give an overall picture of the characters and personalities of the men who made possible the successful operation of both the railroad and the lumber company.

Progress

Over the years the personnel of the machine and engine shops became more and more proficient in maintaining the equipment, not only of the mill machinery, but of the railway. Back in January 1891 when No. 2 had gone into Cypress Swamp, the only part that had to be purchased was a headlight reflector, all other parts could be either repaired or made locally. Fortunately, in this case, it was mainly a matter of completely dismantling the locomotive, cleaning it thoroughly, and reassembling it. In March 1894 the same locomotive was retubed and a new tube sheet installed. Two years later a new frame was purchased for No. 8 but a bit later, when some of the personnel became proficient in the art of gas welding, engine frames were patched and repatched. They were also capable of making welded boiler tubes and the task of putting on new tires on driving wheels was routine. To accomplish this, an acetylene gas ring-type tire heater was fashioned out of perforated gas pipe and fitted with clamps to hold it in position. In fact, they made several sizes of tire heaters, one for each size tire in use.

To do their own wheel and tire turning, a medium size wheel lathe was installed. This lathe could handle the driving wheels of all the engines except No. 2, whose drivers still had to be sent to Petersburg for turning. Later, a larger lathe was installed which could take the driving wheels on all the locomotives. Cylinders were bored by hand, a hand-cranked machine being used which was slow but when properly aligned and tightly clamped in place would do a satisfactory job. In a small brass foundry behind the machine shop, journal brasses were cast as well as other small brass and bronze parts. The brasses turned out by the foundrymen lacked the finished appearance of those purchased elsewhere but they were satisfactory so far as wear was concerned. By this time the repair facilities had outgrown the original lean-to and were properly housed in buildings at the south end of the Dendron yard.

In an effort to increase the draft of No. 2 and the moguls, smoke box extensions were purchased from Baldwin in the fall of 1898 and installed by the shop crew. These engines had been giving trouble due to the fact that steam could not be maintained when they were on the road. When using cured wood, they steamed satisfactorily, but cured wood was not always available and when the fireman tried to get by with green wood, he was in trouble, generally requiring frequent stops to blow up steam.

Richard T. Waters, the chairman of the board of directors, and literally the owner of the Surry Lumber Company, and the railroad, died on April 21, 1900. His son, Francis E. Waters, was immediately appointed to fill the vacancy as he inherited his father's interest in the two organizations. Young Waters continued the policies followed by his father for about two years before he began to introduce a program of expansion and modernization which he had been advocating for some time. By April 1902 plans were on the drawing board for the enlargement of the Dendron plant by the erection of two mills, several sheds, and the necessary trackage to serve the new structures.

As of July 1, 1900, there were ten locomotives in service; the second No. 1 being grouped with the donkeys although she was considerably heavier; the mail train engine, No. 2; the donkeys 3, 5, 7, and 9; the moguls 4 and 6; and the jacks 8 and 10. Rolling stock consisted of the combination car, a coach, ten boxcars, and twenty flatcars. This was the equipment admittedly owned by the Railway Company and did not take into account the various pieces of equipment used strictly for logging and were considered to belong to the lumber company. It is impossible to definitely identify the freight cars for they were either second hand or had been built in the car shop. When additional equipment was required, it was readily available from second hand dealers or other logging companies. During the early years of operation, flatcars were used to haul logs as well as cordwood and just when such use ceased is pure conjecture. It must have been at a fairly early date for in 1895 there were 35 or 40 standard log cars in service. The changeover was undoubtedly rather gradual. These log cars were all fitted with short standards but later on, a long standard was used. At first these long standards gave considerable trouble by jumping out of the sockets when the cars were running empty. After one had jumped out and hurt a brakesman, a locking device was fashioned and applied. From then on there was no more trouble of that nature.

The maximum number of flats owned was thirty, in 1889. The following year ten were dropped from the roster and by mid-1903 the number had slowly decreased to ten. The number of boxcars was increased from two to three during fiscal 1894 and to nine during 1898. After that the number increased rather rapidly for the lumber company began to use them to haul kiln-dried pine lumber, in which the company specialized. Where formerly the lumber went to the river on flatcars, this new type of drying required that the lumber be kept as dry as possible. In addition to this, the peanut traffic increased considerably and this required boxcars. The only thing that these cars had in common, it seemed, was that each had two trucks under them. By this time the shop was not only repairing cars, but building car bodies. All of the early freight cars had their couplers rigidly fixed to the end sills but the couplers of the newer cars were spring mounted. During fiscal 1900, which means somewhere between mid-1899 and mid-1900, the company purchased the secondhand coach which has already been mentioned. Prior to this the combination car had been the only piece of passenger equipment. To further describe this combination car built by the Barney & Smith Manufacturing Company of Dayton, Ohio, and which replaced the original car, it might be said that the smoking compartment was fitted with three seats on each side and the baggage compartment was about square and without windows.

During February of 1901 a duplicate of No. 10 was tested at the Baldwin plant and delivered to the company in March. The arrival of No. 12 eased the transportation problem considerably and made possible the eventual retirement of the second mogul to extra duty and shifter service, working with No. 4 in the mill yard.

It wasn't too long before the new mills were an actuality. They were designated Mill C and Mill D, the latter being a shook mill. Mill C included a large dry kiln in a separate structure and it was to transport the product of this kiln that the boxcars were acquired. Thus, the Dendron plant was nearly doubled in size and capacity, particularly as Mill C had a double saw. This saw had teeth on both sides of the blade and could cut when the carriage was traveling in either direction. To supply the enlarged plant, a new section of timber was opened, some tracts which had been owned since 1886 but never cut over. The main line was extended in a southeasterly direction from Dory for a few miles and a large logging camp named Vicksville erected at its terminus. The camp consisted of about 25 permanent houses and a commissary.

A branch was built east from Vicksville into the woods, its length being extended as the need arose. It eventually passed around behind Berlin to the southeast, crossed Round Hill Swamp, followed Seacock Swamp, and terminated up around Sandy Hill Church. It literally butted up against the Ivor-Berlin road at a log-loading yard. The route was something like nine miles in length although there was considerably more trackage than that, considering the fairly long line to the northeast off the upper end and the various woods tracks. So far as is known, this branch was never given a definite name although it was referred to at times as the "Berlin Branch". It was strictly a logging line and was never used for any type of common carrier service.

To work the expanding system, three donkeys and a fourth jack were ordered from Baldwin. The donkeys numbered 11 and 15 showed a boiler test date of August 1902 and the 17th of September of the same year. The jack, No. 14, showed a date of the following November, and upon arrival was used mainly as a relief engine. Although rumors are heard ever so often concerning a donkey No. 13, actually there never was an engine so numbered. Superstition was responsible for that.

Although No. 8 had been delivered with a Radley & Hunter stack and a short front end for burning wood, and the other jacks with a straight stack and an extended front end for coal firing, the four engines were supposedly identical in design. For some reason the 14 proved to be a poor steamer although her engineer claimed that it was because of the firemen as much as anything else. When she arrived, her fireman was

Dawsey Purcell who had come up from Norfolk. He had gained his experience firing on the Norfolk & Virginia Beach narrow gauge, along with his brother Gene, and he seemed to have no trouble keeping the jack hot. When he left for greener pastures, the 14 apparently resented his replacement and trouble started. She just wouldn't steam and after she had been in service about six months she was put in the shop and had her cylinders rebored and bushed. That helped but there were still times when keeping up steam was quite a job. When she died out on the road, Sam Atkinson, her engineer, and the fireman would go to work on the fire. As soon as it was burning properly, Sam would climb up on his seat, pull out his dog-eared Bible and read until the needle was on the mark. Sam claimed that most of his time on the 14 was spent waiting, for one reason or another, and he spent that time reading. The 14 practically wore out that copy of the Bible. There is no explaining the individual idiosyncrasies of supposedly identical pieces of machinery.

The new donkeys were modern editions of the earlier series and reflected their "newness" by the presence of several improvements, mainly a redesigned main frame and a strengthening of the bunker frame. Since the delivery of No. 9, the method of getting logs out of the woods had changed to the extent that front ends and bunker frames were frequently broken by loaded log cars slamming up against them. Where formerly loads had been hauled out of the hollows by adding more power until they were lugged out by brute force, now the idea was to depend on speed to make a grade. This method of railroading naturally subjected the draft gear and frames to considerable abuse. When a donkey went into the shop with a broken front end frame, Higgins made liberal use of strap iron in rebuilding it as far back as the cylinder saddle, giving the front end a springiness which absorbed a goodly portion of the shock transmitted to the frame when violently closing the slack in a string of loads being shoved. Additional braces were put under the bunkers and the frame made more rigid at that end. The altered design did not cure the trouble but it did alleviate it. Baldwin tried to overcome the trouble by increasing the weight of the frame forward of the saddle and by bracing the strikerplate at the bunker end but, again, that did not entirely eliminate broken frames. In October all three of the new donkeys had Baldwin property plates bolted to them. They had to be purchased on time.

When No. 11 was delivered and ready for service, No. 3 was pulled in for an overhaul and the new engine handed over to Emmett Williams. He was admonished to be careful with her for she was new and stiff. Maybe it was because of that stiffness, or maybe it was because of the track, but anyway, he turned her over between Assamoosick Swamp and the Plank Road crossing the next day. No donkey remained unscarred very long, irrespective of the attention it received.

With three new donkeys in service, No. 1, the Loco engine, was sold to a logging firm. It was taken into the Dendron shop, the rods taken down and was made ready for shipment. She was then towed to Wakefield, loaded on a flatcar, and shipped to the new owner.

When the company first began to haul men into the woods, it used a flatcar. In the winter it was sometimes a very unpleasant experience, that trip to and from the woods. The men would sit on the deck with their legs dangling over the sides. If it was bitter cold, dirt would be thrown on the deck and a fire built on that. Dangerous? No, not particularly, when you consider the slow speed at which the trains ran. In later years the company converted at least six boxcars, two for each of the three camps, into labor cars and these replaced the flats. These cars had seats built around the sides and a stove in the center with the pipe stuck through a hole in the side. Although the cars were far from comfortable, they were warm in the winter and dry in wet weather. All six of these cars did not go into service at the same time, but as they were required. At first the white labor rode in a converted boxcar and the colored on a flat but this practice was discontinued after the first winter that converted boxcars were used and each race had its own car. Still later the company purchased second hand passenger cars for this service.

The procurement of all equipment fell on Higgins, as purchasing agent. Periodicals having to do with the lumbering industry were received regularly at the Dendron office and carefully scanned by Rogers, the advertisements receiving particular attention. When rolling stock was offered for sale, and it appeared to be something that the company could use, Rogers would suggest to Higgins that he go look it over. Distance made no difference if the price was right. Of course, Higgins occasionally sent home some surprising items, but he also picked up some bargains. The fly in the ointment was that when Higgins was well "lubricated", he was apt to purchase almost anything.

An amusing account is told of a trip Higgins made to Suffolk, Virginia, to purchase log cars from the Suffolk & Carolina when that line was being broadened out. Rogers learned that the S. & C. had a number of such cars which they wished to dispose of and as the line was narrow gauge, it seemed that this was an excellent chance to pick up some much needed equipment at a bargain price. So Higgins was sent down to look over the cars and to purchase them if they appeared to be in fair shape. Rogers actually expected the price to be near that for junk and it would be no problem for the car shop to rebuild the frames if the cars were just that for they had been rebuilding cars for some time. Higgins duly arrived in Suffolk, contacted the S. & C. official who was in a position to dicker, and was shown the cars. They were in excellent shape and were being sold only because the road was changing its gauge. However, something didn't seem just right. Higgins checked again. The cars were narrow gauge, fitted with link and pin couplers, were equipped with hand brakes, and were of the four-stake variety, but that feeling persisted. He checked a second time and again they checked out. He gave up and headed for the office to sign the sales agreement. On his way he started across the main line, which was three-rail in the yard, taking a long step to clear the near rail and put his foot in position so that his second step would take him over the far rail of the narrow gauge and just short of that of the standard gauge. It was done subconsciously from long experience, but to his surprise, when he took that second step he put his foot down smack on top of the far rail of the narrow gauge. Then it hit him, the gauge was wrong. The S. & C. was 42-inch gauge, just six inches wider than his road. The deal was not consummated, naturally.

As has already been said, a goodly number of the log cars were actually built in the company shop although the iron required for their construction, such as wheels, couplers, journal boxes, and such items, were purchased already fabricated from various firms dealing in logging equipment. Quite a bit of the iron for these cars was purchased from The Tredegar Works in Richmond, Va. Many of the smaller iron castings were cast by the company foundry. This equipment, being the property of the lumber company, was hauled at so much per car mile, on paper. They were not declared as rolling stock by either the railway or the lumber company, but were classed, for all practical purposes, with the swing carts used in the woods. Just how many log cars there were at any given time, or the largest number ever owned, it is impossible to say, but we do know that at the peak of the logging activities about 400 such cars were in daily use. According to the report filed for the year 1903, which extended from mid-1902 to mid-1903, the company hauled 80,000 tons of forest products with the next largest tonnage being peanuts, 2,475 tons. This report should eliminate any doubt that the S.S.&S. was strictly a lumber road.

During the early summer of 1902, ten flatcars were added to the fleet. Later on a secondhand, and so-called second class, passenger car and thirteen boxcars were procured. The following year eleven additional boxcars were put in service. In the fall of 1904 a baggage car and five boxcars showed up. The baggage car was second hand and possibly so were the boxcars. During this time the fleet of log cars was steadily growing but we find no mention of them. Odd as it may seem, it appears that the logging cars were not numbered, and, for that matter, it has been said that the passenger equipment carried no numbers. Indications are that it did, certainly inside if not out. Such numbers were undoubtedly those assigned by the original owner. Just what the company considered a second class passenger car is hard to say, but it possibly was a coach provided for the colored patrons, or maybe it was the first coach purchased to be used on a labor train. On the other hand, back in those days a coach provided for the conveyance of any passengers was officially considered to be second class transportation. First class transportation was provided by the use of club, chair, or sleeping cars.

In November of 1902 the necessary parts to convert the earlier donkeys to coal burners were ordered from Baldwin. The new engines had been delivered fitted to burn that fuel and presented firing difficulties for none of the firemen had ever fired with coal, or so it seemed. After asking around it was found that only one man, Charlie Wrenn, an ex-Norfolk & Western fireman, had ever had any experience with coal and he was promptly given the job of teaching the other men the art of firing with it. The conversion from wood to coal was rather rapid, once it had started, for the management recognized the potential market value of the wood formerly used as fuel. Then, too, coal firing was more satisfactory as it tended to give an even heat for a longer time between stokings, and it was less apt to set fires along the right of way. During the fiscal year ending June 30, 1902, the company used 3,970 cords of wood and no coal. The following June the report stated that 1,525 cords of wood and 2,807 tons of coal were used, but the report for the year ending June 30, 1904, showed that the conversion had been completed and only a very small amount of wood had been consumed.

The increased activity in the woods naturally required a larger labor force and this was not available locally. The company imported about 150 Russians, bringing them down from New York to Scotland Wharf by boat. They were then loaded into three boxcars and hauled on the end of a string of empty log cars to Straw Hill. In anticipation of their arrival, a number of deserted farm dwellings were fixed up to house them. These were located between Zigler's Trestle and Straw Hill. To take any overflow that might occur, tar paper shacks were erected at Straw Hill. To welcome them, a feast of cheese, white bread, and other foods considered to be typically Russian were prepared.

When they were signed up, they were lead to believe that they would be housed in various towns along the railroad and transported to and from the woods each day. Basically that is exactly how the company planned it, but the further they went the smaller the "towns" became and when the train finally stopped at the point where the "reception" had been prepared, they were completely disillusioned and there was considerable grumbling. By the time the engine was turned at Straw Hill, had picked up its train and was starting back to Dendron, several of the newcomers were already walking the ties on their way back to civilization. It was the beginning of a general exodus. In an effort to hold as many as possible, a general order was put out that no Russian was to be allowed to ride in an engine cab, but trouble finally reached the point where it was decided to ship out the new help. A special train was made up and all who wished to leave, left.

It was during this prolonged embargo on hauling foreign labor that a train overtook one of them staggering down the track. Repeated toots of the whistle failed to swerve him from his eradic course, so the train was stopped and the engineer walked forward to see what it was all about. He was fairly sure that it was just another case of the man being too drunk to know what he was doing but there was no odor of whiskey and all he could say was, "Me sick, me very sick." Obviously he was, and rule or no rule, he was loaded into the cab and taken to Dendron where he was turned over to the company doctor. Although he received all of the attention possible, he died, the first local victim of what became known a year or so later as the dreaded "flu".

The company learned from experience and later on when more Russian labor was brought in, they handled everything differently by settling them in the logging camps, more or less with the other woods labor. Of course, some of them left but a large number settled in the area, married, and raised families. There was quite a settlement known as Russian Church located south of the Double-Barreled Road Crossing, as it was called. This road crossing was roughly three-quarters of a mile south of Hunting Quarter Branch and three and a half miles north of Yale. The Russian settlement was on the road between the crossing and Yale, a little over a mile north of Yale, and consisted of the church and a few scattered houses. The Double-Barreled Road Crossing, or as the company generally shortened the name to the Double Crossing, was nothing unusual except for the fact that the railroad crossed two county roads within a matter of feet and the crossing whistle had to be unusually prolonged. The crews were generally very careful when approaching the crossing and although both roads were fairly well traveled, no one remembers there ever having been an accident there. That isn't saying that none occurred for there generally has to be a reason for such caution.

The Russians kept more or less to themselves for they naturally preferred to associate with people they understood and the ways of the local inhabitants were beyond their comprehension when it came to everyday living. That difference naturally bred suspicion. When they first arrived the men wore the dress of the typical Russian peasant; leather boots, caps, baggy trousers, and heavy coats. They were steady workers and grumbled only moderately at the very worst conditions, which were really bad at times. Some saved as much of their wages as the company commissary would allow and bought little patches of land, working in the woods during the day and tending their holdings when they could. Some of them were excellent farmers and as such were gradually accepted by their neighbors, but it took many years before you ceased to hear "that Russian family". In fact, you can hear it now, once in a while, after sixty years. Some of the older inhabitants still chuckle at the memory of a booted Russian sitting in the sun on the edge of the West Hope commissary porch, chewing on a hunk of raw salt pork cut from a slab with his hunting knife and apparently quite content.

Improvements and expansion had cost considerable money, all of which had been supplied by the lumber company. To make paper compensation and to show an increased valuation of the railway company property, 500 shares of stock were issued and taken by the parent company in payment. This doubled the amount of outstanding stock of the railway company but did not require an increase of the capitalization of $500,000, of which $400,000 still remained in reserve. On June 30, 1904, the company reported current liabilities of $527,991. Against this they listed the cost of the road at $306,640, cost of the equipment at $85,023, cash and current assets at only $213, and a profit and loss account of $136,115, that amount representing the accumulated deficit. As the owners considered the railway part of the business to be merely a part of the overall operation, they were extremely lax in maintaining separate accounts or in reporting the financial condition of the subsidiary. It might be said that a deficit was deliberately shown on the books for tax purposes, not that one didn't actually exist. If there had been a profit from operations, it would have been absorbed by the parent company as rightfully belonging to them, and that would have been the end of it.

As the lumber business continued to boom, the amount of finished lumber hauled to Scotland Wharf increased in quantity. The company finally came to the conclusions that the amount being transported by the mail train was insufficient, and that No. 2 was too light for the run. She was still a lively little kettle, with a light train, for she had been kept in excellent shape, including the installation of new grates for the burning of coal in December 1902. She was just too light on her drivers to be hauling a mixed train. With a replacement in mind, the management began looking around for a heavier locomotive, something second hand in a relatively good condition, and reasonably priced. In the late summer of 1903 Higgins located a Baldwin Vauclain compound ten-wheeler that had been made available by the broadening out of the narrow gauge Pittsburgh, Johnstown, Ebensburg & Eastern at the time of its consolidation with the New York & Pittsburgh Central. The engine was purchased and shipped to Wakefield, unloaded, towed to Dendron, and made ready for service. So far as tractive effort was concerned, the engine was everything that could be desired for it was apparently impossible to stall it. On the other hand, the compound idea, being something entirely new so far as the shop personnel was concerned, was none too popular. Then, too, there were certain mechanical weaknesses, possibly brought on by the light, rough track.

When the ten-wheeler was ready for service, the smoke box number plates were swapped with the eight-wheeler and the new No. 2 went to work hauling the mail train. The little American was then offered for sale and in 1912 we find her working on the Rocky Mount & Northern, a logging line operated by the Tar River Lumber Company at Rocky Mount, N. C. This line paralleled the Atlantic Coast Line's Spring Hope branch for a short distance, swung north to cross the Tar River on a wooden trestle and terminated in what was known as the Red Oak Section.

After B Mill was erected, water for the boilers became a problem during protracted dry spells and after the size of the plant was practically doubled, the water problem during the dry months occasionally became downright acute. The first effort made to obtain sufficient water when the Blackwater River dropped and the impounded water in the company's pond was exhausted, was to ditch water from the river bed to a point where it could be reached by the pump suction. If the dry weather persisted, the water level would frequently drop below the suction strainer and no amount of ditching would solve the problem. On the other hand, there seemed to always be water in Cypress Swamp, at Sexton, for the swamp was partially fed by springs.

Syphoning water from the swamp was fairly easy for there were natural holes in which the water collected. About 200 yards above the trestle was a rather large hole, the water from which was made available at the trestle by opening a ditch in the stream bed. Below the trestle was a stretch known as Dixie's Run in which water collected. This was also ditched, bringing the water upstream to within reach of the suction hose. Even so, on occasions every available hole was syphoned dry and the crew had to sit and wait for them to fill.

To transport the water from the source of supply to the mills, three or four rectangular pine boxes were made of four by six timber, each box being approximately five feet high, seven feet wide, and twelve feet long, and strengthened with iron rods. The tops were open and slosh boards, in the form of non-watertight partitions, were installed. The boxes were slid onto the deck cars when in use and off when no longer required. They were not fastened down in any manner, their weight being sufficient to hold them in position.

A water train usually consisted of an engine and one car. It was invariably run at night after all other traffic had ceased, for the main line was blocked while the train set on the trestle and waited for the tank to be filled. The process of filling a tank was both effective and simple, almost as much so as emptying it. On occasions a crew would work all night and the main problem was for at least one man to stay awake at all times. When the car had been spotted and the syphon rigged, and was functioning properly, it was strictly a case of keeping up steam and waiting for the tank to fill. One brakesman perfected a system whereby he could lean up against the tank and sleep with his hand dangling down inside. When the cool water reached his hand, it would awaken him and he would wake the engine crew. The syphon would then be disconnected and they would pull out for Dendron. On one occasion when the entire crew went to sleep, the steam dropped to the point where the syphon failed to function. The engineer was the first to rouse and found a partially filled tank, a dead syphon, no steam, boiler water so low that it wouldn't run from the bottom try cock, and practically no fire on the grates. It was an embarrassing situation, to say the least.

On arrival at Dendron the water car was spotted as near the cistern to be filled as possible. These cisterns were enormous brick and concrete affairs almost completely buried in the ground and the water was normally pumped into them through a network of buried pipes. When discharged the water ran through a wooden trough from the car to the cistern. Each wooden trough could be moved slightly to simplify the spotting of the car. The tanks had a valve on one side at the bottom, three or four inches in size, which when opened let the water shoot out and into the trough. If the crew wanted to hurry things along, a gravity syphon made of pipe was filled and hung over the side of the box, thus adding about a three-inch stream to the discharge.

To put pressure on the fire plugs located throughout the property, water was pumped into the smallest of three overhead tanks and to increase the pressure, steam fire pumps were installed. The fire pumps were strictly on a standby status for the height of the tank was sufficient to put enough pressure on the lines for flushing and washing down. An intricate system of piping and valves interconnected all tanks and cisterns although during dry weather no attempt was made to keep the two larger tanks filled. Water was piped from one of these to the mills and shops, and to two of the many residences, that of the general superintendent and the mill superintendent. Water was not furnished to any of the other residences, the stores, or the hotel. All that could be said for this water was that it was wet, for it was strictly brackish, untreated, swamp water. It was not used for drinking or cooking, such water being obtained from an excellent spring until the general superintendent fouled it by an overfall from his cesspool. Wells were then driven. The water tank across the track from the station, from which the engines took water, was filled by an independent pump pulling water from a driven well.

Speaking of putting pressure on the fire plugs brings to mind the periodic fire drills. Oil came in barrels, as did salt fish, pickles, flour, sugar, and a number of other items. As the empty barrels accumulated out back of the Dendron commissary, they were eventually set on fire as a means of disposal. It was then that the mill whistle let go with frantic bleats and the hose crews vied with each other to hook up and get a stream on the blaze. The oil-soaked barrels made quite a blaze and the boiling smoke added a bit of realism to the event. It was very spectacular and rather exciting. Salt, fish, sugar, flour, and a number of staple foods, as well as oil, were purchased by the carload lot and distributed to the other commissaries from Dendron. They came cheaper that way.

Water for the mules and men in the swamp, or woods, when not available from streams, was obtained from open wells dug at convenient locations. Occasionally these wells ran dry and it was then necessary to haul in water, the tank car being used as a storage tank at the camp.

It is impossible to state definitely the length of any branch, when it went in or when it came out. Nor is it possible to say how many branches were in service at any given time. All that can be done is to quote the approximate total mileage of probably all of the branches at the time the yearly report was made, a most unsatisfactory approximation at best. For instance, on June 30, 1900, a total branch mileage of twenty miles was given. The same mileage was given two years prior. These two mileages must have covered the remains of the Slabtown line and the track west of Dory. As of June 30, 1891, the total mileage was given as only six miles for the branches, which was undoubtedly the Slabtown line and other short branches. From this we can deduce that the Slabtown line was pulled out during the fiscal year ending June 30, 1901,

as an increase of only a mile and a half is shown as of that date
and we know for a certainty that steel was still being pushed
towards Prince George County, thus making such a small increase unreasonable unless something came out to offset the
increase in length of that line. Even so, just exactly what happened and what went in and what came out, and when, is impossible to tell with any kind of accuracy.

The following year, 1901-1902, six and a half miles were reported as an increase over the previous year, making a total
of 28 miles of branch lines. This was undoubtedly largely accounted for by the West Hope Branch and was possibly its maximum length. This supposition is strengthened by the fact that
only an increase of 1,320 feet was reported the following year.
This does not mean that the track wasn't shuffled constantly,
for it was, neither does it mean that only that amount of new
track was laid. It is simply the reported increase in the total
length of branch line track over the previous year and it does
not include the donkey tracks.

The end of fiscal 1904 saw an increase of seven miles
of branch line mileage which could have been the extension
of the main line south from Dory to Vicksville, and of the beginning of construction of the Plank Road Extension from a
switch where the West Hope branch crossed the old toll road
between Assamoosick Swamp and Chub. Although the line
south from Dory was an extension of the main line, it was considered to be a logging branch. There has always been considerable speculation as to why the railway company did not extend common carrier service south as the main line was extended over the years but there has never been an answer other
than the fact that possibly the estimated common carrier traffic did not warrant the trouble of altering the charter.

Logging operations north of Straw Hill reached their peak
around the early part of 1904. By 1905 considerable logging was
again being done to the south. Several fairly long woods tracks
were laid between Straw Hill and West Hope, one of which left
the branch right at the south end of Peeples' Bridge and
followed the south bank of the river for some distance southwest through the bordering swamp. The line east from Vicksville was also being extended northeast. Like most of the

logging lines, this branch just grew, reaching further and further into the woods as the timber was cut and new stands acquired. Although the branch was eventually quite long, Vicksville was always the camp from which it was worked.

Due to this gradual extension, the branch was not sanded until it was of some length. The track was simply laid down on a cleared right-of-way, more or less like a donkey track, and prior to the time the company got around to improving it, the jacks did not venture beyond the main line switch. Donkeys brought the loads out to the switch and left them there, standing on the main line to the south, where the jacks could couple onto them without having to come in over the light track. Trains coming south always turned at the Dory wye and backed down to Vicksville. Twice a day empties were brought down from Dendron and kicked into the branch so that a donkey setting on the main line south of the switch, against the loads, could run up after the jack had pulled up out of the way, and back into the branch against the empties. It would then shove them on up the branch and distribute them where needed. When the donkey had cleared the switch, the jack would back down on the loads, couple up, and leave for Dendron. The rear brakesman would drop off, throw the switch for the branch after the last car had cleared, and climb on again. This was done more or less as a courtesy to the crew bringing out the first cut of loads off the branch.

One winter morning Henry Billings brought down a string of empties with No. 10, turned his train at Dory and backed down past Vicksville to the switch. Cornwall, with the 15, had brought out the last cut of logs required to make up a train and had backed them down against the other loads. He had cut loose and was waiting for Billings. The string of empties arrived, was shoved around into the branch clear of the switch, and then Billings cut off and eased up far enough for Cornwall to run up and back in against them. Everything went according to plan, up to a certain point.

The 15 leaned against the string of empties and got them moving, the 10 drifted on down against the loads, coupled up, and got ready to leave but when Billings opened the throttle, the train refused to get rolling as it should. There was ice on the

rails and the 10 couldn't get a grip. Sanding didn't help very
much. After some see-sawing the train began to move, after a
fashion, and the last car cleared the switch. The brakesman
threw the switch for the branch, ran, and climbed on. The 10
was still having trouble staying on her feet.

The grade to the north was fairly heavy and Billings coaxed
his charge nearly to the top but it just couldn't make it and
finally stalled. The driver brakes were set and Billings
whistled for hand brakes but before enough of them could be
set to hold the train, gravity took over and began dragging the
whole works down the grade, the locked steam brakes having
no effect on the icy rails. Billings then tried to hold his train
with reverse lever and sand but the speed slowly increased.
Under normal conditions the brakes would have been released
and the train allowed to run free until the opposing grade
stopped it, then the throttle would have been opened and a run
made for the grade, but there was no opposing grade, just a
dead end, and there was that open switch into the branch. Billings knew that if the jack was dragged into the branch, it was
a sure thing that the light rail would collapse under her. Once
on the ground it would be impossible to get her back on
the main line without practically building a new track.

Something had to be done, and fast. He told his fireman to
climb back over the tender and when he released the brakes
and nudged the cars to take the strain off the link, to pull the
pin and let 'em roll. He silently prayed that the 15 had managed
to shove the empties far enough up the branch to be out of the
way when the loads came charging into the woods spur. With
brakes set, there was little doubt that the train would stop on
the first upgrade, but unbeknown to Billings, the 15 was
having its share of trouble on the first grade in from the
switch.

The pin was pulled and Billings got his engine stopped. The
loads barreled through the switch and around the curve into
the branch with the brakemen sailing off like birds. In
the meantime, Cornwall was sawing back and forth, trying
to get the little donkey to stay on its feet long enough to get the
cars over the top of the grade. He happened to glance back towards the switch just as the loads swung in on him. He and his

fireman hit the ground running. As far away as possible was going to be too close when those loads hit the donkey, and hit they did. That donkey was a thoroughly messed up little engine. The logs stripped it clean from the front end to the steam dome, and the empties stripped her clean from the rear. Those empty log cars rode up over the coupler, crumpled the bunker like paper, smashed the cab into kindling wood, and climbed up over the boiler head. The donkey was literally buried in logs and smashed log cars. They eventually got the mess cleaned up and the shop was able to rebuild the equipment but it was quite some time before Cornwall stopped looking back over his shoulder at the track behind him. You couldn't blame him.

He was very much like the newly hired brakesman who was helping unload some l.c.l. freight from the mail train when it was hit from the rear. It scared him so badly that he walked off the job right then and there and didn't even bother to come back for his pay. Railroadin' just wasn't for him.

Southward

By 1906 all logging operations had ceased north of Straw Hill and the track was up to that point. Logging was still being done north of West Hope and cutting had begun between there and the Nottoway Trestle. As rail was in demand elsewhere, it was decided to abandon Straw Hill and begin stripping the line back towards West Hope. The inhabitants were loaded on passenger cars, their household furnishings into boxcars, and everything, including the commissary, was moved to a new camp known as Upson. This camp had been built in anticipation of the move and was located around the point where the branch crossed the Plank Road for the first time, a mile west of Assamoosick Swamp. It was at this point that the Plank Road Extension switched off the branch and headed south. The new camp consisted of the inevitable commissary and numerous houses strung out along the west side of the road both north and south of the crossing and along a street that had been laid out parallel with the railroad to the north and east of the crossing. It was on this street that the Russian woods labor lived.

Upson was strictly a logging camp, temporary in nature, being rather dead during the day but alive in a subdued, tired way at night after the logging crew had returned from the woods. The camp was named for Ernest Upson, the company's bookkeeper at Straw Hill, a well liked person who was eventually forced to retire because of poor health.

As soon as Upson was established, logging was begun in earnest along the Plank Road Extension which was gradually extended south until it reached beyond what became the Virginian Railway in 1907, west of Sebrell. During the first year or two of operation, the line was sanded for only a distance of about five miles, at which point a siding was installed where empties could be put to clear the loads brought up from the south by the donkeys. Trains were assembled there for the jacks dared venture no further over the rough track.

At the end of June 1906 the Surry Lumber Company, not the railway company, made a report in which they listed 15 locomotives and 202 cars as the total amount of equipment in use.

Obviously this included all of the equipment in use on the railroad, or was supposed to, but one item is open to doubt. Whoever made up the report either could not count or there was a
standard gauge locomotive in the company's lumber yard at
Norfolk, Virginia. In later years there was a four-wheel gasoline shunter in service there and we do not know when it was
purchased. However, so far as the narrow gauge motive power
is concerned, we can count only fourteen locomotives. A report
for 1905 states definitely that there were two shifting engines,
which would be the 4 and 6, four freight engines which would
be the jacks, and seven tank engines, the 3, 5, 7, 9, 11, 15, and
17. No mention was made of the No. 2 but it would have been
included to make 14 locomotives. Maybe whoever made that
report forgot that No. 1 was gone. The report further stated
that the shifting and freight engines were fitted with American
Brake Company steam brakes but that the tank engines had
no brakes of any kind. The report of 1903 stated that there were
four freight engines, nine shifting engines, and one passenger
engine. The moguls and donkeys were grouped together to
make the nine shifting engines.

So far as the 202 cars are concerned, that would be about
right for the number of log cars but as they listed the railway
company's locomotives, we have to take it for granted that they
also listed their cars. This would leave 139 cars, the majority
of which were undoubtedly log cars.

This seems as good a place as any to comment on one thing
that merits attention and that is the colloquialism as found on
the narrow gauge. Apparently every railroad had a certain individuality in speech as well as everything else and Surry
Lumber Company's railroad was no exception. Undoubtedly
the reader has already wondered about the frequent apparent
incorrect use of the term "donkey" when referring to one of
the small tank engines. That term was purely local and its de-
rivative has already been explained. Then, there is that
"brakesman" which was possibly derived from the fact that
one man was responsible for more than one brake but it
doesn't explain the plural "brakemen". Nor can we explain
the pronunciation of "coach". It was "coe-ach", almost two
words, and it was applied to all passenger-carrying convey-
ances hauled in the mail train as well as the labor coaches. We

also have the term "No. 2" which was applied to the mail train, be it Train 1, 2, 3, or 4. This is easily explained for from the very beginning to very near the end, the mail train was hauled by a locomotive carrying the road number "2". Those are only a few of the more obvious variations of speech but they serve to illustrate the differences encountered on this extremely individualistic railroad.

A hard summer rain had fallen just before dawn on that July morning in 1906 and was just tapering off when the donkey took the labor train west from Upson, crossed the Nottoway and climbed the grade leading up from the river towards West Hope. Water was literally pouring down the ditches on both sides of the track, but, so far as anyone could see, the track was still solid. No one thought anything about possible scours or washed out ballast. Sydney Barker, with No. 12, was following the labor train at a respectable distance with the morning's supply of empties.

Dan Presson was firing extra on the jack that morning, being third choice, for Merritt Bishop had gone off to get married and his regular replacement, Hodman Conway, could not be found. When the call boy went looking for him, Dan's mother said that he was off partying but that she would surely tell him when he came home. It was quite late when he got home, but he was told, and he was riding the footplate that morning. Dan had trouble staying awake and after they left Dory he prevailed upon the head end brakesman to spell him while he took a nap on the brakesman's seat up beside the left side of the firebox.

The train cleared the trestle, crossed the truss bridge, and began the climb up out of the bottom. It happened without a second's warning. The track simply dropped out from under the left side of the locomotive and it pitched over on its side, crushing Presson between the boiler and the left side of the cab. He was killed instantly. An investigation showed that the water rushing down the grade had scoured under one side of the track and had softened the grade to the extent that it squashed out when the weight of the heavy jack was applied. The donkey had not been heavy enough to cause the track to settle.

Presson's widow was given the house in which they lived at Dendron for the rest of her life, rent free. In addition, the company kept up the property, free of charge, and paid the taxes. There was no insurance or cash settlement, but she was guaranteed a place to live. That was a company policy and even today descendents of the original occupants still maintain residence in houses left their mothers, although the free rent policy ceased when the lumber company went out of business. At that time the occupants were offered the property at a ridiculously low figure, averaging around $500 a dwelling, and most of them took advantage of the offer. Yes, Dan's mother lived with him and his wife.

In the early part of 1906 survey stakes crept across Jerusalem District of Southampton County, south of Vicksville, definitely locating the route of the Tidewater Railroad. This standard gauge line was being built from Norfolk to the West Virginia state line and was to be strictly a coal hauler. The company immediately went into high gear and began leveling off a grade in a direct line with and from the stub end of the extended main line at Vicksville. The idea was to get the grade completed and the track laid across the Tidewater grade before the contractor could complete the grade of the standard gauge and lay track on it, thus blocking the narrow gauge from timber tracts purchased by the Surry Lumber Company as far back as 1888. Christmas of 1906 found the lumber company graders within sight of the proposed crossing and Tidewater construction gangs were bearing down on them from two directions. To complicate matters, steel was advancing rapidly from the east, close on the heels of the graders. It was a close race but the lumber company won, thus requiring the standard gauge to pay for the special work for the crossing. The narrow gauge gang couldn't very well drop their tools as soon as the track was past the proposed crossing, so they kept going for some distance, far enough to insure against the standard gauge shifting its location slightly and building around the south end of the logging line. The crossing was guaranteed.

There wasn't any race to get the Plank Road Extension across the Tidewater's grade but the company lost no time in doing so. The Plank Road Extension had been gradually extended south for some distance, far enough to necessitate the construction of a wye for turning the jacks. At the same time

The original attempt at something resembling a motor car. Although it was referred to generally as the 600, it is very doubtful that she carried a number. The second 600 was clearly numbered.—P. B. Owen

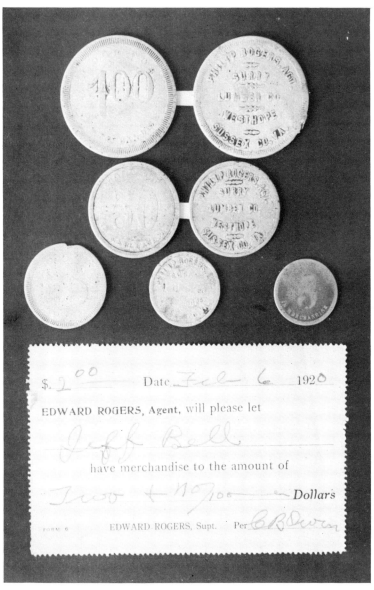

A complete set of company "money" as issued during the regime of Philip Rogers, up at West Hope. Later on Causey had a set issued from Sedley. The slip at the bottom is a credit chit authorizing so much credit at a company commissary.

Surry Lumber Company's "A" Mill and its dust collector
taken around 1921. Dendron. Va.

To assist in preparing the letterhead and large engraving generally
framed and passed around as a publicity stunt, two general views were
taken from the water tank. This view shows B Mill in the immediate foreground, then A Mill and D Mill in the distant background. The section
known as "Egypt" and the main outdoor storage yard is shown in the left
background. The view was taken looking almost due south. About 1921.

This is the second of the views made to enable the engraver to do a fairly accurate job and shows C Mill, better known as the shook mill, and a storage shed. The main line entering town from the north can be seen at the extreme left. We are looking a bit west of north from the water tank. About 1921.

A very general view of A Mill and the storage building for finished lumber. Dendron, Va. About 1916.

Loading barge *Cecil* at Scotland Wharf with dressed lumber. Standing in front of lumber skids: left to right, F. P. Seward (with hands in pocket—visiting farmer). Dick Goodson (in immediate foreground—dock superintendent), P. G. Chapman (with high pants—lumber inspector), A. R. Chapman (extreme right—lumber inspector). Standing behind lumber skids: left to right, Henry Gill (left side to camera—lumber inspector), J. J. Seward (facing camera—lumber inspector). The others are not known. This was taken in 1910 or a bit earlier.—Joseph Seward

The burning of H Mill on January 23, 1925. It might have been a spectacular fire but it doesn't make much of a picture.—Joseph Seward

The donkeys 7 and 5 wait at Sedley for Monday morning and the beginning of another week in the woods.—P. B. Owen

Car house, commissary, and highway equipment, taken at Sedley in 1922, or at least that is what the license plate says.—Mrs. P. P. Causey

A log train hauled by the 5 and 7 coming up out of the woods
to the south of Sedley.—C. B. Owen

Donkey No. 11 with her crew at
Surry.—R. L. Edwards

A section gang poses for picture. P. C. Cox, the only one sitting down, was the section foreman.—M. H. Ferrell

The third of the jacks, No. 12.

The Master Mechanic and some of the shop personnel proudly pose
with the second No. 2 that has just had Southern Valve Gear installed.
The engine shop is in the background.

Loading logs. This could have been taken on any of the
many logging spurs.—Mrs. R. L. Edwards

The last of the jacks, the 14. The engineer on
the ground is Sam Atkinson.

One of the Percherons introduced by Causey to replace the mules. Here
we see a really beautiful animal, the prize horse in the work horse class
at the 1918 Four Counties Fair at Suffolk, Va. James C. Causey is the one
holding the reins.—Geo. L. Barton, Jr.

James C. Causey—Logging Superintendent
from 1915 to 1927.

Dr. P. P. Causey, the company doctor. and his private
"car", the 600.—Mrs. P. P. Causey

The entire mill personnel assembles for
picture at Dendron.

A builder's picture of the 16.—Baldwin
Locomotive Works

The newly arrived 16 and her crew proudly pose for their picture. Left to right, we have Nealey Hawkins, brakesman; Thomas J. Bain, engineer; Hugh Hargrave, fireman, and, of course, the 16.—T. J. Bain

"The 600 clear at Indigo Siding." So, Causey reports back to Dendron that he is in the clear for an opposing log train. Taken between Dory and Vicksville in July 1920.—Geo. L. Barton, Jr.

The mysterious 18 entertains visitors on a Sunday afternoon. Of the three visitors, we know only Clyde King at the right, engineer of the third No. 1 at Central Hill. Apparently this is the closest the bashful 18 ever came to getting her picture taken.

Willie Lewis oils his 19 at Dendron while waiting for the Rotarians to complete their personally conducted tour of the mills. The Suffolk Rotary Club had come up in response to Causey's invitation. A special train was run for their accommodation.—Geo. L. Barton, Jr.

The Suffolk, Va., Rotary Club members line up beside the 17 for their picture. The man second from the right in the front row, holding his hat under his arm is Amadio Obici, the acknowledged peanut king of the world and certainly one of the most philanthropic men Virginia ever had.— Geo. L. Barton, Jr.

The argument in 1915 at Dendron between the Atkinson brothers, tied up the main line as well as the yard tracks. Here we have Archie's No. 10 on her side . . .

and to get him out of the cab they had to dig a trench
under it. He wasn't hurt, just bruised a bit.

During the whole affair Sam just sat and waited in the cab of his No. 14,
for he couldn't go anywhere with that derailed tender.

No. 4 after being converted for use as a shifting engine
in the Dendron mill yard.—Joseph Lavelle

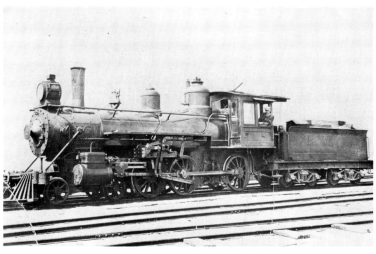

The rebuilt second No. 2 waits on the dock
at Scotland.—E. T. Atkinson

A Sunday School excursion loads at Sedley. The car is the all-purpose car kept at that place for use of the paymaster.—P. B. Owen

Employees of the Surry Lumber Company at Vicksville, Va. In the back row, left to right, Nat Williams, engineer of No. 17; Act King, loader; W. H. Kitchen, fireman; Joe Hancock, track man; Bill King, foreman; Caesar Temple, engineer; H. W. Taylor, foreman. In front row, left to right, Herbert Turner, sawyer; J. T. Joyner, track man; Richard Owen, Vicksville Superintendent; a man named Travis; Herbert Ellsworth, foreman; another man named Travis who was a teamster; and finally a stranger.—P. B. Owen

The wreck at Airfield when the train of empty log cars, left, locked horns with the mail train coming up from Dory. That lowside behind the jack was loaded with coal for the donkeys in the woods.

A Sunday excursion ready to leave Sedley. The main item of interest in this is the trailer. This was used to haul men to points along the line, such as a bridge gang or section crew.—C. B. Owen

There was a colored brakesman on the S.S.&S. who felt that it was bad luck to have his "pitcher tooked". P. H. Whitmore carried his camera with him on the daily run for three days before he got a chance to use it; just to prove to the brakesman that he was wrong. But, the following day the brakesman fell between the rails at Dendron and was killed by a log car. "Maybe he was right." Whitmore said later on, "for he never got a chance to see the picture."—P. H. Whitmore

The No. 20 as the builder saw her.—
Baldwin Locomotive Works

Engine No. 22 at Surry.

A proud engineer poses with his newly assigned locomotive at Newtown. T. T. Squires and his 22.—Mrs. T. T. Squires

The 24 in the Dendron yard. The car over behind her is the saw filer's car. Sept. 1, 1930.

SURRY, SUSSEX AND SOUTHAMPTON RAILWAY
CONDUCTOR'S DAILY REPORT

Date __Nov. 20__ 192_5_

No. Train	No. T. Passes	No. Y. Passes	No. Fares	No. Tickets	Total No.	Amount Fares	Amount Tickets	Amount Freight	Total Freight and Passengers	Back Charges	Pouches Mail	Miles Run
1	1	1	1	1	1						3	14
2	1	1	3	1	4	1 00	10	35	1 45		12	30
3	2	1	7	3	8	65	60	4 54	3 79	1 51	27	30
4	1	1	2	.	2	40	-	1 56	1 96	4 15	4	14
TOTAL	2	-	8	4	14	2 05	70	6 45	7 20	3 73	43	88

TIME REPORT

STATIONS	No. 1 A	No. 1 L	No. 2 A	No. 2 L	No. 3 A	No. 3 L	No. 4 A	No. 4 L
Scotland								
Surry								
Moorings								
Elberon								
Dendron								
Wakefield								
Manry								
Dory								

Time on No. 1 ____ Time Lost ____
" " 2 ____ " " ____
" " 3 ____ " " ____
" " 4 ____ " " ____

Engine No. __30__   Engineer ____

REPORT CARS HAULED

Train No.	Coaches	Baggage	Shanks	Lumber	Empty Cars	Ties	Lathe	Shingles	Coal	Grain	Lime	Plaster	Peanuts	Mdse.	Hay	TOTAL
1	1	1														1
2	1	1		5	4								1			6?
3	1	1		4	4											2 0
4	1	1			6										2	

EMPLOYEES

	POSITION	AMOUNT EARNED
E. I. Atkinson	Conductor	
Leon Bland	Brakeman	
Richard Cote		

TIME MADE ____

TOTAL ____

A close study of the above report will tell, more than words, why the road went broke.

A general view of the Dendron yard with No. 20 more or less in the way. The combine in the distance was the pay car but here it is the caboose on a string of flats. Labor Day, 1930.

The wharf at Scotland as it
appeared in late 1930.

The interior of the cab of No. 20. The round disc at the top
of the cab is the rear headlight. September 1930.

A practice that caused a number of deaths on the narrow gauge—sitting on the tie ends. However, in this case there was no immediate danger as the last train had run a few days before. Freight cars on the station siding at Surry in early September of 1930.

The passenger train equipment at Dendron all ready for the engine that will never come again, except to haul the cars to scrap. The first and third cars eventually became summer cottages at Scotland while the middle car was the lunch room for the Surry school. Dendron, Va., September 1930.

The highway overpass at Scotland Wharf. This structure has been removed and a new road built down the bluff. December 1930.

The 20 coming into Dendron yard
from the south.

Engine No. 20 stuck on the grade north of Cypress Swamp at Sexton. Although they don't show too clearly, there are several cars of steel rails behind the engine. November 1930.

Train of rails and track iron on the way to Scotland during the stripping of the line. November 1930.

The No. 20 after being abandoned
at Scotland Wharf. 1930.

The 24 abandoned at Scotland Wharf in 1930. One of the two
last engines to see service. This was the standby.

The scrap piled along the main line at Scotland Wharf
after stripping had been completed. January 1931.

Abandoned equipment at Scotland Wharf on January 28, 1931. Left to
right, we have the baggage and mail car sitting on blocks. Next are engines 20 and 24. Behind them is a loaded lumber car and two lowsides of
coal. In the foreground is a passenger train coach and two push cars. The
track is the main line down off the bluff, the wharf being out of sight to
the left.

the line, as far as Urquart's Wye, as it was called, was sanded and the track made safe for the operation of the heavier engines. The line from Upson formed the base of the triangle which pointed to the southeast. A line continued off the point for a mile or two before it died in the swamp. The main branch continued on a short distance, just far enough to provide room to shove loads back out of the way. It was this line that was extended on southwest and a siding put in to accommodate the loads. This second crossing of the Tidewater right-of-way was also at grade and was located just east of the standard gauge's long trestle over the Nottoway River and west of Sebrell.

When finally put in service, both crossings were protected by a throw-off, as a derail was called, on both sides of the standard gauge. In neither case were logging operations begun south of the Tidewater until sometime after the crossing was in. In fact, it is said that the company owned no timber below Sebrell at the time the crossing was installed but was playing it safe, just in case standing timber was later purchased in that locality.

Right after the beginning of the new year, a town was laid out where the two railroads crossed below Vicksville, on the south side of the Tidewater, and named Sedley after a character in a novel by Scott, the name being suggested to Philip Rogers by Dora Bradshaw, according to the way it is remembered. Irrespective of how it got its name, the new town was carefully laid out by the lumber company and H. F. Watts of Petersburg, Virginia, and is still considered to be the best planned village in the county. The streets running east and west, parallel to the standard gauge, are all named for trees, naturally, the first one being Sycamore, then comes Elmwood, Maple, Walnut, Oak, Cedar, Poplar, and Hickory. The streets at right angle to the railroad are numbered, beginning at 9th Street, West and going east to 6th Street, East, there being two 1st Streets, East and West. First Street, East is the main street north and south while Sycamore Avenue is the main east-west street. All streets are sixty feet wide and all blocks are bisected east and west by a sixteen-foot alley. All except one odd lot are of a uniform size, 48 by 136 feet, the long dimension being north and south. Sewage and water lines were laid but the shallow wells from which the water was drawn caused a certain amount of sickness until deep wells were driven around 1917. It is obvious that the company had great plans for its town, but unfortunately it was always a company town and that it remained.

Philip Rogers moved his home and office to Sedley as soon as a combination home and office building could be completed on Sycamore Avenue. From then on all logging operations were controlled from there. The railway continued to be controlled from Dendron. It wasn't until several years later that the reorganized Tidewater, then known as the Virginian and now part of the Norfolk & Western, built a station in the village. There being no common carrier service offered by the narrow gauge, no station was ever constructed. The combination office and residence was built so that it was possible to hand up orders from the southwest corner of the side porch without stepping out into the weather, if it happened to be raining or snowing. The company never bothered with an elaborate spread so far as shop facilities were concerned but erected only a blacksmith's shop set in the throat of a wye about a tenth of a mile from the crossing. Later on a car house was built in which was kept a second hand combination car used as a sort of private car and as a pay car. This structure set between Sycamore Avenue and the Virginian track, west of the narrow gauge. The wye and blacksmith's shop were not put in until around 1909 when logging was begun down near Courtland. The car shed was erected much later. The wye extended east from the main line and was located in the block bound by Maple and Walnut Avenues and by 1st and 2nd Streets, West. The block was bisected by a stream which the stem of the wye crossed on a trestle and from which the engines syphoned water. This eliminated the necessity of erecting a water tank. Today the stream is still there but it is hard to believe that it ever contained enough water to supply the needs of the locomotives.

After some time the line west of Sebrell was built south four or five miles along the high ground to the east of the river bottom and eventually petered out in the low ground formed by the confluence of Assamoosick Swamp and the river.

While this line was being gradually extended, a line to the east of the swamp, the so-called main line south from Sedley, was built in the general direction of Franklin and eventually reached a length of two or three miles. As soon as the timber was cut out, a switch was put in a mile below the crossing at Sedley and the track built southwest and then west. This line eventually reached a point on the east side of the swamp just across from where the crew from Upson was cutting. Irrespective of indications and statements to the contrary, the two lines were never connected by means of a trestle across the swamp, only audibly, for the two operations were so close together that the sounds made by one could be clearly heard by the other. The crew working the west side of the swamp was quartered at Upson while that working the east side was quartered at Vicksville.

Coal for the donkeys in the woods was stored in a low-side spotted on a handy siding. There the car remained until all of the coal had been transferred, by hand, to the engine bunkers, then it was hauled out and another loaded car put in its place. All of the engines on the entire system were coaled in the same manner, irrespective of where they were working. A crew going west from Dory dropped a lowside of coal at Upson for the donkeys working down at the extreme southern end of the extension and the first crew going down there was to take it along. That happened to be Tom Bain hauling a string of empty log cars with the 12. He hung the car of coal on the rear of his train and continued on south, giving the added weight no thought. At Urquart's Wye he turned his engine and continued on south with the tender leading and his train on the nose of his engine. When coming back out he would have the loaded train behind the tender, having run through a siding and leaving the empties for the donkeys to pick up.

When crossing the Tidewater track, for it has been ascertained that this happened during the pre-Virginian days, it was the rule that all trains were to come to a full stop, but rarely was this done. The train would be slowed sufficiently for the brakesman to drop off, run ahead, make sure that nothing was in sight on the standard gauge, and only then did he throw the two manual derail levers. He would then climb on with the train still moving slowly ahead and away they would go. After crossing the tracks, the train would be slowed, the rear brakesman would drop off and throw the levers and climb on again. Bain shut off, Nealy Hawkins dropped to the ground and ran for the crossing while Bain checked his speed with the steam brake. The slack promptly bunched and it was then that the added weight made itself felt for the engine didn't slow down as quickly as it usually did. In the meantime Hawkins had checked the crossing, thrown the derail on the far side, and started back for the near derail but he didn't make it. The tender was right on top of him and he didn't dare get close enough to throw the lever. By the time Bain finally got stopped, both tender and engine were on the ground, with the rear of the tender fouling the Tidewater track. There is no explaining why Nealy didn't first throw the near derail and then check the crossing before going over to throw the far one except for the fact that his method could be accomplished with less walking. True, the rule was to check first, but the rule also required that the train be brought to a complete stop. Rule or no rule, the trainmen generally worked out a method to do everything in a way that required the less effort and that was the way it was done.

An effort was made to rerail the engine, using the derailer as a rerailer, but the train was too heavy for the derailed engine to move. She would simply slip her drivers and chew deeper into the ties. A brakesman was then sent to the nearest 'phone box to call Dendron for help. While the crew was sitting around, waiting, a Tidewater mixed train came up from the east. After ascertaining what was holding them up, the Tidewater crew eased their train up to the crossing and stopped. The first question to settle was if anything could be done to let them by. By sighting down the side of the train it was found that there was just enough room to get by if the coupler on the rear of the tender was removed, so off it came and the Tidewater train squeezed by. After some time a donkey came up out of the woods and provided the added push to move the train. Without too much effort the engine and tender were coaxed back over the derail and onto the track. As the track hadn't been damaged, the derail was removed, the train went on its way, and the incident was forgotten, almost.

Another type of accident occurred on the Plank Road Extension whose repercussions were spread over a wide area, a collision on the one curve in about six miles of track. Bob Wellons was bringing a string of loads north on the nose of No. 3, running bunker first. John Williams had already taken a string up to Upson ahead of him with No. 7 and had started back for the woods, running light and bunker first. Bob obviously expected John to stay at Upson until he arrived and then both would run light back into the woods. John just as obviously thought he would be able to get back to a siding before meeting Bob, or maybe he thought that Bob would stay in the woods until he had returned. As Bob told the story, we will never know John's thoughts on the matter. Anyway, the result was that the two engines came together, bunkers first, on the curve. The two crews saw each other at about the same time and both engineers reversed their engines and went out of their gangways with their firemen going out of the opposite ones. The engines hit, but not hard enough to be derailed, and on the rebound No. 7 took the bit in its teeth and lit out for Upson. No. 3 had a heavy train to hold her so she just set and churned until Bob climbed back into the cab and closed the throttle. His fireman then pulled the pin on the train, climbed into the cab with No. 7's crew right on his heels, and they took off after the runaway engine.

They ran just as fast as Bob dared push the donkey, but it wasn't fast enough. The 7 went barreling around the Upson curve, rattled through the switch, but when she hit the Plank Road crossing, the accumulation of dirt over the rails was too much for her. She jumped the track, rolled across the road, and toppled over. There she lay, churning away until the crew came up on No. 3, ran over and managed to close the throttle. The derailed engine lay as though she was tired from the dash north, sort of panting from the exertion, and the stack was showing more water than steam for the drier pipe had been flooded when she went over.

With Straw Hill abandoned and the track up beyond West Hope, logging operations were concentrated in the area encompassed by the bow of the river. Porter's Wye was put in and a branch built west for some distance, ending at the

Stony Creek-Jarrett road. Several other short spurs were put in and taken out as timber was cut from various small tracts. It was on one of these woods lots that an extremely embarrassing situation took place.

The piece of track involved in the incident was not unlike many others, it just left the main branch and ran into the woods directly to the section being logged. However, this particular track ran down into a gully and tailed up over a rise on the far side. From this track, donkey tracks switched off and ran up and down the gully. Empties were shoved back on the tail of the spur until needed at which time a donkey would go up and bring down the number required. When it became necessary to clear the loads out of the donkey tracks, an engine would bring down all of the empties, shove them into a convenient spur, shove the loads up on the trailing track, and then shove the empties back up against them. Thus, the empties were always available and the loads were back of them, up on the rise. Three donkeys were working the spurs at that time, the 3, 5, and 17, and each in turn shoved loads up the hill and brought down the needed empties. No one paid too much attention to the loads.

The first loads had been shoved to the bitter end of the track but as their number increased and the number of empties decreased, the weight of the train hanging over the edge gradually overcame that of the anchor cars and it took a little something extra to hold them in place. No one added that something extra and while the crews were busy down below on the donkey tracks, the loads began to inch down the grade, the brake shoes slipping just a fraction of an inch at a time. Finally all of the slack was out of the couplings and the cars on top of the hump began to feel the urge to move. The imperceptible movement became a crawl and the crawl a walk, with the brakes shoes screeching in protest. Due to this protest, the cars sort of eased down the grade and came to rest in the bottom, effectively blocking all of the spurs. Several men admitted having seen the cars moving but paid no attention to them, thinking that they were again being shuffled by some crew. Finally it came time to shove more loads up onto the tail track. A brakesman walked out to see what was holding up the crew with the string of loads and found no crew, just the loads. Not only were they effectively blocking his switch but they had all the others tied up tight, too. No donkey could get out to move them. Efforts were made to move them with chains and poles but they were ineffective due to the grade and the angle.

There was only one thing to do, so the woods boss walked out to the branch line switch and reported by phone to Dendron that all logging operations had been brought to a halt, and why, then sat down to wait. Eventually No. 8 came along with a string of loads and was promptly flagged. The situation was explained, a certain amount of kidding took place, and then the engineer cut off his train and carefully, oh, so carefully, eased back into the branch. He coupled up to the string of cars and brought them out, still being very careful until the engine was back on the main branch. The loads were backed down onto the train and then the engine pulled up again to allow a donkey to come out, gather up the empties that were coupled to the recalcitrant loads, and shove them back into the woods. The jack then coupled up again and went its way. Conditions returned to normal in the woods but thereafter when the loads began to accumulate up on the far grade, not only were the brakes given an extra twist, but the wheels were chocked, and you can rest assured that someone kept an eye on them.

Of course, the narrow gauge had to get involved in the last public hanging in Surry County, that of Jack Davis for knocking Charlie Pittman, a groceryman at Dendron, in the head. The fact is that there were very few important events taking place in the three counties served by the railroad that it didn't get involved in, it being that important in the lives of the people. Prior to the introduction of private executions by electrocution and the carrying out of all death sentences at the prison in Richmond, each county sheriff had the unpleasant responsibility of performing all executions ordered by law in his territory and all such executions were by hanging at the county seat. Although such executions were open to the public, by law, it had been the custom to hold the Surry hangings, of which there were extremely few, over in the woods to the southeast of the court house, out of sight of the dwellings and the roads, but the burning of the court house in 1906 and the holding of this particular trial in the general store might have had something to do with the decision to change the location. Anyway, it was decided to build the scaffold in the southeast corner of the court house square, behind the jail.

The crowd was on hand early that March morning in 1907 for word had been circulated that the execution would take place early and there are those who will swear that No. 2's whistle had a more than usual mournful tone as it came through on the six o'clock train. Just as soon as the train had departed, the main actor in the tragedy was brought out and quickly hung. When the train returned to Surry around eight a. m. there was a long, pine box waiting at the station, and so, the narrow gauge hauled away the body of the last person to be legally hung in Surry County.

In 1907 or '08 there was trouble down in Assamoosick Swamp on the West Hope line due to a wandering bull. Each evening a donkey ran through from where the logging was being done west of Chub to Upson and Vicksville, hauling a deck car upon which the loggers rode on their way home, a sort of abbreviated labor train. On this particular evening No. 7 had the run and about twenty men rode the car. The engineer lived at Upson, so when the train reached there he dropped off, the fireman moved over to the right side, a brakesman took charge of the shovel, and the train continued on its way. Maybe the replacement was in too great a hurry or maybe he didn't realize how fast he was running, anyway he went down the grade east of Upson like falling down a well. When a bull suddenly showed up in the middle of the track at the west end of the swamp trestle, he simply could not get the train stopped in time. The donkey hit the critter a resounding blow, knocking him into the swamp and diving in after him, both landing with their feet in the air. The deck car nosed down the fill, tobogganing its human cargo into the mud. No one was hurt too badly, just thoroughly shook up, and muddied.

To get the engine out, a skidder was sent down and the donkey set on its wheels. The skidder was made fast to a convenient tree, a long line was run out and made fast to the frame of the engine and she was literally dragged to high ground. Once clear of the swamp, it was only a matter of time and work before the engine was back on the track, a sad sight but not badly damaged.

An accident of a like nature, but not with such drastic results, took place some time later when Sam Atkinson hit a young bull on the Airfield trestle with No. 14. Sam was coming down to the trestle at a moderate rate of speed and could see the half-grown youngster standing between the rails at the end of the trestle, watching the approaching train as only a member of the bovine family can. The whistle was blown several times but it apparently only aroused his curiosity and instead of going down the fill as Sam expected him to, he just stood there and stared. The steam brake was applied and the speed checked but there was no chance of getting stopped. Just as the engine seemed about to hit him, the bull wheeled and started across the trestle but almost immediately stepped between the ties. The cowcatcher rolled him under the front end, across one rail. As the front truck rode up over the carcass, both men in the cab were sure that the engine was going over but the truck wheel dropped back on the rail and the following front driver completed severing the carcass in half. For a second conditions were rather tense but the only casualties were nerves and the young bull.

When telling of the incident, a former fireman said that no engineer in his right mind would deliberately run into a flock of sheep, or even over one sheep, if he could possibly help it. So far as he knew, no engineer on the narrow gauge had ever done it, but he was very sure that to get a sheep rolled under the front end was to end up in the ditch for the natural oil in the wool acted as a lubricant and the wheels could not get a grip on it. Bulls were a different and constantly recurring story. Odd that no trouble was had with cows. Maybe they had more sense than to argue with a locomotive.

During 1908 the company embarked upon a program of replacing the original iron of the main line with heavier relay steel. This was made necessary by the fact that the jacks were beating the light track to pieces and it was requiring too much attention to keep it in repair. There was also the fact that the light rails were beginning to show considerable wear. The weight of the new rail varied slightly but averaged 35 pounds per yard, and it wasn't until the late summer of 1909 that the work was completed. The original iron went into the woods, replacing rail that was completely worn out. Nearly all of the rail formerly used in the woods had been purchased second hand, anything being acceptable as long as it was light and cheap.

Due to operating conditions, the single-slide crosshead guides installed on all of the locomotives had been giving trouble, causing excessive wear of the cylinder rod glands and bushings, and the crosshead slippers. Higgins installed a double-slide guide on one of the woods engines and it gave such satisfactory results that in September 1908 he ordered standard double-slide guides for the four jacks from Baldwin, and installed them. The new type crossheads were gradually installed on all of the engines and worked very well.

Passenger service naturally varied slightly over the years but basically it was the same, two round trips a day, six days a week. That was all that was ever required for passenger business was never heavy, and it met the requirements of the post office people. These runs were generally mixed, certainly between Dendron and the river, although straight passenger trains would not be called rare. In the mid-'20's the first run of the day, Train No. 1, left Dendron at 6 a. m. and reached Scotland Wharf at 7, an hour later. After a layover of 25 minutes, No. 2 left the wharf and ran through to Manry, arriving at 9:38 a. m. Officially this was the end of the run but it was necessary to run on to Dory to turn the train. Train No. 3 originated at that point, leaving at 9:55 a. m., and ran on north to the river, arriving at 1 p. m. but on its way it lay over practically an hour at Wakefield and 15 minutes at Dendron. The running time on this trip averaged around 15 miles per hour, according to the timetable, but speed was, in truth, about the average 30 miles per hour. The extra time was taken in discharging freight at each station that had been loaded during the hour layover at Wakefield. This trip was the revenue run of the day for it was the only northbound run from the Norfolk & Western connection at Wakefield. River traffic by this time was beginning to drop off and a goodly portion of the freight coming into the area came via the standard gauge connection.

The final run of the day, No. 4, left Scotland Wharf at 2 p. m. and an hour later tied up at Dendron. If there was nothing particularly wrong that had to be taken care of before the crew signed out, they were home by 4 o'clock. They had probably left to get ready for the day's work a little before 5 that morning, so it is safe to say that they were away from home for eleven hours, six days a week. Working conditions had improved over those experienced during the '90's.

The pay train was late getting to West Hope with the Christmas 1908 pay. The paymaster had forgotten the money and had to go back for it. The pay was computed at Sedley, put into envelopes, loaded on the pay car, and the one-car train set out on its round of the camps. The men were paid at Vicksville, then at Upson, and next would be West Hope but when the paymaster got ready to set up to pay off, there was nothing to pay off with. He had forgotten to load that lot of envelopes when the other payrolls were put aboard. There was only one thing to do and that was to go back for it. One of the men in the pay car hurriedly attracted the attention of the engine crew by heaving chunks of coal at them over the back of the bunker, the train was stopped, and back they went. Sure enough, there were the envelopes, just as they had been made up. No one knows why Vicksville or Upson wasn't called so that a donkey could be rounded up and sent after the money. Possibly it was a case of being ashamed at the oversight. Anyway, the "lost" payroll was gathered up and the pay train again left Sedley.

In the meantime the men sat around the West Hope commissary, wondering and waiting, for their Christmas depended on that particular pay. The train arrived around 11 p. m. and by midnight the last man had drawn his pay. No explanation was made for the late arrival but you couldn't keep the engine crew from talking. Imagine, the paymaster forgetting the pay. There were smiles but the embarrassed Mr. Eldridge said not a word until the last man was paid and then with a "Thank you, men", he closed up and the pay train left for home. On that particular night the commissary remained open until about 2 a. m. for there was money to be spent and bills to be paid, and Christmas was right around the corner.

A post office was operated by the lumber company at both West Hope and Upson, being set up in a corner of the commissary. A strict account was kept of the number of cancellations and the value of the stamps sold so that at the end of the year an accounting could be made to the Post Office Department. No attempt was made to keep the funds separate for the amount received from the mail patrons was not that large, everything going into the common till.

Although the Blackwater River flooded regularly and covered the entire bottom south of Dendron, such floods gave the company very little trouble. The trestle was never washed out although the track north of the trestle was badly washed during the spring flood of 1909. The sand pit was right up against the east side of the right-of-way and the water spilling across the track and into the pit ate away the right-of-way to the extent that it was unsafe to operate trains over the flooded track. The company built a foot bridge across the break, brought a donkey and a boxcar, probably one of the labor cars, up from Vicksville, and operated a shuttle service between the break and Wakefield. A pair of steps were provided at each point to facilitate passengers boarding and leaving the car.

While the flood was at its height, the highway bridge was flooded to the extent that the deck was just afloat. A number of boys went across the railroad trestle, down the bank, and out onto the bridge, where they began to jump up and down to see the water spurt up between the planks. That was all that was needed to cause the deck to break loose from the foundation and start downstream, but it soon wedged between some flooded trees. The frantic yelling of the boys attracted attention to their plight and the fact that the highway bridge was being relocated. Ropes were brought, ends were tossed to the boys who made them fast to the sills, and the runaway was hauled back into position. There it was securely anchored so that when the river dropped back to near normal, the bridge was more or less where it belonged. Once the water ceased to pour across the railroad bank into the sand pit, a little ballast was all that was required to repair the line; ballast and a spell of dry weather.

Darkness had already settled that evening in 1910 as the wives in Upson went about their culinary duties, preparing supper for the men who would soon be home, the time of their arrival being subconsciously timed by the sound of the steady beat of exhausts of the log train coming up from the south.

Suddenly something was missing, the egg timer had clogged, the steady beat was no longer audible. One by one the wives appeared at lighted doors to listen and test the sounds brought up from the woods by the southerly breeze. There were only the usual noises of the early evening; the noises of the camp, the croak of the few frogs in the ditches, and the whisper of the breeze, but not a sound which could be attributed to a log train, nothing. There had been no slackening off, the sound had simply ceased, and a single thought occurred to every listener, there was trouble down there. That wasn't unusual but it was exasperating for now suppers would have to be kept warm and for how long, no one knew.

There had been a wreck, not a bad wreck, just another wreck. Jack Honeycutt and Caesar Temple were anxious to get home for it was late and they were stepping right along, the seven loads, that had accumulated down in the woods after the last train had left for Dendron, bouncing and swaying behind No. 9. Caesar didn't like either the speed nor the idea of having the lead engine. No. 5 was known as the "floating donkey" at that particular time, a donkey that was sent where needed and now was taking the place of the donkey assigned to work with the 9 down on the Plank Road Extension. The 5's flanges had been worn sharp and when the train had been made up, Caesar had suggested that Jack lead with the 9, but Jack would have none of it, claiming that there were only two places to be, on the track or on the ground, so there was no need to worry. Caesar soon found himself in the unenviable position of driving a donkey with sharp flanges on the lead end of a log train with an impatient engineer nudging him along faster than he knew it was safe to run.

Suddenly his donkey jumped the track, as he muttered, "I knew it!" Throttles were closed and the crews went out of the gangways, hoping that they were jumping clear of the pile-up that was sure to follow. The loaded log cars slammed up against the derailed engines as everything came to a jarring halt. As soon as everything settled down, the crews gathered in the light of the headlight of the lead engine to count noses and bruises. The last to arrive was Cresley Travis, Temple's fireman. He hobbled up, looked around, and collapsed. A broken leg.

One of the men hurried to the nearest telephone booth and called Dendron. Dendron then called Vicksville and ordered a donkey to run extra to Upson and then to Dendron to bring in the injured man. The run was made and Dr. Devaney set the leg. Eventually Cresley was back in service, practically as good as new. Yes, just another derailment, but suppers were late in Upson that night.

When Ulysses Temple was sent to Vicksville as a donkey driver, he was boarded over top of the commissary with the other engine crews. When he moved in, one of the other boarders asked him his name and on being told that it was Ulysses, it gave him something to think about for it was the first time that he had ever run across anyone actually carrying that name. It rang a bell, though, and he asked the men present if there wasn't a man named Ulysses back in history somewhere. One of the men said that he thought that he was a sort of Roman king, or something. Another man, not to be outdone when it came to knowing things, volunteered the information that Roman kings were called Caesars. The first man then said that Ulysses must have been a Caesar, so Ulysses Temple became "Caesar" Temple, and the name stuck.

In good weather the labor train into the woods from Vicksville consisted of a donkey and a flat car, generally. The men rode as usual, sitting on the deck and with their legs dangling. The speed of 12 to 15 miles an hour appeared deceptively slow, as one Russian found out. There was this cow standing very close to the track, cropping the grass and minding her own business. She failed to even look up as the engine passed her for the cattle that roamed the woods had become used to both men and equipment. The snorting donkey was nothing to get excited about. The Russian, apparently thinking to give her something to really be startled about, stuck his leg out like a jill-pole and let the momentum of the train ram it into the creature's rump. It startled the cow, all right, sending her crashing through the brush, but it also dislocated the Russian's hip, which was far from funny. There was bound to be a certain amount of horseplay and occasionally it got downright rough.

Eastward

The logging branch east from Vicksville switch was being pushed further and further into the woods and eventually the company got around to sanding a section east from the switch, permitting the jacks to reach in for loads and at the same time shortening the donkey hauls. It was still customary to turn the jacks on the Dory wye and back to Vicksville with the engine hauling the train on its nose. From there the train continued on around the switch into the woods, eventually reaching a siding where the empties were dropped and the loads picked up. In a matter of time the branch became so long that a wye was installed up near the end of it and it was no longer necessary to turn the jacks at Dory when they ran through to that point.

The line passed through an area known as Raifordtown, a settlement of self-styled Quakers who had built themselves a school, a rather good school, and a church. They farmed the land for a living and only asked that they be left alone to live life as they saw fit. The head of the Raiford family was the acknowledged head of the movement and his word was law. Although he had sold the standing timber to the lumber company and knew that it had to be cut and hauled out, the community did not look with favor upon the arrival of the logging crew. There was occasional friction between the two groups but nothing serious happened until a rash of open switches broke out. Although there was absolutely no proof as to who was tampering with the switches, there were some rather pointed speculations. When it first began, the first engine crew in from Vicksville would find one or two switches thrown but as time went on, the number increased. It was not only a nuisance, but a decided danger for if one of the jacks suddenly found itself turned into one of the light woods tracks, there would surely be trouble before they could get stopped.

On this particular Saturday evening, quitting time had caught a track gang before they could remove the switch to a dismantled spur. They had taken up all of the rail, right up to the frog, but the points were still in place. To insure against any tampering over the weekend, the switch was lined up for the branch and the points spiked in place.

Monday morning Sam Atkinson came south with the day's supply of empties, turned the 14 at Dory and backed on down past Vicksville and into the branch. The donkeys had been waiting for him at Vicksville and would follow the train on into the woods. It was still dark, that sort of heavy darkness that comes before the false dawn and the first rays of the rising sun. As he passed the camp he could see that everything was ready to move and that one of the donkeys had the labor train while the other was running light and would start to spot the empties as soon as he had dropped them and moved back out of the way. There was some good-natured banter yelled back and forth as the jack clanked past and then some short toots of the donkey whistles to let any laggards know that it was time to go.

Sam went on down to the switch, swung into the branch and began working steam. During the weekend someone had gone to work on the spiked switch, pulled the spikes, and thrown the points for the non-existent spur. The first intimation that anything was wrong came when the tender suddenly swerved, began to bump violently over the ties and to tilt to the left away from the branch. The throttle was slammed shut and the steam brake set but before they could stop, the 14 was on the ground and slowly began to tilt with the tender. The fireman lost no time unloading on the high side of the engine and the engineer was right on his heels, taking to the air without paying too much attention, or caring, where they were going to land. Both men were convinced that the engine was going over, although she didn't. It just so happened that the engineer landed in a rather deep puddle of water which had been frozen over during the night but the ice wasn't thick enough to stand the shock of his landing, and through he went.

Some of the empties had piled up on the nose of the engine when it had come to a sudden stop but most of the train was still on the track, standing on the branch and still hidden by the darkness. Sam's first thought was of the donkeys that would possibly be following him into the woods and the chance of them piling into his stalled train. If they followed him, they would be backing in, running by feel as much as anything else, and when the engineers couldn't hear his exhaust, they would take it for granted that he was in the clear waiting for them. They had to be stopped, so Sam crawled out of the water and headed back towards the switch, running as best he could in the dark. The legs of his overalls quickly froze and soon it felt as though each leg was in a nail keg, but luck was with him. He found both donkeys setting just south of the switch, waiting for him to come back out.

Dendron was called and the accident reported, leaving the next move up to them. No time was lost in assembling the wrecking crew. Nothing ever caused quite the consternation and anxiety among the railroad families in Dendron as did the prolonged single blast of the whistle of the spare locomotive or the deep-toned, bull-blast of the mill whistle. Either told all within hearing that there was a worse than average wreck somewhere on the line and summoned the men assigned to the clean up gang. Families of the men out on the road gathered at the office almost as rapidly as did the men called for the relief run, each asking about a particular person and showing increasing distress if the desired information was not immediately forthcoming.

No. 8 was soon on her way with the necessary tackle and men to get the equipment back on the track. The first job was to right the engine and tender, jack them up, and put rails under them, more or less relay the short section of the dismantled spur, after which it was an easy matter to clean up the wreck. This time both the relaid spur and the switch came out and from then on the company had a man walk the track each morning before the first train went in. The trains would wait for him to complete his inspection before venturing in, cooling their wheels at the Vicksville switch. The man not only took a look at each switch, but he did not ignore each rail joint. This didn't put an immediate stop to the switch-throwing, but it did discourage the practice, and it prevented further derailments caused by tampering.

Forest fires, the bug-a-boo of all logging operations, visited the company only occasionally. Timberland was burned over but in no case was the railroad line damaged. Precautions were taken to ensure against that. A strip 50 feet wide, measured from the center of the track, was kept cleared of trees and brush. It was periodically burned over and all dead trees cut up and removed. Such precautions paid dividends in two ways, they prevented fires from damaging the track and the cleared strip acted as a fire break. There were times when a fire was running before a high wind that it would jump the fire lane but invariably the track, itself, was not damaged.

During a certain period, fires had a habit of occurring over the weekends along the branch east from Vicksville and were invariably blamed on the company's locomotives. There was no proof but there was considerable doubt that the engines were setting the fires for there was a pattern to the blazes. Why were the fires always over a weekend? No one ever admitted having to put out a blaze during the week. Again the Raifords came under suspicion but nothing could be done unless one of them was caught setting a blaze. Finally a fire watch was set, the track being constantly patrolled, and although they never had to put out a fire, the fact that there were suddenly none to extinguish, caused added speculation.

One particularly bad fire swept through the timber tract in Blow's Swamp, between Assamoosick Swamp and Dory. It was apparently set by lightning and from a distance the smoke had the appearance of a menacing, black, rolling thunderhead as it boiled and tumbled in the hot up-drafts created by the heat of the fire eating its way through the thick, dry underbrush. The fire was so intense that the bark was burned from the pines, insuring their eventual death.

As soon as the area had cooled off sufficiently, track was hurriedly laid and the sawyers moved into the burned area to cut the timber before the sap fell. In the evenings the men came out of the woods as black from the soot and ash as if they had been dipped in tar. When the logs were run through the saws at the mills, the sawlofts were filled with a fine, floating black fog. Burned timber is not necessarily damaged timber, if it is cut immediately, but it is an extremely dirty timber to handle.

By the end of June 1910 a switch had been put in a short distance south of the Surry station and two miles of track laid to the southeast where construction ceased while extensive excavating and filling was done to get the track across College Run. When completed, the fill was said to have been the highest on the entire system and the grade leading down to it from the northwest one of the steepest. A camp, known as Newtown, was constructed east of the main line switch and parallel with the new line. To this new camp was moved the entire West Hope installation.

Winter found the fill completed and the track being built steadily to the southeast. Two switches were installed in the new branch, the first being known as Appel Switch and the second as Shady Grove Switch. Secondary branches were laid from these two switches in a generally south-southeast direction. These lines became longer and longer as logging was done further and further from the main branch, and the maze of woods tracks running off them became more and more complex. Due to their frequent relocation, even less than usual attention was paid to their construction. Getting loads out to the main branch where the jacks could pick them up became increasingly difficult due to the many short, but very sharp grades, and the number of broken engine and bunker frames was alarming. From the railroading point of view, it was an extremely difficult section to work.

As activities were stepped up east of Surry, the track between West Hope and the Nottoway River crossing west of Chub was gradually removed as the timber supply was exhausted and the rail was required elsewhere. The track came up across the truss bridge but that on the trestle was left in place so that engines working to Chub and Upson could get water from the Chub tank. It was around early 1910, or soon thereafter, that a branch was laid north up the west side of the Jerusalem Plank Road from just west of Upson. That was followed by a branch up the east side which worked its way up to and around behind Littleton, and terminated beside the Plank Road. Neither line was in service very long.

With the establishment of a camp at Newtown, Surry took on added prestige and, to a certain extent, became a railroad town, for the woods engines laid over at the adjacent lumber camp during the night. The main line trains were nearly always late going south but you could set your watch by the shrill donkey whistles in the early morning. The first scheduled train of the day was known as the "six o'clock train" for a quite obvious reason. It was northbound. Returning from Scotland Wharf it was due at 7:20 but later on the time was changed to 8, after which the train was generally on time, unless a grade had to be doubled between there and the river. This returning morning train always had a fairly long layover at Dendron, the passengers passing the time by gazing at the mills and the scuttling yard engines, and watching the people, lots of people, passing back and forth. There was an air of hurry about Dendron back in those days. It was like a city, almost, for there were actually sidewalks, and there were two banks, a drug store, the movie house, a policeman in uniform, and as far as you could see from the coach window there were houses built close together.

The event of the day at Surry was the arrival of the noon train, the "mail train", northbound for the river. It looked as though nearly everyone was at the station. You could hear the deep-toned whistle of No. 2 as she blew for the crossings and stations to the south; Cockes' Crossing, known officially as Elberon, and Moorings, ten or fifteen minutes before she came in sight, puffing smoke and steam, and with her bell ringing. Cap'm Gladden would step down from the last coach just before it came to a stop, call out "All out for Surry", and the passengers would begin to file out. They were drummers, lawyers, and homefolk returning from the city, and, in the summer time, city cousins and friends coming for a visit. Occasionally there would be a stranger no one could figure out for strangers came to Surry, too, it being the county seat. They were men, women, and children, colored and white, and they had straw suitcases, Gladstones, satchels, and pasteboard boxes tied with string, and some untied. There were buggies, carts, wagons, and an automobile now and then to meet some of them, but most of them walked home, or to the hotel or the Green boarding house, where dinner was waiting for them. It was a disappointing day when nobody got off the train, but it happened now and then when court wasn't in session.

There was always some shifting to be done, one or more boxcars to be placed on the siding near the freight platform. Ice was quickly unloaded into Mr. Joe Green's cart and trundled off to the stores. The mail bags, loaded in a push cart, were pushed to the post office, two doors from the depot, and the main part of the crowd drifted on after it for now the center of attraction had shifted to the post office, except for those who were journeying to Scotland Wharf, and they waited around the station while the shifting was completed and it was time for the train to depart. Freight shipments originating outside of the state and destined for Surry, or any point along the narrow gauge, had to be shipped to the consignee at Wakefield. Upon notification of its arrival, the consignee sent the S.S.&S. agent there a form constituting him agent to receive the shipment and forward it to him over the narrow gauge. In this manner the S.S.&S. kept itself clear of regulations as an interstate carrier.

Finally the engine would back down on the train, a brakesman would drop the pin, and Cap'm Gladden would walk rapidly towards the rear, calling " 'Board! 'Board for Scotland!" The passengers would climb aboard while the Cap'm would stand beside the rear platform with one foot on the step and grasping the grabiron with his right hand. As the last passenger scampered aboard he would look around for any stragglers, call " 'Board!" again and slowly raise his left arm. Up front the engine bell would clang a time or two, the exhaust would snort, and the train would progressively jerk into motion as the slack was yanked out of the links. Cap'm Gladden would swing up the step, look around again, and go inside to lift the tickets. Mr. Arthur Chapman would then lock up the station and go home to dinner.

The layover at the river wasn't too long and for the passengers waiting for the "POCAHONTAS", or the "SMITHFIELD", or the "MOBJACK" coming down the James, it passed quickly. They would watch the men unloading lumber and box shooks from the cars brought in by the mail train, the lumber and shooks being passed along chutes into the holds of barges tied alongside the wharf and tallied by Mr. Putnam Chapman. Tiring of that, there were always passing boats and ships, often large four-mast schooners under full sail, and there were tugboats pulling barges. Always there were rowboats and launches. But, of course, the important and most exciting moment was when the steamer came into view as she rounded Swann's Point with smoke pouring from her stack and her paddles thrashing, even if she still had to dock over at Jamestown Island before coming across to Scotland Wharf. There was still quite a lot of activity on the river even then.

Returning from Scotland Wharf, the noon train was back at Surry around 2 p. m. and so was naturally known as the "two o'clock train" but quite frequently it was late for it had to wait for that down-river boat. Even after the boat had docked, freight had to be transferred to the cars, which took time, and there was the mail to be loaded. This early afternoon train was the last one of the day, unless a log train came on the line for Dendron, and it ran only as far as the mill town. If passengers wanted to continue on from there, they took passage in one of Mr. Leonard James' Model T Ford jitneys. If this is a bit different from the procedure set forth in a previous chapter, it is because it is as it was remembered by one who watched the trains come and go at Surry.

From the first to the last day of operation, the company used only paper tickets attached to stubs, both of which had to be dated and signed by the local agent before the ticket was valid. Some of the tickets were printed with both points of origin and destination left blank, others were printed with only the destination left blank, while others were printed in their entirety. All tickets were numbered at Dendron before being issued to the agents. No interline tickets were sold by the S.S.&S. agents. When traveling beyond Wakefield it was necessary to purchase a ticket to that point and purchase one from there to the final destination from the N.&W. agent.

The company made it a practice to issue annual passes to all doctors and ministers who had cause to use the railroad as well as to officials and employees, and to officials of other railroads who might request them. Passes were always issued to officials of the N.&W., whether requested or not. Of course, trip passes were issued to employees traveling to their jobs and to relatives of employees. Children traveling to and from school generally traveled on a season pass. At one time when Rogers was signing a batch of annual passes, he commented that during all the years he had issued passes, only one person had ever written to thank him, and that was a colored minister who resided in Wakefield and traveled to and from churches along the line to hold services.

Like all small railroads, the S.S.&S. was the butt of many jokes, crude and otherwise, which expressed, in a backhanded way, the feelings, the affectionate as well as less affectionate feelings, of the people served by the line. Thus the line was referred to as the "Slow, Sad, and Sick", with variations, among other things. And, there was the one put to every stranger, "Did you hear that No. 2 and all of the cars ran off Scotland Wharf this morning?" You were supposed to say, "No! That's awful! Was anyone killed?" And then would come the punch line, "No, it ran off this end on its way back to Dendron." If you laughed, it was understood that you were laughing at your own stupidity, not the railroad.

Naturally, it was described as the longest railroad in the world for it ran from Scotland to Jerusalem. However, when a lawyer arguing a case in court referred to the line as "a cowpasture between two streaks of rust", it didn't go over at all well for although they might joke and kid among themselves about their very own railroad, Heaven help the outsider who tried it.

Perhaps the railroad was in the limelight more on August 2, 1910, than on any other single day in its history for it was on that day that the company had to press into service every piece of passenger equipment it owned and run just as many trains as it possibly could to bring to Surry a considerable part of the throng of 3,000 people, including many dignitaries, who came to witness the unveiling of the Confederate monument.

The company had taken an active part in the erection of the monument for the components had been brought in on flatcars. To get the huge stone blocks to the court house square, a temporary track was laid up Main Street from the depot and a team of horses, assisted by a number of men, hauled and pushed the cars over it, one by one. It is impossible to realize the effort required to move a car even the short distance from the depot to the location for it was up a steep grade. Even a donkey could not be used for most of the short spur was laid on loose sand and it would shift and settle under even a single loaded flatcar.

It was a beautiful day and people began to arrive by eight o'clock in buggies, wagons, and automobiles. At ten o'clock that morning the first of the several special trains arrived from

Wakefield, bringing in the first arrivals from the cities. Specials from Sedley, Wakefield, and even from the river, arrived continuously from then until it was about time to begin the ceremonies. After each train had discharged its passengers, it was backed around into the Newtown wye for turning and to get it out of the way. The lack of sufficient passenger cars had to be overcome by the running of frequent trips.

At 11:30 the special of the day arrived from Wakefield, bringing in United States Senator Claude A. Swanson, twenty-five delegates from the Confederate Veterans Robert E. Lee Camp No. 1 of Richmond and ninety delegates of the A. P. Hill Camp of Petersburg, with their drum corps. At the station, waiting for the train, were the remnants of Companies G and K, Cavalry, 13th Virginia Regiment, Surry Light Artillery, Surry Heavy Artillery, and other commands, and, of course, the official reception committee. A parade was formed and marched the fifth of a mile from the depot to the court house square. Unless the drum corps had an agreement among themselves as to who would play what and when, the din during that march must have been terrible. Next came a huge picnic followed by much speech-making, both political and topic, and finally the unveiling. Then followed the mad scramble to leave town. The first train out was, of course, the special with all of the dignitaries for there was a connection to be made at Wakefield, but before dark all of the visitors had departed. Surry was back to normal, except for the stone soldier standing in the court house square, and the railroad was ready for another normal day.

We are told by Judge Willis Bohannan of Petersburg and Scotland Wharf, that to fully appreciate the narrow gauge during the early part of the century, you should have been a small boy living not far from the tracks, and he was one of those small boys, but, let's let him tell it:

"Everything was new, and one of the most important things in life was that wonderful railroad. You must have heard the shrill whistle of the special train in the dead of night as it hurried a very ill person to a hospital. You must have watched the clanking old locomotive No. 2, as she rolled by the depot, followed by her train of cars—flats, lumber cars, boxcars, baggage car, and coaches—in that order. There was about her the smell of coal smoke, pine lumber, and hot metal; and there was the engineer, Mr. Bernard Seward, leaning from his cab window, perspiring and waving to the people in front of the depot. And, there was Captain Gladden, the conductor, with his neatly trimmed mustache, resplendent in his dark blue uniform and visored pill-box cap, a man of small statue but very important looking to us as he handed papers to Mr. Chapman, the agent, or as he swung up on the steps of the last car as the train got off to a noisy and jerky start, bound for Scotland. There were flower beds, protected by board fences, on each side of the front door of the depot, planted there by Mr. Chapman to relieve the general drab appearance around the depot. It was the **dee-po,** not **dep-po,** or station.

"There was the excitement of getting up at daylight in the winter time, the long walk to the depot, buying tickets, and finally boarding the train, just as the sun rose. Then we would be off on the first leg of the trip to the city, and there was always the feeling of leaving the world behind when we looked from the coach window as we passed familiar landmarks such as our house, and, in doing so, get a cinder in our eye.

"Never to be forgotten are the locomotive whistles with their varying tones. Old No. 2 had a deep, almost hoarse, tone that distinguished it from the log jacks and donkeys. Long before daylight on winter mornings there was the long, shrill whistle of the donkey about to leave from Newtown, pulling cars loaded with workers headed for their jobs in the woods of cutting and loading logs. Later in the day, there was the series of long blasts from the log-jack asking for orders, which came by telephone to the company's store nearby. There was the blowing of whistles for station and crossings, and the short, excited blasts that told that a hog or cow was standing, or more likely running, in front of the locomotive. In those days the country-side reverberated with echoes of the whistles of the S.S.&S. trains. There was silence only on Sundays when no trains were running. It is the same silence that old timers sense today when their thoughts turn backwards to the far-away past."

But, let's get back to the mundane things concerning the "Three S's". In the yearly report of June 30, 1911, there were four miles less branch trackage listed then previously which was due entirely to the change of location of operations in the woods. This reduced the branch mileage to 39 miles with two miles of sidings. The maximum branch line mileage was in mid-1913 when 51½ miles were officially reported, or to be exact, that was the official maximum.

It was after the fill at College Run was completed that there was a spectacular pile-up south of Appel Switch. It was no worse than some of the other wrecks but in this case three donkeys were involved, the 11, 9, and 5, the three being on the head end of a log train in that order. It was time to knock off for the day so the loads were gathered up into a train of twelve loads, and the three donkeys working the tract hooked onto them. Arthur Rollison, who had the lead engine, considered himself quite a runner and although Maddox and Temple were as anxious to get home as he, they were more cautious. Rollison kept hurrying the other two men and finally said, "Let's go, boys", climbed in his cab and yanked the slack out of the train, leaving the other two no choice but to start working steam. Gradually all three engines picked up the beat.

They gained speed rapidly but had gone only a short distance when the 11 jumped the track and momentum did the rest. The two trailing donkeys shoved the lead engine around, end for end. That derailed the second donkey and it went into the bushes on the opposite side of the track. That, in turn, derailed No. 5, which went off and nosed up against the derailed No. 11. The loaded log cars went everywhere. The track literally ceased to exist. No one was hurt, nor were the donkeys badly damaged, bent rods being the most serious damage, but everything was in an awful mess.

As soon as noses were counted and the crews had looked over the wreck, one of the men walked out to the nearest 'phone box and reported the derailment to Dendron. At around six that evening, No. 6 left Dendron for the scene of the wreck with Archie Atkinson running and Philip Whitmore firing, and shoving the flatcar used when cleaning up wrecks. It was dark when they reached Appel Switch, between seven and seven-thirty, and Atkinson eased his train into the woods track very gently for he had considerable doubt that the light rail would support the mogul. Then, too, the light from the oil headlight was far from adequate for such precarious railroading. The train eased down into a hollow and when they started up the far side, they stalled. The engineer didn't dare try to swing the train out of the sag so there they set while the brakesman walked up to the wreck and explained the situation. The logging foreman, who had walked down to the wreck from the other direction, had his mules harnessed and sent down to the stalled train. They were then hitched to the flatcar and hauled it on to the scene of the wreck.

The crew still didn't trust the engine to negotiate that light rail in the dark so decided to purchase food from a local farmer and try to make themselves as comfortable as possible until daylight. The fireman and brakesman set out and eventually reached a farm house but the farmer didn't trust them and refused to part with either cooked or uncooked food. Preparing food would have been no problem if there had been any to prepare. Actually, the rebuff came as quite a surprise for it was known that other crews had purchased food there before, eggs in particular.

There being nothing else to do, the two men tramped back to the engine, told their story and the crew spent the night hungry. As soon as it was light they surveyed the situation and decided that they had no alternative but to try swinging the engine out of the bottom. It was then that the farmer, his wife, and his daughter showed up, each carrying a huge basket of food, much more than the crew could have possibly eaten, and offered to sell them anything that they had, but the crew was still smarting from the rebuff of the previous night and would have nothing to do with them. After hanging around a while and finally being convinced that the men had no intention of purchasing anything, the family headed for home, still toting the loaded baskets. The crew then got busy and managed to get back to Appel Switch without further trouble.

In the meantime the donkeys were rerailed, one by one, by hauling them with mules up to the end of the undamaged track leading towards the switch. When the last donkey was again firmly on the rails, mules hauled each one of them to the switch. First, of course, the wreck car had to be hauled there and hung on the nose of the mogul, then came the three donkeys, one by one. As soon as the train was assembled, it left for Dendron, arriving there shortly after noon for it was necessary to run rather slowly. The log cars were left in the woods until the track was rebuilt, that being done immediately.

When that particular log train was made up in the woods, the 11 should have been the third engine rather than on the point. If made up in this manner, the spring-mounted coupler of the leading log car would have eased the hammering administered by the rigidly mounted coupling on the rear of the engine. The rear couplings of the 9 and 5 were spring mounted and could have absorbed some of the shock transmitted by the fixed couplings on the front sills of the following engines, but no one paid any attention to such things as that. This caused most of the broken bunker and front end frames of the donkeys. When the 3, 5, 7, and 9 were built, spring-mounted couplings were installed on the rear of each because at that time a large number of the cars had their coupling castings mounted rigidly on the end sills and the floating coupling would partially protect the engine from the battering received when coupling, and starting and stopping a train.

When the 11, 15, and 17 were built, practically all of the rolling stock was fitted with spring-mounted couplers and it was no longer advantageous to fit the engines with them, so those three engines had their couplers bolted to the rear buffer plate. Incidentally, this type of installation came cheaper. When two or more donkeys were working together and the lead donkey had a rigid coupler, the bunker frame of that engine was subjected to a violent battering. In some cases the stud-bolts which fastened the frame to the firebox were strained to the point where they leaked and cases have been known where they sheared off completely. However, the operating personnel claimed that the Dendron shops were for the purpose of making repairs and so rarely paid the slightest attention to the order in which the donkeys were marshalled in a train. We won't say that the position of the donkeys in this particular train had anything to do with the wreck below Appel Switch for it was possibly caused by speed and a bad rail joint. We seem to have drifted into the subject of rear couplers on the donkeys because of the way those particular donkeys were lined up.

When actuating the brakes on most of the log and lumber cars, the latter actually being log cars with long stanchions, a removable T-handled brake staff was used rather than the conventional shaft and wheel. When loading and unloading, the conventional rig would not only have been in the way but would be quickly battered beyond use. Some of the cars had the brake wheel shaft mounted horizontally across the center beams but the company favored the recessed ratchet wheel type where the removable T-handle shaft fitted into the recess of the ratchet wheel well below the load level. However, when applying the brakes, care had to be taken that the shaft was properly seated before exerting a twisting motion to the handle.

When actuating the hand brakes on a grade, a brakesman had to move rapidly, setting the brakes promptly and releasing them just as promptly so that the descending speed was restricted but not to the point where the opposing grade would have to be doubled. It took smart work on the part of the brakesman and there was considerable danger involved.

At one time the mail train was headed north between the river and Surry, and was made up of cars of lumber, the baggage car, and two coaches. George Smith was braking at this time and as the speed increased, the engineer called for brakes. Smith promptly went about setting the required number but he was in too great a hurry. He rammed his brake staff into the socket of a ratchet wheel on one of the lumber cars and heaved before making sure that the staff was properly seated. It slipped out, causing him to lose his balance and fall between the moving cars. Fortunately he was seen as he fell and the train was stopped as quickly as possible but not before he was badly hurt. He was carefully lifted into the baggage car and the train hurried on to the river where the accident was reported. No freight cars were picked up this time and the engine and baggage car, with the coaches, headed back for Wakefield, making stops only for mail and passengers. They couldn't very well have omitted such stops. Dendron had called Wakefield to make sure that the N.&W. train would wait for them. The run was made in excellent time and the train arrived before the N.&W. train did, but Smith died in the baggage car while waiting.

Another unfortunate accident occurred one night when John Inghram was shoving a boxcar of lightwood splinters in the yard at Dendron with No. 4, the engine running tender first. Sam Fields, the brakesman, was told to take his lantern and go back to the leading end of the boxcar but he got no further than the rear of the tender when No. 6, with Archie Atkinson at the throttle, loomed up out of the darkness, running without a headlight. Neither engine was moving at a speed greater than a fast walk but Fields only had time to yell, stoop down to grab the lip of the tender to steady himself before they came together. The boxcar rode up over the tender sill and amputated Field's fingers as neat as you please. Although he was given immediate medical attention, he was found dead in bed the next morning by his wife. The doctor had declared that he would be all right but those were the days before such a thing as shock was known.

A complete carload of nothing but lightwood splinters might seem unusual but during one particular period of the lumber company's existence, it was far from it. It will be remembered that logs unfit for lumber were cut and split into cordwood and engine fuel. The first to go was the wood for the engine fuel, in 1903, when the engines began to burn coal. Then cordwood sales began to drop off as more and more coal was used for domestic fuel until sales were negligible. The company began cutting up the cull logs into dunnage and shipping it out, but there were logs which proved unfit for even that. These were split up into stove and kindling wood and sold for $5 a boxcar full, the company considering themselves lucky to get that for otherwise worthless waste. Later on the company went into the barrel stave business, then the manufacture of wooden boxes but stove wood and kindling they always had on hand.

So far as actual logging was concerned, prior to World War I the company was interested only in pine, and it had to be prime timber, although a log unfit for lumber did slip in now and then. Precautions were taken that nothing unfit for the saws was cut but there was no way of telling what was under the bark until the tree hit the ground. No oak or holly was cut for commercial use. A small amount of cypress was cut but there was practically no market for it. A little walnut was cut but only if it was from an exceptionally good stand. The market for this was as limited as it was for cypress, in fact, when the mills closed in 1927 there was considerable walnut stored in one of the sheds, boards as wide as eighteen inches, all a full inch thick and sixteen feet long, thoroughly seasoned.

Prior to World War I the grade crossing at Wakefield was protected by a tower in the northeast quadrant. The tower was Norfolk & Western property and was the charge of Mr. Robert Lane whose salary was a joint proposition. Both lines were protected by derails and stop signals on each side of the crossing, all interlocked so that the action of a single lever manipulated all four derails at the same time. It was impossible to clear both lines at the same time and it was the rule that the N.&W. was to be kept clear at all times except when a narrow gauge train was actually approaching and the N.&W. line was clear. The narrow gauge trains had to whistle for the clearance so that Lane could clear the line.

On this particular afternoon, Lane was napping rather soundly, which was nothing unusual, and the lever was set as it should have been, the derails being set against the narrow gauge and leaving the N.&W. track open. No. 4, one of the N.& W.'s crack passenger trains, came down from Petersburg, stepping right along as it was want to do, and as she approached the crossing the engineer blew for the station. The whistle woke Lane suddenly and being momentarily confused, he mistook the whistle for that of a narrow gauge jack calling for the crossing. It was also the rule that the log trains were not to be stopped unless it was absolutely necessary for sometimes it was rather difficult to get them rolling again due to the grade up to the crossing. Lane jumped up, yanked the control lever, and slammed the derail right under the pilot of the passenger train. The engineer didn't have a ghost of a chance to get stopped but the wonder is that the resulting wreck wasn't worse than it was. The engine hit the derail, pitched over to the left and slid down the bank on her side, narrowly missing the narrow gauge coal dock. A head end car followed her but the passenger cars remained on the track, being stopped by the locked brakes. The pile-up did not tie up the narrow gauge but it sure brought traffic to a dead stop on the N.&W.

That same level crossing saw a mishap that had all of the potentials for a major pile-up due to a log train negotiating the diamond at too great a rate of speed. The towerman was watching the string of loaded log cars pound over the crossing when, suddenly, he saw a truck jump out from under the end of a car and roll down the fill. Other than that, nothing happened and the train continued on towards Dendron. He grabbed his 'phone and called in to report what he had seen. From here on there are two versions of the story. One version has it that a brakesman was attracted by the frantic signals of the towerman and eventually was able to attract the attention of the engine crew. The train was stopped, the engine crew walked back to survey the situation and, after agreeing that there was nothing they could do about it, proceeded cautiously on to Dendron. The other version has it that the train continued on to Dendron with the crew totally ignorant of the missing truck and were surprised when they were met by all of the brass as they headed into the yard. Whichever happens to be the way it actually happened, it is a fact that the coupling link supported the end of the car all the way from Wakefield to Dendron, six miles.

In early 1913 the same three camps were feeding the Dendron saws: Upson, Vicksville, and Newtown. Each turned out two trains a day of 25 loads, that being the estimated timber it took to keep the saws busy. Although donkeys laid over at Sedley, there was no camp there, it being considered a part of the Vicksville installation. The mail train continued to shuttle back and forth between the river and Wakefield and Dory. The main line extension south to and beyond Sedley was still considered to be a logging line. Locomotives working west from Dory continued to turn on the Chub wye although there was no traffic west of Upson other than the free train.

Due to the way the track west from Dory had been built, and the fact that it had been allowed to get into a rather poor condition, trains coming east from Upson were restricted to 24 loads when negotiating the grade up from the Assamoosick Swamp flats. If the train consisted of more than the prescribed number of cars, which it supposedly always did, it was to be split into two sections, the second section to be left standing on the main line while the first section was hauled up the grade and left on a siding provided for that purpose. The engine would then return for the second section, haul it up the grade, tie the two together, and proceed on its way. Just why the tonnage was not set at the usual 25 loads rather than one less, it is impossible to say unless the idea was that it was physically impossible for a jack to haul its prescribed train up the grade if run at a reasonable speed, or what the company considered a reasonable speed, and the company was not making a hard and fast rule as to how many cars were to be brought up at one time just so long as the average train was split. Practically all of the crews took a chance, however, and as long as they made the grade safely, there was never any indication that they had not doubled the grade. If something went wrong, there was always something to blame it on, other than fast running.

In describing the grade, one engineer stated that he never thought of splitting his train, irrespective of the number of cars he had, and he always got away with it. When crossing the trestle, he would ask his fireman how his fire was. The expected answer was that it was in good shape. He would then ask how many cars he saw. The fireman would lean out and apparently count, then say "Twenty-four", irrespective of whether there were twenty or thirty. The engineer would then say "Let's go!" and begin to lean back on his throttle. The fireman would jam his shovel in the coal pile and climb upon his seat beside the boiler for when they got to rolling over that rough track it would be absolutely impossible for him to stand on the bouncing deck and the tender and hit the firebox door with his hat, let alone a shovel of coal. The train would gradually pick up speed and go blasting up the grade.

At one time a crew wasn't so lucky for a car jumped the track and a brakesman was killed. The regular brakesman had refused to take the run that morning for he claimed that while asleep the night before, he had a "vision" in which the train was wrecked and he had been buried under a pile of logs. He was given his choice, take the run or be fired. He had too much faith in his vision and his replacement had been killed, just as he had seen it happen the night before.

"JC" Arrives

Philip Rogers' health hadn't been but so good for some time and it was gradually getting worse. Brother Edward decided that it was time to get him an assistant and began casting around. The logical man was Dick Owen, logging foreman down at Vicksville, but he had contracted tuberculosis and was sent to Saranac Lake in New York State. Although he eventually recovered and came home, a man was needed right away and so James C. Causey was brought in from down in North Carolina. Causey was no stranger to the company for the Cumberland Lumber Company, another outfit owned by the Baltimore interests which owned the Surry Lumber Company, had been dealing with him as the head of Causey Brothers for some time. Causey Brothers had been operating the Norfolk Lumber Company at Wallace, N. C., and were selling practically all of the lumber they could produce to the Baltimore people. This lumber was shipped to the Surry Lumber Company at Pinners Point, Virginia, and paid for by the Cumberland Lumber Company of Baltimore with checks made payable to the Causey Brothers. On Friday morning, the 13th of October 1913, the Wallace mill caught fire and in an hour or two there was nothing left but a pile of hot ashes. The loss was covered by insurance but there were no funds to keep the labor force intact until the mill could be rebuilt so when Baltimore offered James C. the position of assistant logging superintendent at Dendron, he took it. This liquidated the unofficial firm of Causey Brothers but Norfolk Lumber Company continued in business and was eventually absorbed by Camp Manufacturing Company of Franklin, Virginia.

"JC", as he was called, was used to a different type of logging; faster, more modern methods, than were employed by the local management of the Surry Lumber Company, and it took an effort for him to fall in line with the easy methods practiced by Philip Rogers. The new assistant had been used to being his own boss and now found himself more or less shackled and held down, for his authority was limited and all changes that he wished to make had to be first approved by both Philip and Edward Rogers to insure against conflict with the organization's conservative policies. The period from the date of his employment to the date of Philip Rogers' final retirement in 1915 must have been rather trying for "JC".

Prior to his arrival, rail motor cars had been used on the narrow gauge to some extent. Motor section cars were used but not extensively. These were the usual small affairs such as were built by Fairbanks Morse with a seat down the center from end to end over the engine and would carry four persons comfortably. To start it you pushed until it was rolling right along at a good trot, then you jumped on and threw the switch. If you were lucky the engine would catch and away you would go. These little motor cars were capable of speeds up to sixty miles per hour, or so it was claimed, but no one had ever actually tried seeing how fast they would run, except once. It was not at all unusual for one to jump the track and dump its riders in the ditch but rerailing them was no problem. Only rarely was one so badly damaged that it wouldn't come in under its own power. One such motor car was regularly assigned to the telephone linesman.

A second type of motor car was built in the company shop and had two seats crossways which, if you crowded a bit, would seat six people. There was only one of these built and it was hard riding and downright unpopular in cold or wet weather. It was open to the elements and there wasn't even a windbreak to partially protect the driver and passengers. Due to its size and riding qualities, it occasionally gave both its driver and passengers unpleasant moments. Ashby Whitmore, the railroad stock clerk and serviceman for the company telephone system, was directed to take some of Rogers' friends up to Upson for a day of bird shooting. After leaving the party at Upson, he headed on over to Chub to turn the contraption and to wait in the clear until the party was ready to return to Dendron. He had the car running right along when it hit a bad rail joint and went into the ditch, turning over on top of him and breaking his leg.

While he was still hobbling around on crutches, Ashby was again called upon to make a special trip with his own motor car, the section car he used when out working on the telephone lines. There had been a breakdown in one of the mills and it was necessary to send the broken part to Norfolk for repairs. It so happened that there was not enough time to make Wakefield for No. 3 on the Norfolk & Western for Petersburg, where the work could have been done, but by fast running a connection could just possibly be made with the Virginian at Sedley. Higgins asked Ashby if he would attempt to make the connection if he cleared the line and gave him someone to push and act as ballast to hold the car down. Whitmore never was one to turn down a chance to really run his motor car and readily agreed. He had 25 minutes to get to Sedley when his colored helper pushed off and jumped on as the motor caught. Away they went, as fast as Ashby dared run, and that was faster than would have been considered safe by anyone else. It was cold that day and Ashby wore a Halloween mask to protect his face while his companion spent his time hanging on, clutching the seat and Ashby's crutches which stuck up like a pair of stub masts.

The mail train had been sidetracked at Manry, below Airfield, to let Ashby by. When the motor car hit the road crossing just north of the Manry switch, it took to the air but fortunately came down on the rails and continued on its way. Whurley Faison, the engineer on No. 2, was watching and commented to his fireman, P. H. Whitmore who was Ashby's brother, "That damn fool is goin' t' kill his self." He didn't, though, and managed to reach Sedley with a minute or two to spare, approximately eighteen miles in less than 25 minutes. For a narrow gauge section motor car, that was right good time, particularly when you consider the condition of the track. When the country finally got into the first European War, Higgins suggested that Whitmore join the army and become an aviator, for as he put it, he had been trying to fly that thing long enough to give him the necessary experience. His broken leg never did heal correctly, leaving him with one leg two inches shorter than the other, and the army let him stay with the company.

Higgins, himself, was no slouch when it came to running a section motor car, particularly when he was partially lubricated. P. H. Whitmore came up from Norfolk one day and when he stepped off the train at Wakefield he happened to meet Higgins, who asked if he was headed for Dendron. Whitmore 'lowed that he was, so Higgins said that he had his motor car there and Whitmore could ride with him. Fine. So they got started and as soon as they were rolling, Higgins handed his passenger a poke in which were four quarts of additional "oil" and told him to hold it and hang on. Whitmore admits that it was a ride that he will never forget.

On Sundays, Ashby would occasionally take out the big motor car for an unofficial trip to Scotland Wharf and back. On this particular trip he had his girl in the front seat with him and a friend, Garland Spratley, and his girl in the rear seat. As usual, Ashby was running right along, giving the girls a thrill, as he expressed it. Just before reaching Elberon they hit a road crossing that was covered by quite an accumulation of dirt and trash. The motor car jumped the track, reared up, tossing Spratley's girl over the rear of the seat, then snapped end for end, pitching Ashby off into the bushes. The girl was right badly hurt but Ashby came out of it with only bruises. No more Sunday jaunts.

After JC took over, the so-called 600 series of motor cars were put in service, converted Model T Ford touring cars. The conversion of a unit or two was done by the Dendron shop but at least one was done by the Berkley Machine Works in Berkley, Virginia. It is fairly safe to say that Berkley converted the pilot model, the unit to which was given the road number 600, and Dendron copied it when converting the other units.

The numbering series was suggested by that of the high-stepping 4-4-2 passenger locomotives then in service on the Norfolk & Western. These locomotives were the pride and joy of the road and were noted for their speed and ease of handling, which was also the case with the motor cars, but unlike the locomotives, the motor cars lacked weight on their single pair of drivers. To run with them, a series of open trailers were built, light four-wheel affairs that were used to haul men, tools, and later on, ice.

During the summer a rail motor and passenger trailer were occasionally used on a Sunday, or a holiday, for a general outing to Jamestown Island, the motor and trailer being left on the wharf at the river while the passengers and driver spent the day eating, playing games, and generally enjoying themselves across the river. Another type of outing of a less joyous nature was the operation of "funeral trains" for the transportation of groups attending a funeral. It was the policy of the company to make available, free of charge, the necessary equipment for such trips. Crews worked without compensation. Other than these special trains, either gasoline or steam, nothing ran on Sundays, it being literally a day of rest. After a moving picture theater known as the Eldon Theater, was opened at Dendron, the company occasionally ran "theater trains" on a weekday evening when some spectacular was playing, such as "Birth of a Nation" or "The Ten Commandments". Like most everything else in town, this theater was either owned or financially supported by the lumber company.

The years 1914 through 1918 were years of expansion for both the lumber company and its subsidiary. The national demand for lumber for construction purposes made itself felt at Dendron in 1916 and reached an all time peak in 1918. During that period every sawmill in the country, irrespective of its size, could dispose of every piece of lumber of any grade that came off the carriage, so this burst of prosperity for the Dendron plant was not a local condition. The company did its best to keep pace with the demand and to fill all orders. Increased business caused the Norfolk & Western to begin double-tracking its main line between Norfolk and Petersburg in 1914 and in so doing brought about a relocation of the narrow gauge at Wakefield. This relocation eliminated the grade crossing and made necessary certain alterations to the station trackage. The track affected was a little over a mile in length. The alteration consisted of shifting the main line west slightly to lower ground so that it could pass under the standard gauge with a minimum of excavating. All narrow gauge trackage north of the former crossing remained intact but that on the south side was removed from the old crossing to the point where the relocated track joined the former main line.

Southbound passenger trains would come into Wakefield over the old line to the station but would swing around into the "down" side of the interchange track, as it was referred to. When departing they would back on out to the main line switch and then proceed south, passing under the N.&W. tracks. Trains running north would back into the station and head out. The old crossing diamond was removed but the track past the station ran right up to the N.&W. tracks so that the coal dock could still be used to load the lowsides.

The beginning of hostilities in Europe in 1914 had their repercussions in Dendron, oddly enough, for the shook mill specialized in barrel staves, the majority of which were shipped to Germany to be made into beer barrels. With the European market closed to them, the company was faced with two alternatives, find a new market overnight or close the mill. The mill closed down and the men began to drift away, some finding jobs with the Norfolk & Western. Fortunately, the shutdown was of a temporary nature but it lasted long enough for the company to lose some of its best mill hands.

It was in the summer of 1915 that the Atkinson brothers tried to disprove the theory that two solids could not occupy the same space at the same time. Archer had his No. 10 which, oddly enough, had the tender of the 12 at the time, and Sam had his No. 14. It was one of those wrecks that happened irrespective of rules. Sam was backing his engine out of the storage track on which it had been sitting overnight, for the company never owned anything resembling an engine house, and was going down to the machine shop to fill his tank from a hose that was kept connected to the water line for that purpose. His fireman, Willie Hendricks, wasn't on the engine at that time, just Sam.

Archer Atkinson had brought a train of logs from Newtown but had been forced to double the hill between Sexton and Dendron. He had already brought in the first half of his train and was coming in with the second half. In the meantime the mill was running short of logs and Rogers went out to intercept Archer and waved him on ahead to bring the loads up to the log deck rather than put his train together and then come on up, which was the way it was usually done and what Sam had every reason to expect him to do. No one paid any attention to the 14 which was slowly easing out to the main line until suddenly the fireman on No. 10, Lawson Bradshaw, realized what was happening. He yelled and jumped, but Archer waited to set the engine brakes and then it was too late for him to get clear. The back corner of Sam's tender literally laid up against the side of the 10 and pushed. The tender went one way and the engine the other. The first intimation that Sam had that something was wrong was when his tender started to tip over. It went only about half way but Archer's engine went all the way. Archer was caught in the cab and it was necessary to hurriedly dig a trench under it so that he could drop down into it and crawl out, but he was not hurt. That was the closest anyone came to getting hurt and no one was called on the carpet. Rogers claimed that if he had tended to his own business and let well enough alone, nothing would have happened, and he let it go at that.

It took four years of piece-meal construction before the company had reached far enough to the east from Newtown to warrant construction of another camp. In 1915 Central Hill, in Isle of Wight County, was completed and ready for occupancy. The standing timber down the Plank Road Extension, south of Upson, and that between Upson and Dory, had been exhausted and new tracts below the new camp were being opened. Upson was abandoned practically overnight. Cars were sent up and loaded with everything that was to be moved out. The mules were loaded in boxcars, the two-wheel log carts were loaded on flats, household effects went into boxcars, and the people went into the combine and coach. No. 6 with a green engineer and a greener fireman then hooked onto the string of cars and set out for the new camp. P. H. Whitmore had just been promoted to extra engineer and it was his first trip alone. His fireman had just been hired and it was his first trip. It was almost an instantaneous exodus for practically everything went out on that one train. Stripping of the line between Chub and Dory was begun as soon as the Plank Road Extension had been dismantled, the rail being used in the woods below Central Hill. The trestle and bridge were dismantled under contract while the company moved the tank and pump to Airfield.

Discontinuance of the freight and passenger service between Chub and Dory presented no problem as it had been furnished free of charge. The company simply nailed a notice on the station bulletin board stating that after a certain date all service would be discontinued, and on that date it was. A day or so later a gang of men arrived from Dendron and began dismantling all of the structures. As soon as the material had been hauled out, they went to work on the track, dismantling that, and it wasn't long before Chub was a place in name only. Upson shared a like fate although it did last a few days longer than Chub.

From Central Hill the track was laid in a southwesterly direction for about a quarter of a mile, then curved sharply towards the southeast, following the contour of the ground. At this point a wye was put in for turning the jacks. From the western leg of the wye was then built a line to the northwest and north that crossed Vellines Swamp and terminated at the Broadwater Road, about a half mile west of Stott's Corner, or Stott's Cross Roads as it was sometimes called, a total distance of from three and a half to four miles, by rail. This line was known as the Sycamore Crossing Branch and was in service until the early part of 1918.

Philip Rogers was finally forced to retire in 1915 and James Causey moved up, becoming logging superintendent for the lumber company and assistant superintendent of the railway. Now he was in a position to sell his ideas direct to Edward Rogers on the basis of higher gross income at less cost and he lost no time doing it. Gradually he was able to modernize the logging operations, bringing in chain saws, improved skidders, and mechanical loaders. So far as the skidders and loaders were concerned, Rogers would not stand for the cost of new machines but agreed that such units be built in the company shop. Upright boilers and hauling winches were purchased and mounted on flatcars which could be moved from one location to another by locomotives. Eventually there were four skidders, one each assigned to Newtown, Central Hill, and Vicksville, with the fourth one being kept at Sedley as a spare.

To locate a skidder, the track was "broken" and the end moved over to end up against a large tree. A notch was cut in the trunk at the height of the coupling and a gill-pole set between it and the coupling, thus anchoring the skidder. All work was done so that the strain would be against the tree. A tall tree was not topped, but the guys fixed at a desired height up the trunk, four guy lines, held the trunk rigid. Smaller trees were topped and the guy lines ran from the top of the trunk. Special tank cars were built to serve as feed water storage tanks for the boilers. The loaders were not too much different from the skidders except that they depended upon four legs, one at each corner, for their stability and could be "walked along" when changing position slightly. Long moves were made on a flatcar.

Causey was a great lover of horses and he stoutly maintained that a horse could do anything that a mule could and do it better. He managed to get Rogers to agree to try horses and eventually Percherons replaced all of the mules. Whether they were actually better than the mules that they replaced is doubtful for some of the mules had been in service so long that they had learned their job to the point that they needed no driver and would respond to a spoken word. If it was necessary to step up the tempo of the loading process, a sharp "Ha!" or a whistle would cause the mule to step out at a more lively pace. A sudden slacking off of the strain on the hauling chain would cause him to stop for the log had rolled into position. A slight tug on the chain would cause him to back up for another hitch. The mule and driver were a pair that worked hour after hour as a team without a spoken word. In fact, it was not unusual for the driver to go off and leave the mule to work entirely by himself.

However, Causey brought in some really handsome animals, actually prize-winning work horses, and they were pampered and looked after better than were their drivers. The quickest way to get fired was to be caught mistreating a horse, but, as an incentive to take care of their charges, a yearly prize was given for the best cared for horse, or team. Drivers were directed to take a horse out of harness immediately if a galled place was found and the animal remained out of service until the place healed. If a horse showed signs of being affected by the heat, out of harness he came right then. Even so, during one particularly hot spell three horses were overcome and it is said that Causey was fit to be tied. Their feed was carefully watched, the amount of oats and corn being regulated by Causey, and the stableman held strictly responsible for the proper feeding. A mule has sense enough to eat only sufficient corn to curb his appetite but a horse will eat until he founders. It is said that if a mule was mistreated by a driver, that driver was in for trouble from the mule, but he would respond to kindness and attention just as quickly.

At one stable it was noticed that the consumption of corn was unreasonably high. When questioned, the stableman swore up and down that he was not overfeeding his charges and, in fact, Causey realized that it was practically impossible for the horses to eat all of the corn sent in and continue to work. Where was it going? The corn was sent to the camp in a box-car in which it remained, the car being used as a storage bin. When practically empty, another car load was sent in, the remaining corn transferred, and the empty hauled out. Under normal conditions a car of corn would last for quite a while but something definitely was not normal.

It wasn't too long before another car of corn was required so Causey ordered it loaded and sent up, but this time he went along with it and didn't let it out of his sight for a second. After being placed on a siding, the remaining feed corn was transferred to it, the engine crew coupled onto the empty car and headed back to Newtown. The men who had transferred the corn dispersed but Causey continued to watch the car. He was determined to stay there until the entire load was consumed, if necessary. However, as if on cue, a local farmer drove up with a dump cart, jumped down and opened the door on the off side, backed his cart up against the opening, and began to rapidly shovel corn into it. Causey descended on him like a cat on a mouse.

Causey prided himself on his ability to handle any situation without outside help, and he considered this to be no exception. He laid into the farmer and gave him a verbal lashing. As the corn had been stolen as needed and as the farmer was in no financial position to make restitution, the company could not regain either the corn or its value in currency if the culprit was taken to court, so after the tongue lashing, the matter was dropped. No more corn disappeared.

Two other incidents took place which will serve to illustrate Causey's methods and his boasted ability to handle any situation. The first had to do with a false tally of logs cut, and took place in 1917. As the timber was cut off beyond and around West

Hope, the men had moved to Upson and then to Vicksville. A goodly portion of the labor was Russian, it will be remembered, hard workers but easily led. A gang was cutting timber up towards Raifordtown on the branch east from Vicksville and it was up in there that the trouble took place. The sawyers were paid 3¢ a cut, which averaged 9¢ a tree, sometimes 12¢ if the tree was tall enough to furnish four sixteen-foot logs. Tally was kept by the foreman who cut a notch in the stump for each log off it.

Gradually the tally crept up to an average of four logs a tree, with an occasional five. The first inkling that anything was wrong came when the supply of logs at Dendron failed to agree with the foreman's tally sheet. The number of logs in the mill yard had not increased but the tally sheets from Vicksville indicated that the log yard was full to overflowing. The mill superintendent began checking and it was found that the logs shown on the sheet for a day's cutting did not agree with what came in by train. The problem was immediately passed on to Mr. Lewis, the general foreman at Vicksville, who called in Mr. Roach from up at Surry to lend him a hand in running down the trouble. A few days in the woods was all that was necessary to prove that some stumps with four notches had actually produced only three logs and those with five had rarely produced as many as four. It was simply a matter of checking the number of little piles of sawdust which extended out from a stump at sixteen-foot intervals, beginning with the first pile sixteen feet out from the stump. If they didn't agree with the number of notches on the stump, something was wrong, and quite a number of them didn't. Causey was notified and he immediately moved in, firing the woods boss on the spot as well as the men known to have perpetrated the swindle.

Causey then informed all of the men that henceforth they would be paid so much a day, a day's work for a camp to consist of a certain number of logs cut and loaded, the total to be two trains of 25 cars each day from each camp. Each train was to bring in sufficient logs to measure a certain number of board feet when cut into lumber. Those who accepted the new scale of wages could continue working, those who did not could pack their belongings and be ready to move out immediately. He then checked the tally sheets against the stumps and piles of sawdust and paid the men according to the number of sawdust piles. That didn't set at all well with a number of the men and a Russian, known simply as "Old Pete", pleaded mightily for a settlement based on the tally sheets. The odd part of this was that "Old Pete" was in no way involved in the affair but argued for what he had been previously told was right. Up until now the tally sheets were the final word in arguments concerning cuts made by the men and now he was told that they were wrong. He just couldn't understand how this could be, for if they were the final word yesterday, why were they not the final word today? The argument got to the point where he was forcibly ejected from the gathering although he was not fired nor penalized in any manner. It must be remembered that only a relatively small number of the men were involved, not the entire gang by any means.

The men who elected to leave were loaded on a flatcar at Vicksville and sent to Wakefield where they were put on the Norfolk & Western train for Norfolk, arriving there in the late afternoon.

While en route to Norfolk, the ringleader got the men together and managed to convince some of them that the lumber company could not just fire them, that they had rights, and that they could force the lumber company to give them their jobs back at the old rate of pay. It was agreed that they would return to Vicksville and force the issue. On arrival at Norfolk they hung around the Union Station until the Virginian passenger train left but the sale of so many tickets to Sedley seemed odd and after overhearing some of the talk, the Norfolk agent realized that trouble was afoot and called the Sedley agent. He got in touch with Causey and told him what was happening down at Norfolk. Causey located the constable, who was on the company payroll, purchased the correct number of tickets for Petersburg via Jarrett and the Atlantic Coast Line, and met the train, which arrived around midnight. As the men climbed off, each was handed a ticket and hustled up the next gangway with orders never to show up again.

There was never any more trouble of that nature although a foreman tried the old dodge of carrying a fictitious workman on his roll. When the paymaster arrived, this mythical person was always absent because of sickness, or some other reason, but the foreman would be glad to give him his pay and get a receipt. He took the jug to the well once too often and was fired. Thereafter, if a man wanted his money, he had to show up in person.

The second incident had to do with a private contractor. On occasions it was imperative that a tract of timber be cut over as quickly as possible and a company gang was not available. It was then the practice to bring in a logging contractor and his crew. They would cut, load, and get out; the length of time required would depend entirely on the amount of timber to be cut and the number of working hours they could squeeze out of a day, plus, of course, the size of the crew. Such crews were generally small and hours were long, if the contractor was to come out ahead.

A North Carolina contractor named Owens had been called in to cut over a section east of Surry. He and his gang boarded at the company camp at Newtown. The company had agreed to furnish transportation to and from the area being logged, but almost immediately trouble arose. A labor train hauled the men into the woods in the morning soon after dawn and brought them out in the late afternoon, the run being made early enough for the train crew to get back to Newtown in time to sign out and not have to be paid overtime, the working hours having been fixed by then. On arrival at the location being logged, the locomotive whistle would be blown as a signal for the men to knock off and board the train. A reasonable length of time had to be allowed for the completion of cuts already started. However, the engine crew noticed that cuts were started after the whistle was blown and eventually they became rather tired of explaining late arrivals at Newtown. Causey finally told the engineer to do as he had been doing but to wait only a reasonable length of time after blowing the whistle and if the men were not aboard, to leave them. Causey then explained the situation to the logging contractor and told him of his instructions to the engine crew. That was on a Friday evening.

The next day was a short day and the train arrived before noon. The whistle was blown and the crew settled back to wait a reasonable length of time. Time passed and the sounds of the logging activities showed no signs of abating. The engine crew decided that they had waited long enough and whistled off. At the sound of the first exhaust, the contractor came running, waving a shotgun and threatening to shoot the first so-and-so who tried to leave before he said they could. The engine crew took one look at the shotgun and decided that it was best not to try to find out if the contractor meant what he said.

Eventually the train returned to Newtown and the engineer called Causey at Sedley, telling him of the incident. Causey immediately came up and terminated the contract with the backing of his own shooting iron, giving the contractor until the next night to clear out. JC remained on location until the last man of the hired crew was gone and on Monday a company crew moved in and completed the cutting.

Some years later, after Causey had moved to greener pastures, which was in 1927, his ability to handle situations fell flat and probably had something to do with his murder. So much for Causey, his ability, and his methods.

The War Boom

By late 1915 the mills were going full tilt, the company having fully recovered from the closing of the stave mill by converting to the manufacture of wooden boxes, one of the larger customers being the Standard Oil Company. A goodly number of these boxes eventually found their way home, packed with cans of lubricating oil for the various gasoline engines in service on the railway and the company automobiles and trucks that were beginning to make their appearance.

The branch, some five and a half miles in length, which ran a little west of south down through Tucker's Pocoson from a switch on the Central Hill line six and a half miles from Newtown was pulled up and the rail sent to Central Hill.

It was down in Tucker's Pocoson that the logging crew found logs in various stages of decay that had been cut and abandoned by Fergusson & Jones who had attempted to log the area in 1880. W. T. Fergusson and his partner apparently encountered unsurmountable obstacles in their logging operations for they worked the area only a short time before moving out. The abandoned logs indicated that their main trouble was of a financial nature and not a matter of having exhausted the supply of standing timber. While working the area they hauled out their timber by means of a so-called bogy track, a light logging railway, possibly laid with wooden rails, over which a small locomotive built by Thomas W. Godwin & Company of Norfolk was used to haul one or more loaded logging bogies at a time. The bogy track ran from down in the pocoson to Fergusson's Wharf on the James River and when the Surry Lumber Company built the branch south from the Central Hill line, they made use of the abandoned right-of-way.

When the timber had been cut out up near Stott's Corner, the track was taken up to a point about a mile west of the Central Hill wye, just to the west side of the Red Oak Road, and another line built from the stub end in a more westerly direction. This new line reached in about seven miles, crossing what was known as Strawberry Plains to Rattlesnake Swamp. This it crossed near its confluence with the Blackwater River and then continued on up the east bank of the river for a mile or two. The company's holdings in this area were quite extensive, reaching north up the east bank of the river nearly to Proctor's Bridge and east practically to Mill and Rattlesnake Swamps. Eventually track was extended up into this area, one line reaching north to just southeast of Pons, about half way between that point and Gwaltney's Cross Roads. There was another large tract east of Rattlesnake Swamp extending to, and practically surrounding, Raynor. Some of the timber in this area was never cut as it was not mature but had to be purchased in order to acquire tracts of timber that were suitable for cutting.

So large a "system" required considerable equipment, particularly since a like amount of timber was being cut northeast of Vicksville and considerable was still being cut between Central Hill and Newtown. In early 1916 six boxcars were acquired. The following year six more showed up but two flats disappeared from the roster, possibly to conversion to company cars of some sort. In fiscal 1918 five boxcars, four flatcars, and a coal car were put in service. All of the boxcars were larger than those already in use, were numbered in the 900 series, and were known as "the large cars". They were long enough to take sixteen-foot lumber at each end and allow three feet for working space at the doors. The fact that the cars appear to have been custom-built gives rise to the theory that they were built in the company shop, flatcars being used in their construction. The regular boxcars were numbered in the 200 and 300 series. All of the regular freight and passenger cars used in main line service were considered to be the property of the railway and they were the only pieces of equipment ever declared in reports to the State Corporation Commission, hence our uncertainty as to what there actually was in use.

It was during this period that the lumber company owned the fleet of over 400 log cars. Although a large number of these cars were built in the company shop, some of them carried the stencil of the Russell Wheel & Foundry Company of Detroit, Michigan. This stencil appeared to have been applied at the time that the beams were lettered "SURRY LUMBER COMPANY", and it would appear that the cars were purchased new. However, that was certainly not the company policy, this purchasing of new cars.

When the Tidewater & Western decided to call it quits during the early part of 1917 and let it be known that there was all sorts of equipment to be had at bargain prices, Higgins naturally had to go up to look over what was offered for sale. He brought home a motor car, the likes of which had never been seen around Dendron before. When asked what he intended to do with it, he said that he was going to use it to haul men between Dendron and Wakefield, run it as a sort of labor train, a round trip in the early morning and another in the late afternoon, and that is exactly what he did with it.

The 700, as it was numbered, was a Model 19 Fairbanks Morse gasoline motor car built by the Sheffield Car Company of Three Rivers, Michigan. It was a large affair that looked like a small four-wheel, battery-operated, street car, more than anything else. Whether it was originally built as an open or closed car is impossible to say but when Higgins got it, it was closed in, being fitted with drop windows and a door at each end on each side. There was a longitudinal seat down each side and the car would seat about 20 passengers, with standing room for about half that number, without crowding. The gasoline engine was under the floor, between the axles, and drove both axles by means of roller chains. There was a hatch in the floor to allow the driver to get at the engine if necessary, and necessity frequently arose. The unit could be driven from either end and would work up to twenty or twenty-five miles an hour, depending upon how heavily loaded it was at the time.

It was a rough riding affair and the men complained constantly but it was a means of getting there and back, most of the time. Quite frequently the driver had to call Dendron and ask that an engine be sent to tow him home for the rig eternally had carburetor trouble. It was said that it could always leave Dendron under its own power but few were the times it got home without help. To house it, a closed galvanized iron shed, little larger than the car itself, was built in the fork formed by the lead-in track and the main line at the south end of the yard, and it faced straight down the main line towards Wakefield. It could be pushed out of the shed, the grade would keep it rolling, and it would practically have to leave town.

The increased activity in the woods naturally caused a demand for additional motive power but new locomotives were at a premium due to the declaration of war with Germany in April of 1917. The general demand for locomotives quickly exhausted the supply of second hand motive power and anything that would pull a few cars went at a premium price. However, in June the company managed to get a ten-wheeler from Baldwin and the following month an 0-4-2 saddle-tank. The ten-wheeler was given the road number 16 and put to work as the extra work engine. Inghram, who had No. 4 at that time and was working the Dendron yard, had been complaining for some time that there was more work to be done than he could handle and that a second engine and crew should be permanently assigned to help work the mill yard. Inghram was considered to be a chronic complainer and no one paid too much attention to him but the arrival of the 16, in addition to taking over the extra board, allowed the 6 to spend most of its time in the yard.

The 0-4-2 saddle-tank was numbered "1" and was the third engine to carry that number. It was, of course, classed as a donkey, the basic design being identical to that of the other woods engines except for minor improvements, which were to be expected after fifteen years of design advancement. When Baldwin was given the order they ran into the new Interstate Commerce Commission rules relative to locomotives to be operated on main lines and to get around them the donkey was listed as being sold to the Surry Lumber Company although after delivery the company placed no restrictions on where it was to be operated.

In addition to these two engines, a Baldwin mogul and a second hand saddle-tank were purchased. These two engines were numbered 18 and 19. The mogul has successfully defied identification due to a lack of company records. In late 1930 Higgins stated that the engine had been built for a sugarcane plantation in Cuba but was not delivered. This statement gives us a choice of two interpretations, either the engine came new to the S.S.&S. from Baldwin, or she was purchased second hand. Opinion is about evenly divided but the indications are that she had seen service elsewhere before arriving at Dendron.

Baldwin records do not show the sale of a mogul to the company in 1917, or anywhere around that year. Available Baldwin

Re-Order Records, that reflect the sale of repair parts, show nothing although it is a known fact that a tender tank was ordered and delivered, an exact duplicate of the original one, even to the extended rack around the lip to increase its capacity of megass, that being the fuel for which the engine was designed. Higgins further stated that due to the fact that the engine was so designed, she was a poor steamer, although Baldwin had changed the grates before disposing of her. After she came to Dendron, Higgins did his very best to improve her steaming ability, even to the extent of installing a new firebox, larger diameter tubes, different front end steam and exhaust piping, and finally, the exhaust nozzles were bushed. That only choked the exhaust and decreased the tractive effort. Odd as it might seem, it appears that no attempt was ever made to bush the cylinders.

Getting up steam when setting still was no problem but once the engine began to work, the needle would drop steadily, irrespective of how hard the fireman worked and cursed. Nothing seemed to work with that engine once she was out on the road. One thing is for sure, though, and that is that the engine taught its crews to swear longer and steadier without repeating themselves than did any of the other engines at their very worst.

There was an oldster who fired for Newell & Bryant at Stony Creek, Virginia, and he claimed that when that firm quit in 1917, they sold an engine to the S.S.&S. and it became No. 18 on that road. But he could not remember the number of the engine that was sold, nor anything at all about her. If the 18 was a Newell & Bryant engine, it can be said with certainty that it was not their No. 5. All we can say about the engine is that she was a Baldwin mogul and was an atrocious steamer.

The 19 was purchased from the Southern Iron & Equipment Company of Atlanta, Georgia, a dealer in used machinery of all kinds. The little saddle-tank had been built in 1880 by the H. K. Porter Company for the Milner, Caldwell & Flowers Lumber Company where she ran as their No. 2 until she was just about worn out. It was then sold to the second hand dealer who fixed it up sufficiently to make her resalable. In addition to being larger than the other donkeys, she was top-heavy to the extent that some of the men swore that she would tip over while standing still on level track. The fact that there wasn't a foot of level track on the entire system doesn't detract from the statement. The instability of the engine was undoubtedly caused by the saddle-tank being set unusually high and there apparently being no longitudinal baffles to retard the sloshing of the water from side to side when the engine began to rock on rough track. Due to its tendency to derail and turn over, or simply turn over, the engine had a bad reputation and once the water began to slosh, and the engine began to roll with it on her springs, the crew would leave it like flies off a hot griddle. The little monstrosity was like a mid-1920 round-heeled flapper with a high bob and a one-track mind but she never quite managed to kill any of her crew, not that she didn't try, repeatedly.

Tipping over was actually nothing unusual for the light track and soft road bed were no support for a derailed locomotive. Of course, all derailments did not end up with the engine on its side but a surprising number of them did. The Baldwin donkeys, with their very low center of gravity, were by far the most stable and could be kicked around quite a bit before they got around to flipping over. The larger engines with their higher center of gravity were another story. The No. 2 broke a rail when backing slowly into the Dendron wye and landed in the ditch with her wheels in the air. The 16 had like trouble while running tender first on a two-car labor train from Dendron to Wakefield at 6:15 one evening. It happened a quarter of a mile south of the Blackwater River trestle, on a curve. The tender jumped first and the engine followed, landing on its side, but the coaches remained on the track and none of the fifty passengers were hurt although the fireman had his collarbone broken. The failure of a tender truck bearing was blamed for the accident.

It has already been said that when the 16 was received they made her the spare engine, having no particular daily assignment but filling in wherever she was needed. The fine difference between a spare engine and a relief engine is hard to define but the spare engine was generally used for extra work while the relief engine was used to replace a unit taken out of service for some reason. Several months later the 16 began hauling the labor train regularly to Wakefield, replacing the 700. The number of men to be transported had reached such proportions that the motor car could not handle them. Higgins then went up to Zanesville, Ohio, and purchased three second hand coaches. All of them were without seats. On arrival at Dendron, one was found to be absolutely worthless and after setting around for a while, was scrapped. Both of the others had crude seats installed and, at first, one was used behind the 16 on the twice daily trip to Wakefield, the other being reserved as a spare car. Actually, only the engine made the twice daily round trip for the car was left on a siding at Wakefield overnight.

The purchase of the three cars at Zanesville apparently was the introduction of the use of second hand passenger coaches by the Surry Lumber Company for the transportation of labor into the woods. The converted boxcars and flats continued to be used for some time, at least until more coaches could be procured. The use of such equipment to haul the men in and out of the woods was beginning to be common practice in the logging industry, possibly in an effort to better working conditions and, in a general way, to make logging as a profession a little less unattractive. The procurement of skilled loggers was beginning to be a problem. So far as the Surry Lumber Company was concerned, it gradually procured enough cars to assign two to each of the three camps and to keep two at Dendron, one as a spare and the other for regular use. When two coaches were required on the Wakefield run, it is possible that the spare was used as the second car.

The coaches working out of Newtown and Vicksville laid over at those points overnight. Of the two cars assigned to Central Hill, one laid over there all night but the other was hauled as far as Jones' Crossing, about seven miles beyond Central Hill and a half mile west of Septa, where it remained on a siding until the next morning. At that time, it was tacked onto the end of the first train of empties going south and dropped at Central Hill. The string of empties would continue on into the woods but the coach would wait and eventually become part of the labor train running into the woods from Central Hill. This practice of leaving the coach overnight, or over the weekend, at

Jones' Crossing wasn't too satisfactory for during the evenings it was sometimes used for various purposes by residents of the vicinity, but it was the best that could be done to facilitate the movement of labor from that area into the woods below Central Hill. Locks on the doors didn't work, either. The labor train was invariably hauled into the woods from Central Hill by the standby donkey, after which it simply continued to be available if something happened to one of those regularly assigned the task of working the woods tracks. This arrangement applied to the other two camps as well.

Possibly the most traveled cars on the road were those that Higgins purchased from the Phelps Dodge Corporation at Douglas, Arizona. He apparently purchased the cars in either 1917 or 1918, exactly when, we do not know, and he went out there for the specific purpose of making the purchase, if the equipment was satisfactory. One of his desires of long standing was to be able to say that he had been in every state in the Union and although we can't say for sure that had anything to do with him going so far afield to purchase equipment, he did keep going while he was out there and crossed over into California, thus adding another state to his list. Unfortunately we can't be too sure what he sent home from out there but the general consensus of opinion is that there was a baggage car, a combination car, three coaches, and five flats, the latter "all stacked on a standard gauge platform car like layers of a cake". One thing everyone is sure of is that they came without trucks and when they arrived at Wakefield there was considerable scrambling around to find enough to mount them on. It is a sure thing that at least one of the passenger cars ended up on logging car trucks.

The history of the cars prior to being put in service on the lumber railroad is also vague. One engineer, who was on hand when they were unloaded, was emphatic about two things, they were lettered "CORONADO RAILROAD", and the passenger cars "had no windows in them, just slatted shutters over the openings". If the first statement is so, then the cars were almost certainly former Arizona & New Mexico equipment that had been relettered and transferred to the broadened out twenty-inch gauge mining railroad. How long the cars had been out of service when Higgins arrived on the scene is another question. We can answer one question, though, and that is why the cars were sent home without trucks. A set of old tariffs provides the answer. Anything on flanged wheels was classed as railroad equipment and the freight rate was extremely high. Eliminate the wheels and the bodies automatically became "hardware". The rate on that was a mere fraction of that on railroad equipment. Higgins figured to save as much as possible on the freight charges and take a chance on being able to pick up trucks for the equipment a bit closer to home. Eventually he was able to find a number of wooden-framed passenger trucks but not in time to go under the equipment on arrival. The passenger cars went into the woods to haul men from the various camps and the baggage car was made into a rolling saw filer's shop, complete with living quarters, if a bunk at one end could be called living quarters. The combination car might have been the one that ended up down at Sedley as the pay car but if so, it, too, had done its share of traveling before coming back east.

When the 700 was taken off the Wakefield run, she was sent to Scotland Wharf every morning and used as a sort of yard engine, shuffling the loaded and empty lumber cars around. This included moving cars around on the wharf, shoving them up the bluff and easing them down, something the builder never dreamed one of the Model 19 motor cars would ever be expected to do. Of course, breakdowns were all too frequent, mainly broken drive chains. The joking statement that she managed to leave Dendron under her own power but had to be towed back now became more truth than joke. Finally she was towed home for the last time, shoved into the shed built for her, and after a time, disposed of. We hear of such a contraption being in service on the Lumber line at Rocky Mount, North Carolina, where the first No. 2 finally landed, and later the same motor car went to the Narron Central out of Kenly, North Carolina, as their sole piece of passenger equipment. It could have been the 700 but we can't be sure. After the 700 was pulled out of service, the shifting down at the river was left entirely to any engine that happened to show up on a train. No unit was ever again permanently assigned to work that terminal.

Caesar Temple's donkey developed a leaking staybolt while working south of Wakefield and it became so bad that it was decided to get the engine back to Dendron while it was still possible to keep up steam. Temple started out with a brakesman firing and overtook the mail train at Wakefield. No. 2 was setting at the station waiting for leaving time before continuing on to the north, but Temple couldn't wait as the temporary fireman was having increasing trouble with his fire. He ran around the mail train and kept going. By the time he had reached the grade leading down to the Blackwater River, steam was so low that it would have been impossible to get up the grade north of the trestle. Temple stopped, there being enough remaining steam pressure for that, put wedges under the drivers, and got busy killing the fire to prevent a burned crownsheet.

In the meantime, leaving time arrived, Whurley Faison brought the mail train out to the main line switch and started for Dendron, not knowing that the donkey was stalled ahead of him. Whurley never was one to drag his feet so he had No. 2 stepping right along as it rounded the curve on the grade down to the river, and there set the donkey. Temple and his fireman saw No. 2 bearing down on them and went out of the gangways like a pair of canaries. The fireman on No. 2 hit the ground while the engine was still doing about 40 miles an hour, to "lighten the engine" as he put it, while Faison did his best to do the impossible. They came together with a resounding crash. The rear end of the donkey rode up over the pilot beam of the passenger engine and completely junked the front end; breaking the frame, messing up the front of the smoke box, and even knocking off the stack. On the other hand, No. 2 walked right smack up to the donkey's boiler head. The odd part of the whole affair was that very little damage was done to the running gear of either engine. The impact caused the donkey to jump the wedges under its drivers and take off down the grade like a scared rabbit. A farmer who was plowing his field beside the track at the time, said he nearly swallowed his chew of tobacco when he saw the engine go flying past with no crew and most of the rear end missing.

Whitmore and Faison surveyed the damaged ten-wheeler and decided that with a little luck they could get it to Dendron, so the broken cowcatcher was hauled out of the way and the train allowed to drift on down to where the donkey had finally come to rest. They eased up behind the woods engine and gently shoved it to Dendron where both engines were left and No. 12 continued on with the mail train. The crew of the donkey? Unfortunately they had to walk in, considering it wise to stay out of the passenger engine crew's sight for a very good reason. They should have reported in at Wakefield.

The winter of 1917-1918 was one to be long remembered for during extended periods of time intense cold made logging impossible. During one particularly cold spell everything was at a standstill for two months. Generally, cold meant little to the men but the operations were iced in, making it actually dangerous to cut timber and impossible for the donkeys to get loads out of the woods. When the sap froze in the trees, they seemed to turn to stone and the saws made practically no impression on them.

Richard Cole lived longer and built up more seniority, if there had been such a thing, with the railroad than any employee on the payroll. No one knew his age, not even he, but it was believed that he lived to be very near the century mark. He remembered the first David Steele and his CORNELIA but by the time anyone got around to talking to him about Steele or his early days with "the company" his mental file had become scrambled to the extent that very little could be learned. At his advanced age, it was to be expected. He was a small colored man who had lived a full life, joyfully, taking things as they came, and he was respected and well liked by "his white folks". He was vague about the number of his children but the number of his grandchildren and great-grandchildren must have been legion. During his time he had held many jobs on the narrow gauge and when acting as a brakesman he had lost fingers while making a coupling inside one of the lumber storage sheds at Dendron.

The fact that he was small and slight of bone structure caused him to be chosen to squeeze through the nine by fourteen-inch firebox doors of the donkeys when there was work to be done in the extremely limited space inside of the fireboxes. It was well known that he had an uncontrollable fear of cats and would go out of his way to avoid one, irrespective of its size.

One day a donkey working out of Central Hill developed a leaking boiler tube and it reached the point where it was impossible to keep the boiler hot. Someone had to go over there, climb into the firebox and roll the tube. Sam Atkinson was ready to leave Dendron with a train of empty log cars, so Cole was issued the necessary tools and sent along to make the repairs. On arrival, he dropped off the engine, climbed into the cab of the donkey, and after putting some planks over the hot grates, squeezed through the door into the firebox and went to work on the leaky tube. Atkinson ran on south, dropped the empties, turned on the wye below Central Hill, picked up the loads that had been left there for him, and came on back to Central Hill where he stopped to pick up Cole, but Cole was still struggling with the recalcitrant tube.

Atkinson climbed down and started over to see how much longer it would take to complete the job for he had to get clearance from the agent at Newtown for the run to the main line switch. On his way, a tiny kitten ambled across his path and suddenly Sam had an idea for a practical joke. The kitten was scooped up, Sam climbed in the gangway of the donkey, and Richard found himself sharing the cramped quarters with a dreaded feline. It is a wonder that the firebox didn't burst for Cole went wild. The luckless kitten was quickly stamped through the grates and Cole's frantic yells brought other employees running. They did their best to quiet him down and get him through the tiny fire door but his fright had caused his body to swell and it was some time before anything could be done. Hard feeling? None was ever shown.

No. 6 had been having flue trouble for some time but when the dryer pipe began to leak, the company realized that it actually needed a new boiler and continual repairs would not eliminate the necessity. The Baldwin people were contacted early in 1918 but they wrote that they were up to their ears in work and could not possibly take on additional orders. After asking for bids from several firms, the work was given to the Capitol City Iron Works of Richmond, Virginia, who required the old boiler as a pattern. Consequently the engine was dismantled, the boiler loaded on a flatcar and sent to Wakefield where it was transshipped and forwarded to Richmond. Upon receipt the Richmond firm stripped the boiler and found, to their surprise, that the shell was in excellent shape, due possibly to the purity of the feed water used, therefore it was not considered necessary to build a new one. The trouble had been with the firebox and flue heads, so these were renewed and at the same time all of the internal steel piping was renewed. To increase the heating surface, all of the tubes were increased in size from one and a half to two inches.

The influenza epidemic hit the Sedley area during the fall of 1918 and spread with alarming rapidity, striking down entire families. It was impossible for the local doctors to administer to all that required attention so Causey contacted his brother, Peter P., who was a doctor but not practicing, and asked him to come up and lend a hand. He came, did a wonderful job, and after the epidemic had run its course, for it was never whipped, remained on as his brother's assistant. Doc Causey, as he was called, was a lumberman as well as a doctor.

At the height of the epidemic, some of the people at Sedley got together and set up a sort of soup kitchen. Large cast iron kettles were set over open fires and into them went whatever was donated and out of them came savory broths and soups which were delivered to the sick. Color and race were ignored, the only prerequisite being that the family be incapacitated and in need of food. During this operation the company was a working partner for a majority of the sick were its employees and no one has ever accused the company of not looking after its own.

Due to the increased demand for lumber and higher prices, the company began to relog their holdings between Dory and Wakefield, and to purchase additional stands of timber that had been bypassed when the company worked south due to the fact that the owners and the company could not agree on a price or the trees were not considered mature enough. In some cases a section had to be again purchased because the price paid had covered only timber suitable for cutting at that time and over the years the second growth had reached marketable size. Naturally the matured second growth on company-owned land was another reason for the back-cutting. It is a fact, too, that the company had cut only the prime timber during the

'90's, but as they worked back it was a different story. Lumber left on the yard because of its poor quality found a ready sale and trees left standing because of defects that would effect the quality of the lumber now came down and went through the saws. All pine measuring twelve inches in diameter ten inches above the ground was cut. White oak, suitable for ties, was also cut but red oak was not touched.

The center of this renewed activity was Airfield, which now consisted of one residence, a store, a dam, and a pond. It is approximately half way between Wakefield and Dory and it was there that orders were received and meets arranged, by 'phone. During the days that the railroad ran through there, a mill was perched on top of the earthen dam, a gristmill, but it is no longer there. The age of the community, if the present location can be called that, is uncertain but it was there many years before the railroad was built. The structure that houses the store shows its age in that few nails can be found holding the timbers together, the main timbers being mortised and tenoned and are of heart pine, hand hewed. After these many years the structure shows neither rot nor damage by insects and is structurally sound. During its known lifetime it has had many usages ranging from a brandy distillery to a post office.

Invariably the store and the mill were owned by the same person, the earliest known proprietor being a Dr. Nickolson. It was during a Mr. Cofer's ownership that the building housed a distillery, while a Mr. Branch used it as a store and post office. A Mr. Barker used it strictly as a store and finally R. C. Morris took possession in 1912. At his death the mill ceased operations and stood idle until the State purchased it in 1935 for $1,400, at which time it was pulled down and the pond, and the grounds around it, became a recreational area. The store became an office, of sorts.

The dam, the concrete spillway, and the wicket remain in their original condition. The mill, which straddled the dam at the south end of the spillway, had an undershot wheel that turned a single stone. From 1886 to 1930, the years that the railroad was in operation, the mill was very much in use and although Airfield was no industrial metropolis, there was a certain amount of activity there. Just how the place came to be called Airfield, no one knows, but it has been suggested that the almost constant movement of air over the pond might have had something to do with it.

In 1916 a line was laid to the east from a point on the main line about a mile south of Manry and ran some three miles into the woods. This line was in service for about two years. In 1917 a line roughly a mile in length was put down from a switch approximately a quarter of a mile south of Airfield and ran along the south shore of the millpond. During the same year a line was run dead south from about the same point on the main line for a distance of about two miles. This particular branch remained in service for only about four months before being pulled up.

Also in 1916 a wye was put in on the main line about three-quarters of a mile north of the Airfield trestle and a line laid from it east along the north boundary of Lightwood Swamp to where it is joined by Bentley Swamp. This line came out in 1918 and the steel was used to lay a line west from the main line, beginning at a point about 500 yards south of the wye, which was known as Barhams. The second line was in service until 1925 and was used to log the area to the immediate west as far as Seacorrie and Assamoosick Swamps. The total mileage of this branch was not laid at one time, but as it was required to reach further and further into the woods. When the main branch was laid it was literally a case of moving the Barhams line from the east side of the main line to the west side, mile for mile, and when the line was completed it was found that a special length of rail cut to fit a gap in the east line fitted perfectly into a like gap in the west line.

This new branch followed the north bank of the Airfield mill-pond for about a mile, crossed the swamp that fed the pond from the north and about a quarter of a mile further on it left the county road it had been following, and forked. The south branch ran about three and a half miles, possibly four, to Assamoosick Swamp, while the other branch ran northwest about two miles to a section known as Birdsong's Quarter. These two lines, as well as the main branch, were well laid and sanded. A siding was put in on the north side of the main branch, ex-

tending from a point 200 feet beyond the throat of the wye to
the trestle over the swamp. Donkeys worked a maze of woods
tracks radiating from the branches and brought the loads down
to the siding, which would hold about forty cars, where they
were picked up by the jacks, and of course it was here that the
jacks left the empties to be picked up by the donkeys.

All of the woods lines in that area were laid with six-foot pine
ties, hand hewed under contract by Lewis Edmonds, and
spaced fifteen to each length of thirty-foot, twenty-pound rail.
The faces of the ties varied from four to six inches, depending
upon the diameter of the trees from which they were cut. They
were smoothed off on the top and bottom only, hence the var-
iance in width. Just why the company contracted for the cutting
of ties for the branches around Airfield rather than furnish
them as they had done for other lines, we just don't know.

As the company worked back from Dory, the logging
branches were not necessarily laid on new road beds. It is more
than possible that some were laid on rights-of-way built and
later abandoned during the '90's, one such being the relaying
of the old West Hope line in 1924 from Dory wye to Elmore's
Curve. This particular branch came out for the second time in
1926.

Charlie Brittle, the section foreman, was not only in charge
of the main line from Wakefield to Dory, but he also had the
job of staking the rights-of-way into the woods for branches
built off his section of the main line. A gang under Phelix Lane
cleared away the brush and prepared the ground while another
gang under Tom Bradshaw laid the steel. Theoretically, only
Bradshaw and his gang were employees of the railroad company, but the chances are dollars to peanuts that they were
paid out of the same pocket. Once the track was in, it was up
to the woods section foreman Jim Stevenson to see that it remained in a fair condition, which means that it was kept more
or less to gauge and the joints were kept in line. As was the
case with the woods tracks elsewhere, the ties were slapped
down on bare ground, irrespective of grade, for they were to
be in use only a short time. Grades were severe, curves sharp,
and the track extremely rough. One man who should know
swears up and down that he knew of track into one hollow where

The body of the combination express & R.P.O. car at Scotland
sitting on blocks beside the main line. November 1930.

The general office building and station at Dendron a few months after
the line was pulled up. The track passed between the viewer and the
building. 1931.

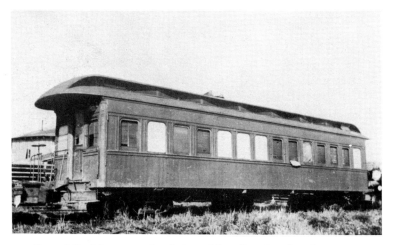

One of the labor cars after being sold to Gray Lumber Company.
The S.S.&S. lettering is still vaguely discernible.

The 7-spot after being abandoned beside the Southern Railway at
Suffolk, Va., by the Planters Box Company. Feb. 16, 1931.

Boiler head of donkey No. 7. This picture was taken well after the donkey had been abandoned at Suffolk, Va., and had been stripped of all brass. Suffolk, Va. April 1932.

Locomotive No. 26 sitting in the Gray Lumber Company siding at Waverly, Va., after she had been purchased from the S.S.&S. The picture was taken in 1930.

One of the two remaining engines of the S.S.&S. No. 26 out of service at the U. S. Overseas Airport in New Jersey. Taken in 1964 and at present, January 1967, the engine is still there.—Edgar T. Mead

The other of the two remaining engines of the S.S.&S. and still in service. No. 6 as she appeared on the Argent Lumber Company railroad at Hardeeville, S. C., in April 1956. She is now out in the Mid-west hauling passengers.—Edgar T. Mead, Jr.

The much rebuilt No. 6 as she appears today, 1966, on the Midwest Central R.R., Mount Pleasant, Iowa.—Harold Plummer

SUPERINTENDENT'S OFFICE

Surry, Sussex and Southampton Railway

Dendron, Surry Co., Va.

July 28, 1930

Mr. J. Q. Hancock, Agent, Dory, Va.
Mr. J. W. White   "   Manry, Va.
Mr. W. B. White   "   Wakefield, Va.
Mr. J. D. Hart   "   Dendron, Va.
Mr. G. W. Noyes   "   Elberon, Va..
Mr. J. O. Chappelle   "   Moorings, Va.
Mr. A. R. Chapman   "   Surry, Va.
Mr. E. Younglove   "   Scotland, Va.

Gentlemen:

      This is to advise you that the S. S. &.S. Ry. will discontinue its operations on Thursday, July 31st.

      Please see that all the freight in the depot is delivered on or before that date.

      Please also post the enclosed notice.

Yours very truly,

Edward Rogers.

Superintendent

ER:IC

SEDLEY
Virginia

- - - - : Streets laid out by the Surry Lumber
            Company.
———— : Streets actually opened.

1. Virginian Railway station.
2. Surry Lumber Company office.
3. Company commissary
4. Commissary store house
5. Shed for "Gausey's Coach" (Pay car)
6. Company smoke house
7. Structure for processing meat.
8. Blacksmith and Repair Shop.
9. Trestle where engine tanks were filled.
10. Home of Philip Rogers and later of Dr.
    P. F. Gausey
11. Church built for white employees.
12. Church built for colored employees
13. House for motor cars.
14. Home for commissary agent.
15. Home of company carpenter, O. J. High.

1920

Scale: 1" = 400'

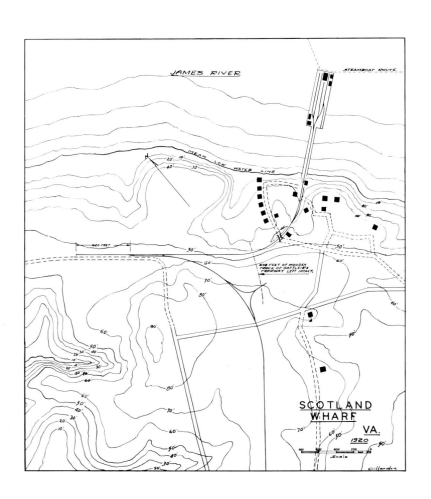

JAMES RIVER

STEAMBOAT ROUTE

MEAN LOW WATER LINE

620 FEET

838 FEET OF WOODEN TRACK OF GOTTLIEB'S TRAMWAY LEFT INTACT.

SCOTLAND
WHARF
VA.
1920
Scale

SURRY, SUSSEX & SOUTHAMPTON RAILWAY — LOCOMOTIVE NUMBER 1 (FIRST)

BUILT BY THE TANNER & DELANEY ENGINE COMPANY, RICHMOND, VA., 1883, FOR DAVID STEELE, SPRING GROVE, VA. AS "CORNELIA".

TAKEN OVER BY THE SURRY LUMBER COMPANY IN 1886. ORIGINAL 4-WHEEL TENDER REPLACED BY THE SECOND OWNER.

CYLINDERS: 7 IN. X 14 IN.

THIS DRAWING IS AN APPROXIMATION, HAVING BEEN PREPARED FROM TANNER & DELANEY DETAILED ILLUSTRATIONS
AND ALL KNOWN DATA ON THIS PARTICULAR LOCOMOTIVE.

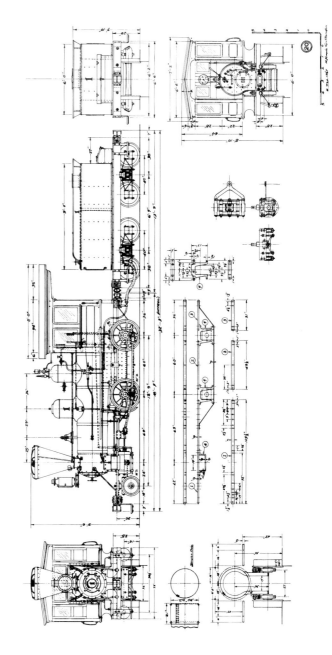

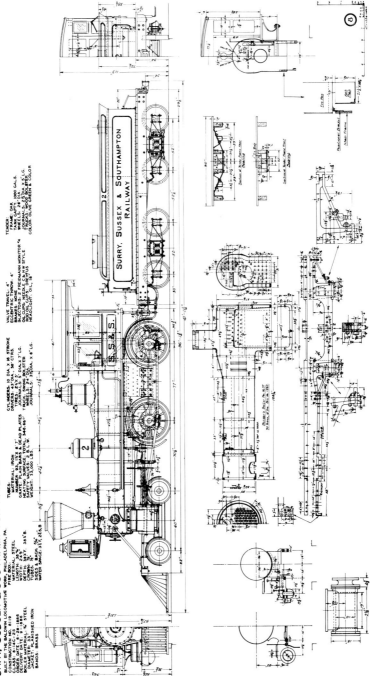

SURRY, SUSSEX & SOUTHAMPTON RAILWAY – LOCOMOTIVE NUMBER 2

SURRY, SUSSEX & RAILWAY

BUILT BY THE BALDWIN LOCOMOTIVE WORK, PHILADELPHIA, PA.
CONSTRUCTION NO. 8119
CLASS. 8–14 C.–3
ORDER DATE. 8–28–1888
DELIVERY DATE.
BOILER MATERIAL. ⁵⁄₁₆″ STEEL
JACKET. PLANISHED IRON
BANDS. BRASS

FIRE BOX.
  MATERIAL. STEEL
  LENGTH. 28⁵⁄₈″
  WIDTH. 24⁵⁄₈″
  DEPTH. 59⁷⁄₈″
  CROWN. ¾″
TUBES. ½″
SIDES & BACK. ⁵⁄₈″
WATER SPACE. 3½″, 2½″ & 8

CYLINDERS. 10 DIA. x 16 STROKE
DRIVERS. 43″DIA., 38″ CTRS.
GRATE. PLAIN BARS & DEAD PLATES
TRUCK. 8 WHEEL
HEATING SURFACE. TOTAL 346.46″
SAFETY VALVES. 2 B.L.W.
WEIGHT. 33,000 LBS.

TUBES.
  MATERIAL. IRON
  NUMBER. 93
JONES & 5′ DIA. x 7′ LG.
JOURNALS. 5″ DIA. x 7″ LG.
TRUCK. SWING BOLSTER
WHEELS. 24″ DIA.
JOURNALS. 3¾″DIA. x 6″LG.

VALVE TRAVEL. 4″
ECCENTRIC THROW. 4″
INJECTORS. 2 F. FRIEDMANN MONITOR ⁴⁄₄
OIL CUPS. NEEDLE, C & N W STYLE
HEADLIGHT. OIL, 18″

TENDER.
  FRAME. OAK
  TANK CAPT. 1000 GALS.
  WHEELS. 24″ DIA.
  JOURNALS. 3¼″ DIA. x 7″ LG.
  COLOR. OLIVE GREEN & COLOR

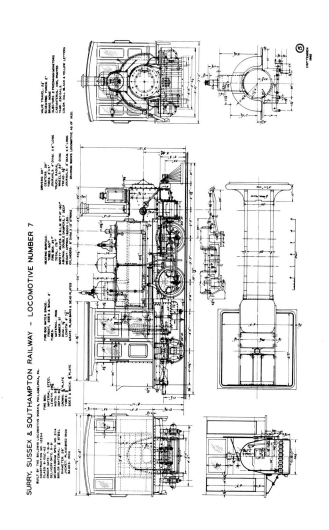

BUILT BY THE BALDWIN LOCOMOTIVE WORKS, PHILADELPHIA, PA.
CONSTRUCTION NO. 12214
CLASS 8-12/D-2-42
ORDER DATE 7-26-91
DELIVERY DATE 9-91
MECHANISM SPECIAL NO. 2114
BOILER MATERIAL ½ STEEL
DIAMETER 42"
JACKET, PLANISHED IRON
BANDS, IRON

FIRE BOX WATER SPACE,
FRONT, SIDES & BACK, 3"
FIRE BOX:
MATERIAL STEEL
LENGTH 29¼
WIDTH 29¾
DEPTH 31½
TUBES:
MATERIAL IRON
NUMBER 57
DIAM. 1⅞
LENGTH 4' 7¼
SIDE & BACK, ⅜" PLATE

HEATING SURFACE:
TUBES 142"
FIRE BOX 25"
TOTAL 16.7"
SAFETY VALVES 2 B.L.W. SET AT 160"
ASH PAN DOUBLE DAMPER, 7" DEEP
WEIGHT, APPROX. 18,000 LBS.
GRATE, PLAIN BARS & DEAD PLATES
CYLINDERS 8" DIAM. X 12" STROKE

DRIVERS: 30"
CENTERS 24"
TIRES 2" X 3"
JOURNALS 4" DIAM. X 6" LONG
TRUCKS, RADIAL
WHEELS 22" DIAM.
TREAD 2⅜"
JOURNALS 3" DIAM. X 5" LONG

VALVE TRAVEL 2¼"
ECCENTRIC THROW 2"
BRAKE, NONE
INJECTORS, 2 FREEMAN MONITORS
CAB MATERIAL, ASH, PAINTED
TANK, 250 GALS.
COLOR, ALL, BLACK & YELLOW LETTERS

DRAWING SHOWS LOCOMOTIVE AS OF 1920.

CRITENDEN
1960

SURRY, SUSSEX & SOUTHAMPTON RAILWAY — LOCOMOTIVE NUMBER 10

BUILT BY THE BALDWIN LOCOMOTIVE WORKS. PHILADELPHIA. PENNA.

CONSTUCTION NUMBER: 16011

BOILER TEST DATE: MAY 1898

BUILDER'S CLASS: 10–22E–24

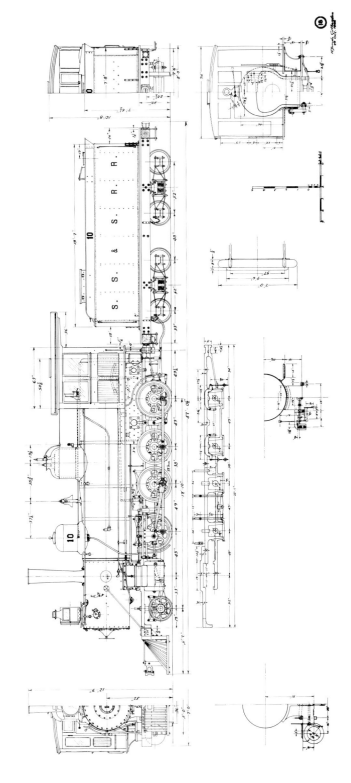

SURRY, SUSSEX & SOUTHAMPTON RAILWAY – LOCOMOTIVE NUMBER 11

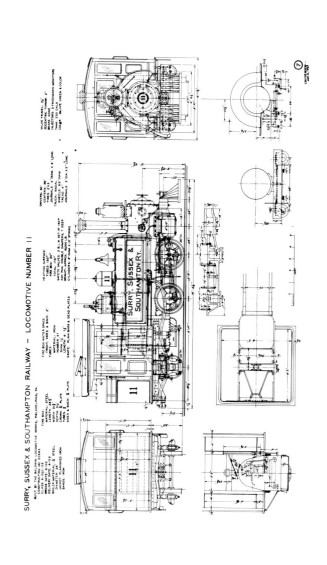

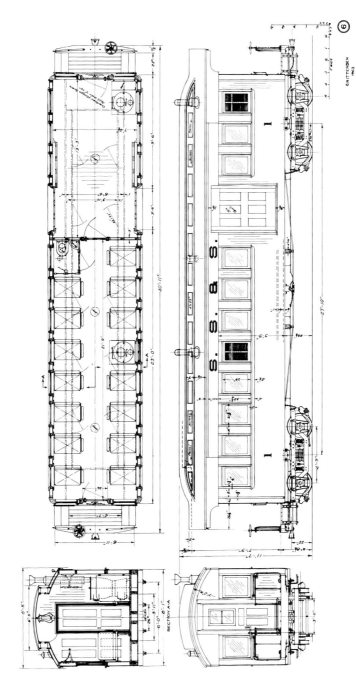

SURRY, SUSSEX & SOUTHAMPTON RAILWAY — COMBINATION CAR NUMBER 1.

BUILT BY THE NORTH CAROLINA CAR COMPANY, RALEIGH, N.C., 1883.

SURRY, SUSSEX & SOUTHAMPTON RAILWAY —PASSENGER TRAIN COACH NO. 3
BUILT BY BILLMEYER & SMALL CO., YORK, PENNA.

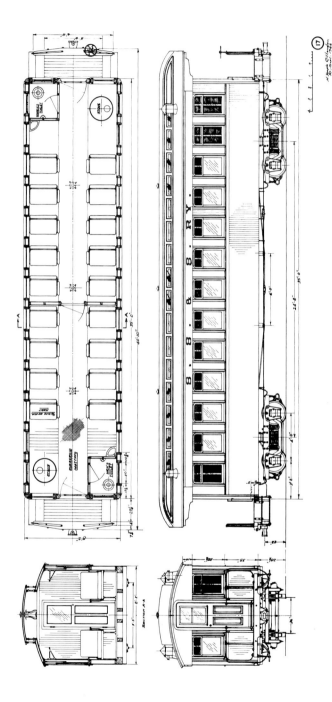

SURRY, SUSSEX & SOUTHAMPTON RAILWAY — COAL CAR NO. 55

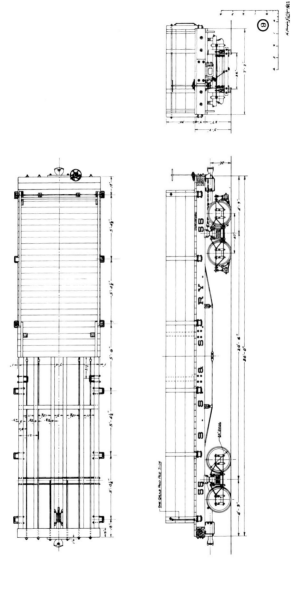

SURRY LUMBER COMPANY
LOG CAR
KILBY CAR & FOUNDRY CO.

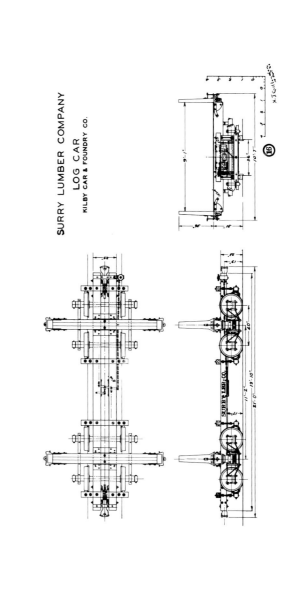

it took three donkeys, working hard, to get out a single car of logs. Derailments in the woods around Airfield were as common as they were elsewhere, there being several a day, but no one paid any attention to them. Quincy Hancock took No. 3 in one day, tank first, and that afternoon he brought her out, tank first. During the day the donkey had jumped the track, flipped over, and landed in such a manner that when they finally got her back on her feet, she had been turned around. He was the same Quincy Hancock who kept his money in the sand dome of his donkey. The idea was that if anything happened to him, his money was safe and no one but he and his wife supposedly knew where it was, but like most secrets on the narrow gauge, everyone knew it.

Prior to Causey taking over the logging operations, the method of getting out the logs had changed very little over the years. In addition to the men, a section crew consisted of two snaking mules used to haul the logs clear of the sawyers, three swing carts with two mules per cart, used to haul the logs to the loading deck, and one mule to haul the logs up onto the cars. When a section was opened, the railroad was laid straight in on one side or the other and trees felled for about 200 yards to either side. When all the trees to that distance had been cut, the track was moved over about 400 yards and the sawyers went to work again. By using this pattern of track laying, it was not necessary to haul by swing carts over 200 yards at any time. There were exceptions, of course. As soon as a tree had been felled, cut into sixteen-foot sections, and loaded, another followed it as closely as possible until the last tree in the section was out. The track was then removed and relaid in a new section, the teams being driven into the new location by road. Willie Lewis was woods superintendent of all of the area between Wakefield and Sedley. After Causey took over, the main difference was the substitution of horses for mules, of course, and the gradual introduction of power equipment.

From around the first of March to the first of May, a track crew followed every engine from Dory to Wakefield, and possibly from Wakefield to Scotland Wharf, to prevent fires being set by the locomotives. This was the outgrowth of the trouble experienced down east of Vicksville. Although considerable care was taken to prevent fires, they did occur along the route now and then. Although the engines burned coal by now almost exclusively, once in a while a donkey would have to resort to the use of wood for fuel, and then there were sparks. The first spark out of the stack was the signal for everyone to start watching for smoke rising from the brush. Early one morning a dwelling between Airfield and Wakefield burned and the owner promptly blamed it on sparks from a locomotive, even though the structure stood well back from the right-of-way. The company replaced the dwelling for they did not want the ill will of any of the people in the area. Replacing a frame structure was considered to be a cheap price to pay for continued amity, but it appeared that they should not have been so eager to keep the peace. Later on a barn south of Airfield burned and the engines were blamed. If it worked once, why not try it again, and again the company replaced the structure.

Although lumber was comparatively cheap, it was obvious that the policy was much too generous and although there was certainly no objection to replacing structures destroyed by fires actually set by the locomotives, the company had no intention of rebuilding all of the delapidated structures in the county. Steps were immediately taken to insure that the engines did not set any fires. In addition to following the locomotives, regular patrols were set up and it can be said that the number of fires suddenly decreased to practically zero.

Post-War Prosperity

From the day that the 16 had been put in service, there had been argument after argument about her ability to haul tonnage. Tom Bain, her engineer, claimed that she could handle a heavier load than anything on the road but the crews of the jacks thought otherwise. Eventually it was possible to settle the argument once and for all.

Down on the Central Hill line a string of fifty-six loads had accumulated and the 14 and 16 were to bring them in as two trains. The crews put their heads together and decided that this was as good a time as any to see just what the 16 could actually do. Bain backed his engine down on the string of cars and after a little backing and filling, got them rolling. Atkinson followed him with the 14, running light and well back to give Bain plenty of room if he should stall. Bain did all right until he had crossed College Run and started up Jack Bell Hill, some two miles east of Newtown, but there he stalled. He backed up and made a run for it but again he stalled. It was obvious that the 16 just wasn't going to take those fifty-six loads over the top of the grade. Sam Atkinson dropped back to a siding and let Bain shove his train back down the main line east of the switch. He then ran out ahead of Bain while Bain cut off and backed into the siding out of the way. Sam backed down on the train, took out all of the slack very gently to prevent breaking any links, and started for the hill with the engine working full out. We won't say that it didn't take a bit of straining, but the train did not stall and ran all the way through to Dendron without stopping. It is also possible that Atkinson was a better throttle artist than Bain, or knew his engine better, but the chances are that the jacks were better suited for hauling heavy trains than was the ten-wheeler. Anyway, there was no more argument although Bain continued to grumble that his engine was the better of the two.

On one occasion No. 2 was running south from Dendron, right on schedule. She went down the hill towards the Blackwater River trestle, picking up speed as she went, swung around the curve leading out onto the fill that formed the approach to the trestle and, lo, there set a donkey, right smack in the middle of the trestle, taking water from the river. There was a frantic effort to get stopped while the donkey's crew scattered in all directions, even overboard, but there just wasn't enough room between the two engines and the donkey got a hefty smack on the snoot which sent it skidding down the track. No one was hurt and only a slight amount of damage was done.

It seems that the donkey had been assigned the job of hauling a ballast train and had shoved a string of empty flats into the sand pit track. While the men were loading the cars, the engine crew had cut off and run out on the trestle to take water. So, they spotted the engine over the main stream, dropped the suction hose over the side, started the syphon, and made themselves comfortable. Apparently everyone had forgotten all about the mail train and the first intimation they had that they were on its time was when it suddenly came charging around the curve, running with the bit in its teeth for the grade on the far side of the river.

Another incident took place on the same trestle which came very close to ending disastrously. One night No. 8 was coming up from the south with its train of loads. While crossing the trestle the engine suddenly lurched sharply to one side but held to the rails and righted herself. The engineer didn't dare shut off for he had no assurance that the structure wouldn't give way under the static weight. The superintendent happened to be riding in the cab at the time and after the engine was again on her feet, and he managed to get back on his, he turned to the engineer.

"Was THAT there this morning?"

The answer was a laconic "No".

That was all that was said but both men, and the fireman, looked back as the loads swayed dangerously as they passed over the sag and snapped back in line. The gods of Fate were with them and the train cleared the trestle without going into the river. On arrival at Dendron, all service south of there was immediately halted and Wakefield was instructed to hold everything there that night that might be coming up from the south.

The next morning the superintendent took his motor car and went down to take a look at the structure. He found that a stringer, that extended from bent to bent, some ten feet, was missing, completely gone, leaving the ties and rails unsupported on one side. The only solution anyone could think of was that a log had rolled from a car in the preceding train and had knocked out the stringer. Just how that could be done and not wreck the train, was something else again. Could it have been that someone held a grudge and deliberately removed the timber? Maybe so, but no one ever found out for sure.

It must be remembered that J. C. Causey was hired after the mill at Wallace, North Carolina, had burned. He had been in partnership prior to that with a F. A. Addington and they had logged for the Norfolk Lumber Company even then. Prior to the consolidation of their interests, Addington had been operating a small mill, using only one band saw, with no re-saw, and had two small 0-4-0 dinkeys to haul in his logs. When the move from Burgaw to Wallace was made, Causey extending the logging line, which more or less paralleled the Atlantic Coast Line Railroad, moved some of the houses over it on flatcars, and set up a new logging camp.

The Wallace mill was expanded and the logging line greatly extended, making it necessary to procure additional motive power. The two engines then in service simply could not cope with the expanded operation. The Norfolk Lumber Company's original motive power consisted of one locomotive, an 0-4-4 Forney built by Vulcan, and Causey had soon found that when run tank-first, as a tenderless 4-4-0, she held the rough woods track much better than when operated with the smoke box leading. Hence, Causey favored a 4-4-0 when it came time to procure new motive power, mainly because of the flexibility, but the Baldwin salesman was under orders to push the fairly new 2-6-2 design for logging roads and finally persuaded Causey to give one a try. Until the new locomotive could be delivered, an A.C.L. engine was rented for $8 a day. When No. 3 arrived in 1910, she quickly proved to be far superior to either the Forney or the rented engine when operated in the woods, and Causey was well pleased with it. Later on, though, Norfolk Lumber Company bought a second Forney, No. 4, from Bowen & Street of Suffolk, Virginia. This engine was formerly off the New York elevated lines and had been purchased by the Suffolk firm, which dealt in second hand logging equipment, for resale. All of this Norfolk Lumber Company equipment was eventually taken over by the Chesapeake-Camp Corporation when that company absorbed the smaller firm.

So, when the Surry donkeys began to show signs of having reached a point where extensive repairs were no longer economical, nor practical, and where actually the small locomotives were proving much too light for the type of logging now being practiced by the company, Causey began to bally-hoo the 2-6-2 design as replacements. Another selling point was that a heavier engine could replace two or three of the donkeys and in so doing reduce the number of employees necessary for train service in the woods. Eventually, two 2-6-2 tender locomotives were ordered from Baldwin but again they ran into trouble with the I.C.C. rules. The engines were ordered fitted with such outlawed equipment as standard fire doors, link and pin couplers, and no train brakes. By now additional I.C.C. regulations had become effective and locomotives so equipped were not allowed to operate on railroads engaged in common carrier service. The fact that all of the locomotives in service on the narrow gauge were so equipped was immaterial. After a certain date all motive power had to be fitted with certain safety appliances and these engines were to be delivered without the minimum requirements. According to law, it just couldn't be done.

Again the order was signed by the Surry Lumber Company, giving the impression that the locomotives were to be used solely for logging. Baldwin didn't care just so long as they had a signed statement from the purchaser to that effect. The two locomotives, sans all frills and items not absolutely necessary for their actual operation, were delivered in late November of 1919. As soon as they were ready for service, one of them, the 20, was sent to Sedley, replacing donkeys 15 and 17, while the other, the 22, was sent to Newtown, replacing the 3 and 5. The four donkeys in the worst condition were then withdrawn from service. The four in the worst condition were not necessarily those four replaced by the Prairies.

During the early part of 1919 three additional large boxcars were put in service, and other than a coal car added to the roster in 1925, they were the last cars procured by the company. This coal car was undoubtedly a flat with side and end boards erected by the car shop. The lumber business was still excellent, riding on the wave of prosperity created by the war which had been brought to a successful conclusion the previous year. There was still a fair amount of marketable timber in the woods although the company was beginning to see the end due to a depletion of the available supply.

Two additional tracts were acquired in 1920 which required the construction of two short spurs just east of Surry off the Central Hill line. One spur was laid from a switch at Newtown and ran southeast into timber purchased from a Mr. Roach. The second spur, about a mile and a half from the main line switch, was laid to the southwest into a tract purchased from John T. Seward. This second branch had at least two woods tracks of some length radiating from it, one cutting off to the right, going in. This line forked almost immediately, the right arm running a short distance to terminate back of Newtown while the left arm more or less paralleled the branch line for about a mile. The second woods track cut off to the left and ran a little east of south for about a mile and a quarter. The timber holdings served by these lines were not very extensive and were cut over in short order. The track was then removed.

The two new engines proved a success although the light woods tracks gave a certain amount of trouble. Irrespective of the longer wheelbase and the greater number of wheels with which to distribute the weight, the Prairies were much heavier and harder on the light track than were the donkeys. These tracks had been laid for nothing heavier than the little nine-tonners and it had a nasty habit of settling under the heavier engines, particularly during wet weather. However, a short time later two more Prairies were ordered from Baldwin but were to be delivered even more stripped down than were the first two. Basically, the engines were exact duplicates of those of the first order. The 24 and 26 arrived in late October of 1920, the 24 being sent to Central Hill where she replaced the two donkeys working out of there. The 26 went to Sedley as a spare engine. Two additional donkeys were promptly retired, again not necessarily those sent home from Central Hill. This left only the 1, 17, and 19 of the once extensive fleet of tank engines. Some of these donkeys were sold and some were scrapped, but which, and how many, found a new home is impossible to say. We know that No. 5 was sold to the Southern Iron & Equipment Company of Atlanta, Georgia, and was subsequently sold on January 29, 1923, to Hendrick & Wade Construction Company of Lilesville, North Carolina. Somewhere around the same time No. 7 was sold direct to the Planters Box Company of Suffolk, Virginia. It seems logical to suppose that No. 5 was selected by the second hand dealer because of the fact that she had a comparatively new boiler.

Somewhere between the delivery date of the first two Prairies and the second pair, the company began fitting electric headlights to their locomotives. The 20 and 22 came fitted with oil headlights while the 24 and 26 came without headlights of any kind. On delivery the company fitted them with electric headlights, both front and rear. Headlights and generators for all of the engines, so fitted, were furnished by the Pyle National Company. Later on the company stated that all of their locomotives were fitted with electric headlights and that they had prevented numerous accidents, but at the time the installation began, there were donkeys which never got the new equipment due to the fact that they were slated to be disposed of.

As of the end of 1921 the total roster consisted of 16 locomotives, 70 boxcars, 12 flatcars, five coal cars, four coaches, the combine, two baggage and express cars, approximately 400 log cars, and three camp cars which were converted boxcars. In addition there were the passenger cars used for hauling men into the woods and swamps, various flatcars with logging machinery mounted on them, and at least three log cars with 18-foot wooden cylindrical tanks on them and used for storing water for the loader and skidder boilers. The tanks were built large enough to fit snugly between the stakes and were fitted with a flap-type cover over the filling hole that served no purpose other than to keep out the leaves and twigs. This unlisted equipment was considered the property of the lumber company and at no time was ever listed in detail. The locomotives in service were the third No. 1, the second No. 2, the 4, 6, 8, 10, 12, 14, 16, 17, 18, 19, 20, 22, 24, and 26.

On a certain day in 1921 the 22 was working over north of the highway between Spring Grove and Surry Court House on the woods branch which left the main line at Moorings, ran in a northwesterly direction, and crossed Pigeon Swamp just west of Loafer's Oak. Spires had picked up a string of 25 loads on the nose of his engine, making it necessary for him to bring them out running tender first. As the engine started down the grade leading into the swamp from the northwest and began to pick up speed with the cars nudging her on, Spires checked the speed with the steam brake and as he did so a pin about half way the train jumped out. To get up the grade on the far side of the swamp it was necessary to release the brake and begin feeding steam and as that was done the front portion of the train began to run away from the detached rear part. A brakesman riding just forward of the break saw what had happened and began making frantic signals to Spires to get going in order to stay ahead of the rear section which was rapidly picking up speed on the steep grade. Spires caught the signal, jerked open the throttle and the sudden lunge of the engine yanked out the draft gear of the first car. The front section of the train quickly came to a stop and then started back down the grade. The brakesman didn't have a chance to jump for there was no safe place to land and while he was trying to make up his mind as to what to do, the two sections came together. Logs and cars erupted like water from a lawn sprinkler. The brakesman was tossed clear and escaped with nothing worse than bruises and scratches, and a thorough dunking. The wreckage of logs and smashed log cars formed a pile some twenty feet high. It was an unholy mess and it couldn't have happened in a worse place.

C. T. Gwaltney, who was operating the skidder at that operation, was sent in with his gang of 21 men to clean up the wreck. His first job was to clear the right-of-way and rebuild the track. The clearing was quickly done by shoving everything over into the swamp. The track was then repaired in short order and trains were again moving in and out of the woods. The big job was to pick up the logs and smashed cars. Gwaltney moved in a log loader and a string of empty log cars and began playing jack-straws with the logs and sorting out the parts of the cars. It proved to be a five-day job for no sooner had he set up his rig than a train came along and he had to tear down and get out of the way. He would then move back in, set up again, do a little work, and tear down again, over and over again. There was no room on the low fill for a second track and to build another fill around the wreck would have taken longer than it was estimated it would take to clear up the obstruction working as they did.

Log loading equipment was used again to clean up a wreck on the Tyus tract between Pigeon Swamp and Moorings, just southwest of where the above wreck took place. Gwaltney was using a skidder to drag logs up out of the swamp and pile them beside the track which, at this particular point, was on a stiff grade and a fairly sharp curve leading up from the swamp. The cars were ready to go so Spires coupled onto them but when he tried to get them rolling, the weight behind the tender was too much and the 22 laid over on her side gently like a tired old horse. Neither Spires nor Freeman, the colored brakesman who was firing at the time, were hurt. Spires immediately called Dendron from the 'phone located in the loading yard, but while he was talking, Gwaltney was looking over the situation. Before he hung up, Gwaltney took the receiver and told Rogers that he thought he could set the engine on its feet with the skidder, if it was all right with him. He was told to try it.

To get a straight haul on the engine, he rigged blocks to various trees, down low, and rove a cable through them, one end being wrapped around the boiler of the engine and made fast, and the other end passed around the skidder haul-in drum. When strain was applied to the rig, there was considerable vibration and groaning but the engine came up and dropped back on the rails just as nice as you please. No damage had been done to the engine and she was able to continue the trip, bringing out the cars to Moorings, a few at a time, before continuing on to Dendron.

Coming out of the woods one evening, Spires had twelve to fifteen loads behind the 22 and was stepping right along. Gwaltney's gang was riding the logs, as the saying went, to get home to Newtown from up near Central Hill. Suddenly a rail snapped under the engine, dropping the drivers between the ties and bringing the engine to a stop as suddenly as if the train had hit the base of a rock cliff. The loaded cars slammed up against the rear of the tender with such force that the center sills buckled, some breaking, catapulting men and logs all over the place. Gwaltney had been riding in the cab, as befitted the boss of the logging operation, and as soon as everything settled down, he began counting noses. All but one man was accounted for and after a short time he was found under a log, mashed down in the mud of a ditch, face up, fortunately. They got him out and upon examination it was found that he had no broken bones, only badly bruised and scared stiff.

The summer of 1921 is famous up around Dendron as the summer of the big drought. At first it was considered to be a dry spell, nothing unusual for that time of year nor anything to get excited about, but as it began to stretch out into weeks, it became more and more serious. Streams began to dry up and the exposed mud of the swamps to dry out and crack. The water in the Blackwater River dropped below the pump suction and gangs of men began ditching to lead what little water there was to it. Soon even that little trickle ceased to run and stood in disconnected, stagnant pools until it evaporated. Wells went dry and conditions became desperate. The mills were shut down and the teams brought out of the woods and shipped to Christiansburg, up in the hills, to wait out the dry weather.

To provide water enough to keep up steam for the generator, fire pumps, and the ice plant, the company again brought in water by rail from the old reliable, Cypress Swamp. A box was made of two by eight inch timbers, and mounted on a log car. This water, in a very limited quantity, was obtained by again ditching the bed of the swamp, connecting pool to pool until the water could be reached by a syphon hose lowered from the trestle. Locomotives drew their water from the same source. All available fresh water was carefully hoarded and when an engine came in off a run, her fire was immediately killed. Any fireman who let a safety valve pop was about as popular as a skunk at a camp meeting. The only regular run maintained was that of the mail train, and of course, the water train. Lumber trains had to be run now and then for there were still orders to be filled, drought or no drought. Water consumption was considered when assigning an engine to any run other than that of the mail train and the talk was always of whose well still had water in it and whose went dry the night before.

The mills were closed for about a month and then the rains came. It was a gully washer but the parched earth drank up a lot of water before any began to run off. It was only then that a trickle of water began to show in the riverbed and pool began to spill into pool. The connecting ditches helped immensely when water began to run in the river and soon the pump was able to discharge water into the cisterns. The teams were brought back and conditions gradually returned to normal but the people never forgot the summer of 1921, the summer of the big drought.

Motor car No. 600 was the one generally used by Doc Causey when making his rounds of the camps and it has been said that he sometimes ran with a heavy hand on the throttle for he knew what the motor car would do, and which was a lot more important, what it would not do. At least he thought so. This was the second No. 600 for the first one had joined its ancestors when the converted Fords put in their appearance. One bright sunny day he was running north from Sedley, where he had his home. When up near Vicksville he ran up on Fennie Bradshaw sleeping in the shade with his head on a rail, and hit and killed him. The doctor said that he was in bright sunlight and the man was unnoticeable in the heavy shadow. When his eyes had adjusted to the sudden shade and he made out the sleeping man on the track, it was too late to stop. It was a most unfortunate accident. On the other hand, the one that could be termed the most ludicrous was when the same motor car ran off and left the doctor.

One rather cold, frosty morning in early 1922, JC and Doc Causey left Sedley in their respective motor cars for Dendron. When Doc went to get his train orders, JC told him that he already had orders for his motor car and that Doc had just as well run on them, as a sort of second section. It was always that way, JC led and his brother followed. So they left Sedley and ran on north, Doc keeping his brother's motor car in sight. When they passed Airfield, Clyde King came out behind them with the 17 hauling a log skidder. He ran considerably slower than the motor cars for the skidder was top-heavy and unwieldy, and the doctor and his brother were out of sight before King had cleared the Airfield switch.

Just south of Seacock Swamp, that being just south of Wakefield, the doctor saw D. C. Branch over on the road and decided that it was as good a time as any to find out how an ill member of his family was doing. He pulled up on the gear lever, stopped the car, and got out, leaving the engine running. King continued to come on north, taking it very easy, and gave the motor cars no thought until he suddenly saw Doc's sitting on the main line and its driver over on the road. It came as a surprise but, actually, it was nothing new for the doctor had a habit of leaving his motor car sitting anywhere it happened to be while he saw a patient. King figured that Doc would climb in and get going as soon as he saw the train coming up behind him and with that thought in mind he tooted his whistle a couple of times and kept coming.

Doc looked up but kept right on talking until the last second and then made a dash for the motor car, jumped in, dropped the gear lever into forward position, let out the clutch and pulled down on the gas lever. King closed the throttle and was coasting but now he opened up again for both he and Doc were confident that the motor car would run off and leave the train. But, there was a joker in the deck in the form of a thin coat of ice on the rails. The motor let out a roar, the wheels spun, but there she set. It was immediately evident to King that he was going to hit the motor car and he locked his drivers but the skidder did exactly that, skidded the donkey on up the track, and although they were slowing down, the distance was about eighteen inches too short. The doctor tried once or twice to rock the motor car into motion but failed, so he pulled up on the gear lever and joined the birds, leaving the engine running on half throttle.

The 17 nudged the rear of the motor car, giving it a hefty boost, exactly what was required to get it rolling, and away she went, the shock of the collision having caused the gear lever to drop into high position. Branch stood and watched the whole thing with a surprised look on his face. As soon as they could gather their wits about them, Doc and the engine crew went into high gear. A brakesman pulled the pin on the skidder, Doc climbed up into the cab of the donkey, and King took off after the motor car as fast as he dared run the little engine. The donkey snorted and bucked, rumbled and rolled, but all they got for their wild ride were three broken springs, which says very little for the condition of the track. They never saw the motor car again.

In the meantime, JC's orders read that he was to cross the mail train at Wakefield, which would also wait in the station track for the 17 and the skidder, so when he arrived he backed into a siding and, as time passed, began to wonder what had happened to his brother. The mail train from the north ran into the station track and began to work the l.c.l. freight and mail. Thus the main line just happened to be clear when suddenly the run-away motor car came sailing through. JC was still looking up the line after it, in wonder, when the 17 came pounding up and Doc blurted out the story. JC immediately called Dendron and reported the 600 through, driverless, and directed that it be turned into a siding against some log cars. It took a few seconds for Dendron to grasp the situation during which time the motor car was getting closer and closer. Finally Jim Hart ordered a switch opened and everyone stood clear to witness the final act of the drama.

The grade coming up from the river slowed the 600 somewhat but as soon as it topped it, she began to roll again, apparently having the time of her life. Fortunately it was only a short distance to the switch, which should have derailed her but didn't, and she went into the end of the string of empty log cars with a bang. The holding-down belts promptly sheared off and the body and the engine slid right on over the coupling onto the bed of the car, all nicely loaded for the trip to the shop, as Hart remarked. The motor car was rebuilt but the doctor swore that it just wasn't the same, that it didn't have the get-up-and-go that it had prior to the accident. The doctor? He finished the trip with his brother while King ran back to the skidder and brought it on up to Wakefield. During all of that time No. 2 cooled its wheels at Wakefield.

The railroad crossed Seacock Swamp on a series of trestles of various lengths. During normal weather a fairly large amount of water flowed under the longest of the lot and if one had the time, and patience, and didn't expect too much, fish could be caught. One morning Sam Atkinson was running south with a train of empty log cars when he came upon two colored boys fishing from the span over the deepest part of the stream. He blew his whistle, but they paid no attention to it, apparently being asleep or just indifferent to the approaching train. Sam kept coming, feeling quite sure that the boys would get off the trestle in plenty of time for him to pass, but they just sat, and fished. Finally they seemed to become aware of the fact that the train was not going to stop but by then it was too late to get clear and both went overboard. One boy got ashore, although he had hurt himself by jumping, but the other hit deep water and apparently hit bottom and stuck in the mud for he did not come up. Sam got his train stopped and the engine crew ran back. One of them went in after the boy but by the time he was located and brought ashore, he was dead. A brakesman was left with the body while the train ran down to Airfield and reported the accident by 'phone to Dendron. There was no logical explanation why the boys didn't get off the trestle. Yes, they had heard the whistle and saw the train. Why didn't they get off the trestle? They were fishing. Did they think that the train would stop and wait until they decided to go home? Silence. Continued questioning failed to solicit a single logical reason why they didn't get up and get off the trestle when the engine blew at them. Could Sam stop? No, not with that train shoving the engine. The best he could have possibly done was to slow down and give them more time. One hurt, one dead, because they wanted to fish.

On a certain morning John Williams, with Clinton Joyner firing and Arthur "Hack" Johnson braking on the front end, picked up the empties on the nose of the 16 that had been left at Central Hill for the day's operation and started shoving them towards Rattlesnake Swamp. The 19 was waiting to follow with the two coaches which made up the labor train, carrying about 85 men, the entire logging crew working in the woods at that time over beyond Strawberry Plains. As soon as the 18 was supposedly a safe distance ahead, the labor train left town. After swinging west at the wye and crossing the Plains, the track approached the Blackwater River and the closer it got, the more undulating it became as it crossed ridge after ridge between small streams flowing into the river. When the line was built, no cut-and-fill work had been done so the grades were short and sharp. Even so, they were long enough and steep enough to make it necessary for a train to drop into a bottom running as fast as the engineer dared to get over the next rise.

Williams had the usual twenty-five empties that morning and he had to build up considerable speed on the downgrades, giving the cars a nudge to start them rolling and then letting them run free with the engine trailing and acting as a brake now and then. As the train started up the first opposing grade, the sudden bunching of the slack when Williams began to work steam, caused a pin to jump out about half way up the train. Naturally no one knew this until the grade was topped and the brakesman, who was standing on the tender looking over the cab roof at the train ahead of the engine, saw the front part of the train suddenly begin to pull away from the rest of the train. He yelled to the engineer that his train had broken in two and that the front part was running away. Williams got stopped just as quickly as possible and started back up the grade with everything he could get out of the 18. He knew that those cars would run out of momentum on the far grade and come back down and up like a streak of greased lightning, and he wanted to give them plenty of room to seesaw back and forth across the bottom until they finally came to rest.

No one had given the labor train a second thought but Williams had just begun to breath easy again when the 19 showed up, running fast to make the grade with the two loaded coaches. Johnson went off the tender like a frightened bird while Joyner went out of the gangway in a flat dive. The engine crew of the 19 left their engine just as unceremoniously. Then they came together, completely wrecking the 19 and derailing the two coaches. The shock was so great that the 19's whistle valve was jarred open and the whistle continued to screech until the boiler was bled of steam. The noise could be plainly heard in Central Hill and as a long, continuous blast from a whistle was officially the call for immediate assistance, the agent had a feeling that the trains had in some manner managed to run together. His worst fears were confirmed when one of the crew finally sent a man to the nearest 'phone to report the accident and to ask for medical assistance.

Nearly everyone was hurt, but by some miraculous quirk of Fate, no one was killed. Some were seriously injured and others just badly shaken up. The company doctor, R. L. Seward, was the first medical assistance to arrive and did what he could until Doctors Roy Parker and Massey could be located and brought in. Those who were able did for those who were more seriously hurt until help arrived. The extra engine, No. 1, was sent in with a boxcar and brought out the worst cases as quickly as possible. After being given treatment at Central Hill, these were sent on to the hospital at Smithfield. After they had been taken care of, the others were looked after in the order of the seriousness of their injury. They, too, went back to Central Hill in the boxcar, but not to the hospital at Smith-field. The 19 was never repaired but was hauled to Dendron and eventually scrapped. The 18 was not too badly damaged for the tender had taken the brunt of the shock, being driven up against the boiler head. Fortunately Williams had managed to back far enough up the grade to be clear of the run-away cars when they rolled back against him.

New Timber and Re-Cuts

Logging over beyond Strawberry Plains was done for about two years before String-of-Logs Pocoson was made available, that amount of time being fixed fairly accurate by the fact that one of the members of the crew of a jack remembered that he and his fireman cut bean poles for two seasons while waiting for their train to be made up over in Strawberry Plains before they moved over to the new location. That tells us that the track was put in during the winter of 1917-1918, being built from the tail of the Central Hill wye southeast in a straight line for five miles to the Blue Ridge Road. It wasn't a case of the logging operations in Rattlesnake Swamp ceasing completely at that time, but that it was curtailed and a part of the logging crew shifted to a new location. Operations were carried on simultaneously at the two locations for a time, certainly as long as there was standing timber available in the former area.

Sanding the new line was made possible by the discovery of a so-called gravel pit between Strawberry Plains and the wye. This new line did not bisect the pocoson but cut through the main portion of the company's 1,721-acre holding in the pocoson. The pocoson ran roughly northeast and southwest while the railroad cut across the northeast end of it.

It so happened that the third No. 1, when still fairly new, was sent up to Central Hill as the spare engine and as such it fell her lot to work the ballast train, hauling loaded flats from the pit to the point where the ballast was being put under the track. Now, it also so happened that this pit was down in a bottom where any engine, particularly a donkey, would have considerable trouble getting out as much as a couple of loads at a time. The engineer who had her at that time found that out the hard way. He had just two loads and when he tried to get them up out of the bottom, they didn't want to come, so he tried swinging them out. Back and forth, back and forth across the bottom he went, gaining a little on each swing, but suddenly the donkey jumped the track. Being wise in the unpredictable ways of a derailed donkey, the engineer wasted no time starting out of the gangway as the loads continued to keep the donkey moving. He missed the step and shot under the engine, landing between the rails, flat of his back, and as the engine rolled over on top of him the wheels dropped between the ties and firmly anchored him, but fortunately that brought the train to a stop. To the fireman's frightened query, "You hurt?" the engineer answered that he didn't think so but that he was in one hell of a tight spot and that engine was HEAVY!

The fireman and the section hands who had been loading sand went to work to get the engineer free but they had to jack up the engine to do it. Although he had been mashed as flat as a pancake, no bones were broken. For quite a spell he walked around, black and blue, both front and back, but he lived to brag that he was one man who had an engine roll over and sit on him, and lived to tell about it.

To reach down into the pocoson, proper, it was necessary to lay a track some two miles in length in a southwesterly direction from the main branch and run woods tracks from that as the need arose. This track approximately followed the high ground down the center of the pocoson, the right-of-way being logged out as it was built. Only the main branch was sanded and considered to be more or less permanent trackage.

Although the acreage to be cut over was large, the supply of standing timber could last only so long and by the early '20's the company was looking to the east of the main branch for additional tracts. The timber on two tracts was eventually purchased, that owned by Doctor Seward, who seemed to anticipate the needs of the company, which was just a bit south of Nuby Ridge and east of the county road that paralleled the swamp, and a much larger tract known as Ross Pocoson, to the east of Cook Swamp. Back in those days that particular swamp was known as Great Swamp and it was a fairly large one. That was prior to the construction of the dam at Everett and the formation of Lake Burnt Mills and its elongated upper reach known as Nuby Pond.

Which of the two lines went in first is immaterial, even if it was known. The logging operations in the two areas seem to have overlapped for a time although the amount of timber taken off the Seward tract does not seem to have warranted the construction of the necessary railroad to get it out.

A switch was put in about two miles north of the end of the main branch at Blue Ridge Road. From this switch a line was built east about a mile, then a little south of east for about three-quarters of a mile, and finally a little north of east for about a like distance. It terminated well within the swamp, a little short of four-tenths of a mile east of the county road which it crossed about a half mile north of the village, if it could be called a village, of Orbit. In fact, it was said that the track crossed the road at Orbit and on the west side of the road crossing a through siding was put in to take the empties shoved in from Central Hill by the heavier engines. This line was sanded from the point where it joined the main branch to Orbit. Later on additional standing timber was purchased which was between the Seward tract and the east-west county road to Nuby Bridge and a line was built northeast from the line on the Seward tract into this new plot. The purchase of this additional timber possibly accounts for the attention given by the track gang to the line into Orbit. This was one of the two branches.

From the main branch to the center of Ross Pocoson was about four miles, as the crow flies, but the route of the logging branch built there followed the route of a stray dog bound for home. It had to cross Nuby Run and what is now the upper end of Nuby Bridge Pond but was then an extension of Great Swamp, and it had to follow a fairly easy route. The grade in and out of Nuby Run was rather stiff although it was eased somewhat by a low fill across the bottom. The west bank of Great Swamp was steep, steep enough to require a cut to ease the grade to the trestle which was about 150 yards in length. Over on the east side of the swamp there was a bit of marshy ground that required a low fill to cross. The track then curved up and into the pocoson proper. The line continued through the heart of the pocoson for about an additional mile and a quarter, then swung north across Bowling Green Road, nearly a mile east of Garner School, on the north boundary of the pocoson, and died in the broken ground bordering Champion Swamp. Another feeder line cut off in the pocoson and crossed the same road about a quarter of a mile west of the school and terminated just north of the road. It appears that logging began in there during the spring of 1922 and continued for at least two years.

They began bringing logs out of there before the line was sanded and this lack of ballast augmented the damage done when a log train jumped the track, one of two wrecks that occurred on the new line within a week during the summer of '22. Which wreck happened first is something else that is impossible to say, it being something like which came first, the chicken or the egg. Actually, it makes little difference as to their order of occurrence or the order in which they are related.

Hugh Barrett was bringing in the usual 25 empties with the No. 8. He turned the train on the wye at Central Hill and backed on down to the switch, then started in over the new line. As it was new track, he didn't drop down on the fill across Nuby Run too fast but took his time. He didn't want any of that unanchored track shifting under him, so when he started up the far grade he had to really work steam. Suddenly, the light log racks buckled, going in every direction, some even breaking in two. Their derailment first derailed the engine and tender, then, acting as a lever, flipped them over to the right, causing them to slide down the fill on their sides. Barrett was pinned in the cab and a broken gauge glass parboiled his back with live steam before he could be gotten out. Bernard Seward was firing and he had managed to jump free. When they got Barrett to the hospital and removed his clothes, oh so carefully, his skin came with them, like peeling a banana. It took time for him to get over it, but he lived.

John Williams was bringing out the day's 25 loads and an empty tank used to haul water for the skidder, with the 24. They came on across the trestle over Great Swamp and started up through the cut, making fair time with the engine holding the rails and working hard. The lead truck of the engine suddenly jumped the track, wedged between the ties and brought the train to a bone-jolting halt. The 24 promptly lost her feet and as the drivers began to spin, the loads started to haul her back down the grade. It was a ticklish situation to be caught in, so Williams and Perley Edwards, his fireman, didn't take time to argue but unloaded right then, not even taking time to close the throttle.

It must be remembered that this was before they got around to ballasting the track and the ties were laying on top of the ground with nothing to hold them in place. That derailed leading truck began dragging the ties along, bunching them together until one would hit an obstruction. The wheels would then jump over the bunched ties and start gathering up another lot, leaving lengths of rail unsupported in any manner whatsoever. The ties on the trestle were fastened down, so it wasn't so bad when the engine was hauled back over them but a number were broken. The ties on the approach were hauled up tight against the first secured one on the trestle.

The train kept going back towards the pocoson until the momentum ran out and then the spinning drivers began to take hold. Back towards the west bank came the train, the leading truck still banging up and down over the ties, but after she passed over those bunched ties it was as if the track wasn't there. The rails collapsed and the engine dived down the bank, the tender and four loads going with her. That stopped the rest of the train. To untangle the mess a log loader was brought out of the pocoson and piece by piece the wreck was picked up. The track had to be completely rebuilt and after that second wreck it was immediately sanded.

Trouble was not confined to the lines south of Central Hill during those years, not by any means. The main line came in for its share of trouble as well. The heaviest grade between Surry and Dendron was that leading up from Cypress Swamp, from Sexton to the throat of the Dendron yard. Quite frequently it was necessary to double the hill and on such occasions the rear end of the train was left standing on the main line just north of the road crossing at Sexton. On one such occasion a jack had stalled on the grade and the crew had cut off the rear of the train and started up the hill with the front half. As the train approached the yard the engineer noticed that a switch leading in from the main to a siding filled with loaded log cars had been left open. He promptly wiped the clock, causing the slack along the train to bunch violently. Just a car or so back from the engine a pin jumped out and most of the train started back to Sexton. The run was too short to allow much time for setting brakes so after a few were wound up, which were ineffective, the brakemen hit the dirt and let them roll. The cars picked up considerable speed during their short run and when they hit the rear section, logs and cars were exploded all over the place. It is safe to say that that particular grade saw more runaways than did any other one on the entire system.

Sexton was the scene of another mishap of a different nature when a part of a log train went through Cypress Swamp trestle. Hugh Barrett was bringing in a train of 25 loads from Central Hill with No. 8 and as he approached the Sexton road crossing he bunched the slack to check his speed, then opened his throttle as soon as he was sure that the crossing was clear. When he bunched the slack, a pin jumped out on the rear coupling of a car some ten loads back. The long link remained in the socket until the engine began to work steam, then it pulled out and dropped down, hitting the ties just as the cars ran out on the trestle. It not only stripped every tie from the trestle but knocked down the bents, causing the cars to pile up in the swamp. About ten loads went through the break before the piled up wreckage blocked the rest of the cars and caused them to stay put. Oh, the things that can happen on a logging road are beyond belief.

C Mill burned again in 1923, but this time the machine shop also went up in smoke. The mill and shop were replaced but the shop was greatly enlarged when it was rebuilt. Both this and the earlier fire had been set by sparks and were repetitions of fires that plagued lumber mills during the days that sawdust and slab siding were used to feed the boilers. The 1923 fire was so hot that it buckled the rails of the main line and the mail train, coming up from the river, had to work its way around through the mill yard to get around the kink.

The wharf at the river was burned twice, the first time being around 1909 or '10, and it was thought that it was set by a carelessly tossed cigarette or an overheated stove. It was at night and before the fire was brought under control, the post office and considerable docking space were destroyed. No barges or schooners were tied up at the time and there were no cars on the wharf. At the height of the fire a tugboat coming down the river saw the blaze and came in close enough to put a stream of water on it. This was the main factor in finally bringing the blaze under control. Incidentally, when the post office was established on the wharf, the Post Office people simplified the name of the locality to Scotland, possibly as a space saver on the canceller, and although it was from then on officially Scotland, it was still Scotland Wharf to the oldsters and the river men.

The second fire was around 1912 or '13 and was set by hot coals dropping out of the ash pan of No. 2 while she set waiting for the down boat from Richmond. It was quite a wait, which was nothing unusual, and the crew went up to the store to pass the time, leaving the engine to look after herself. Finally one of the crew started back to check the fire and water, and noticed considerable smoke coming up from between the planks under the firebox. Obviously some hot cinders had set the lightwood timber ablaze. He yelled for the rest of the crew and lit out for the engine. By the time the crew was able to get the engine rolling, there was considerable fire mixed with the smoke and the best that they could do was to save the baggage car and coach that were coupled to the engine. Several box-cars of lumber and box shooks were completely destroyed and their ironwork fell between the buckled rails into the water where, so far as is known, it still remains.

When it was apparent that the fire was out of hand, the barge that was loading lumber at the time, was winched over against the old Gottleib Wharf piling, the movement being hurried by the screams and screeches of the captain's wife. When finally extinguished, the fire had destroyed the river end of the wharf, including the warehouse, and about half of the docking space as well as all of the rolling stock and freight on the wharf at the time. One of the structures was filled with ice. The fire consumed all of the woodwork but left the ice, still neatly piled and only slightly melted around the edges. The ice had been sent down from Dendron for shipment and was stored awaiting the arrival of the vessel upon which it was to be forwarded.

In addition to owning its own ice plant, the product of which was sold as far away as Baltimore, the company furnished electric power for the lights of all the dwellings in Dendron, at least all of those that were wired, and for the street lights. The lumber company had "entered into an agreement" with the town in 1916 to supply electric current, that being soon after the company had installed a generator and began electrifying some of the machinery in the various mills. They never did get around to what could be called complete electrification. True, Dendron was strictly a company town but due to the fact that it was incorporated, they had to go through certain red tape, sort of making deals with themselves, to fill the letter of the law. The furnishing of current from the mill generators was not unusual but in this case power was supplied only from Monday morning to about ten o'clock Saturday night. At that time the plant was shut down and everyone supposedly went to bed, or got out their kerosene lamps. No current at all was supplied during Sunday. When the mill closed permanently in 1927 the town was without electricity, or fire protection. During the early '20's the company did much to improve conditions in the three counties, even to the extent of building roads. Those were the days of the Model T Ford and roads were becoming more and more in demand.

The operation of the company stores, or commissaries, as they were called, was one of the more important related activities engaged in by the Surry Lumber Company, certainly from the viewpoint of the families of the men employed by both the railway and the lumber company. Commissaries were a common part of all the larger logging and lumber companies for it was an acknowledged fact that if the necessities, and a few of the luxuries, of life were available, the employees were more content and the labor turnover was greatly reduced. The commissary was the center of any logging community and in most cases it was the only center where the men could gather and discuss the news that filtered into the woods from the outside.

The first of the several Surry Lumber Company commissaries was located at Dendron and was opened for business soon after the first mill began operations. A Mr. Doudy was put in charge and the store stocked with everything generally found in a large, well stocked country store, plus many additional items: clothing of all kinds, furniture, shoes, kerosene which was generally referred to during those early days as coal oil, needles, patent medicine, candy, hardware, plows, and many other apparently unrelated articles, including something to wet the whistle. Across the counter went a surprising amount of goods, but very little hard cash. As long as you worked for the company, your credit was good from pay day to pay day, at least up to a certain portion of your usual pay, and of course, there were always men who literally owed their souls to the company store, as the saying goes. This meant that they always used the maximum amount of credit allowed them between pay days, but they were the exception rather than the rule. A strict account was kept of what an employee could afford to pay and this was done at Dendron by the company bookkeeper. When an employee wished to purchase on credit, he requested a voucher for the necessary amount from his boss and this was passed across the counter as we would use a personal check. These vouchers eventually found their way back to Dendron where the bookkeeper debited the pay due the employee for the amount shown. They were then cancelled and when the employee was paid were put in his envelope to show that he had already used that much of the amount due him.

When the commissary was opened at West Hope, the company issued its own "money" in the form of pewter tokens of the denominations of 10¢, 25¢, 50¢, and $1. There was also a brass token worth 5¢ in trade. These tokens passed readily as cash in the area and were not a Surry Lumber Company innovation for many companies, both large and small, used such a substitute for coins in making change during those days. Surely the reader can remember the tokens used by some drug stores which were redeemable in trade.

The Dendron commissary was erected on the east side of Main Street, just south of the freight house. A stub track cut off the main line and ran alongside a platform at the rear of the building. Through the door opening on the platform went all of the stock. For some extremely vague reason, furniture was stored and displayed on the second floor, each piece having to be manhandled up and down a narrow stairway. The general impression appears to be that company commissaries were operated for their employees only, and that the merchandise was sold at, or very nearly at, cost. Nothing could be further from the truth for anyone was welcome to trade there, for cash, and prices were generally a bit higher than at private stores in the area, when there were any. Into the so-called cost went everything conceivable that could possibly be associated with or have any possible bearing on the sale price of the merchandise. In fact, when a private store was eventually opened in Dendron, the commissary lost quite a number of its patrons.

The prices of merchandise sold at the commissary and the privately owned general store during the turn of the century were actually quite reasonable when compared with those of

1965 although they were a bit higher than elsewhere at the time due to the cost of delivery to Dendron. Eggs sold for 8¢ to 20¢ a dozen, depending on the size of the eggs and their scarcity. Bacon, better known as salt pork or side meat, was 6¢ to 10¢ a pound and it didn't come sliced. Beef was available only during cold weather prior to the introduction of refrigeration but could be had at 15¢ a pound for the very best steak. Flour brought $4 to $6 a barrel, sugar 3¢ to 5¢ a pound and it always came in a huge barrel from which it was scooped into paper pokes, as paper sacks were called. A suit of men's clothes could be had for $10 to $20, overalls were 50¢, and a pair of work shoes ranged from $1.25 to $2.25. "Sunday shoes" cost a bit more. In later years, after the company had installed its ice plant, it was possible to get a 300-pound cake of ice for $1, but prior to that ice was considered a luxury, something that the average family did without, unless they cut their own ice from some nearby pond during the winter and had an ice house out back for storage. It was brought down from Maine on lumber schooners as ballast but sold as a paying cargo. Few people could afford the "imported" ice. When the company ice plant began operations, the flow of ice was reversed, the company selling it along its railroad line and shipping it from Scotland Wharf. The price remained about the same, due mainly to the lessening value of the dollar.

After some time Mr. Doudy, at Dendron, was followed by W. L. Gladden, Sr., and finally by W. H. Purcell who remained in charge until the commissary was closed. At that time it was sold to Purcell and he continued to operate it as a private store. During the time that Gladden was in charge, he not only ran the commissary but also the hotel, the operation of the commissary being in addition to the hotel operation. And, he was the company's first notary public.

When Dory was created and a camp erected there, a commissary was established. The stock was not as complete as that of the Dendron store but items not available could be ordered through Mrs. Parish, the manager, who was the daughter of Billy West, the first woods foreman, and the widow of an employee who had been killed in the woods.

A commissary was opened at West Hope in 1898 with Mr. Bobbitt as manager. Mr. Herbert Owen followed him and Mr.

R. L. Edwards followed Owen. In 1910 Mr. Edwards moved with the commissary to Surry, or Newtown to be exact, and remained as manager until it was discontinued in 1927. He then purchased the fittings and stock, moved them to a new location and opened the former Edwards General Store in Surry. It is safe to say that the Edwards establishment was the last of the honest-to-goodness general stores in the county and was literally an extension of the old commissary. The old building at New-town was pulled down. The fourth commissary was at Straw Hill with Mr. J. C. Robinson as manager. In 1906 this one was moved to Upson and Mr. Mathews became manager. Later it was moved a second time, to Central Hill in 1915, where Sam Hedgepeth was manager for a short time, followed by W. D. Joyner until the stock was moved to the Dendron commissary in 1927. Joyner then purchased the building and continued it as a store but had to restock it. Mr. Thornton followed Mr. Math-ews as manager at Upson prior to the move to Central Hill.

The Vicksville commissary was the next in line, with Mr. Turner as manager, followed by Clarence Owen in 1912. Mr. Owen was transferred to Sedley when that commissary was opened in 1920 but Fred Barker was appointed his assistant and was left at Vicksville where he remained until the store was closed. The last three commissaries to remain in business were those at Sedley, Dendron, and Newtown.

Although the men in charge of the commissaries were fre-quently referred to as "agents", they were actually managers for they managed the stores for the lumber company. All goods were billed to Philip Rogers as agent for the Surry Lumber Company and later to J. C. Causey, who followed Rogers. This gave the company more buying power which was reflected in lower prices to the customers, supposedly.

Actual procurement was up to the individual managers, ex-cept in certain cases, who made periodic trips to Lynchburg for shoes, Norfolk for medicine and dry goods, and other nearby places for various items, depending where experience had proven that the best prices were available. One of the excep-tions was pickled herring which arrived in carload lots after being purchased from the lowest bidder.

Twice a year Causey sent certain selected managers and their wives to Baltimore, presumably on a purchasing trip.

Actually it was sort of reward for the profitable management of the selected manager's store for the past six months, so it is reasonable to suppose that each manager strived to show as large a profit as possible. If he failed to be one of those selected for the semi-annual trip, Causey never found fault with him for he was invariably unmercifully chewed out by his spouse who periodically reminded him of his shortcomings until the next list was posted. Woe be unto him if his name was not included. Truthfully, though, rarely was anyone left off over once and such omissions were "necessary" to keep the size of the party within reason, officially. Never a word was ever said about poor management. It wasn't necessary.

Baltimore was considered to be the wholesale clothing center of the east coast and offered a greater selection at less cost than did any other city within a reasonable distance. On some of these trips Causey would go along and at such times the expense account would take a beating. Nothing was too good or expensive for the party and they traveled in style. The party always went by boat from Norfolk to Baltimore, traveling on one of the boats of the Baltimore Steam Packet Company, better known as the Old Bay Line, and would invariably eat supper and breakfast on board.

On one such trip the party was sitting around a table in the dining saloon as the boat left the Old Point pier and headed up the Baltimore channel. The colored waiters in their spotless white aprons and jackets were busy serving the patrons and when a milky white broth was set before each member of the party, Causey eyed his with considerable misgivings. He picked up his spoon and tentatively stirred the concoction. He looked at the hovering waiter and asked, "What's this?"

"Oyster stew, suh."

There was a bit more exploratory stirring and then, "Where the devil are the oysters?" The stirring continued amid a dead silence, and then, "Take it back and let's see some oysters in it!"

The waiter beat a hasty retreat with the offending stew and when he returned there were actually oysters to be found in it. Each bowl made a round trip to the galley and when it returned there was a reason to call it "oyster stew".

Rain began falling during the afternoon of August 22, 1923, and it increased in intensity until it was coming down in sheets. The millpond at Airfield was full and the miller had opened the wicket in an effort to ease the pressure against the dam. When he went home it appeared that the water had stopped rising although it was already at the top of the spillway and putting considerable pressure against the earthen dam. Shortly after dark, with the noise of an explosion, the dam went out north of the spillway and with a rapidly increasing roar, as the break widened, the water rushed out and across the highway. The position of the break caused the water to bank up against the railroad fill north of the trestle, where it boiled and swirled for a minute or two, then the fill simply dissolved and the water continued on its way, leaving the rails and ties hanging in very thin air.

At the time the dam went out, Charlie Kitchen was outside of his home, about a mile south of the mill, and clearly heard the noise made by the bursting dam. After listening to the roar for a minute, he went back inside and told his father that something was wrong down at the mill, but due to the storm they did not go down to investigate until the next morning. At that time they found the pond empty but water still roared down Lightwood Swamp, being fed by the three overflowing swamps at the head of the non-existent pond. The railroad fill and track had ceased to exist by then, the rails later being found downstream a ways. The morning southbound train of empty log cars was flagged, and after reporting the break in the line, the empties were backed around into a logging branch and left while the engine returned to Dendron. Upon checking the rest of the line as far as Dory, it was found that there were two other washouts to be reckoned with but neither was as bad as the one at Airfield.

Every available section hand was put to work to close the break but it was a couple of days before the line was back in service. During the first day, Causey came down from Dendron, where he had spent the previous night, and watched the work as it progressed. He always used a particular coach, which was referred to by the men as "Causey's coach" and it was kept well stocked with cold food in case he was unable to get to a camp, or home, for a hot meal. On this particular occasion the engine crew assisted in depleting the supply in short order, by invitation of course, while they waited until they could ease across the new fill on temporary track.

As soon as the Airfield break was repaired, the other two were taken care of in short order and service was restored. During the time that the line was out of service, the mail train officially ran no further than Wakefield although it had to be run on down to the Airfield wye for turning, the wye being north of the washout.

By this time a fairly decent dirt road practically paralleled the railroad all of the way from Dory to Surry and l.c.l. freight, and an increasing number of would-be passengers who owned automobiles or could cadge a ride with someone who did, began to travel by it. Farm products were still shipped by the narrow gauge and during peanut season it was quite a problem to satisfy the demand for empties. The assignment of the available boxcars was the unpleasant duty of the mail train conductor, W. L. Gladden, and when he died in service in 1925, it was passed along to his successor, E. T. "Sam" Atkinson. It was a thankless task for rarely were there enough cars to go around and invariably every farmer along the line wanted cars at the same time. Peanuts, corn, and pork, but the transportation of peanuts was the big headache. The lumber company didn't help matters, either, for they required a certain number of boxcars for the shipment of lumber and their requirements came first.

It was not unusual for a crew bringing in a string of loads to the mills to have to do some shifting before they could pick up their empties and head back to the woods. Bob Wellons, with the 20, had been caught in that predicament and was late leaving Dendron, shoving a string of empties and running tender first. He knew that Herbert Gilliam was waiting in the woods just north of Airfield for him to arrive before bringing his string of loads out to the main line, but there was nothing that he could do about it but hope that Gilliam wouldn't get impatient and leave before he got there.

Gilliam, with the 26, had been waiting some time back up in the woods on the branch running east from the main line, but as time passed and Wellons did not show up, nor was there any word of him, he figured that something had gone wrong. He couldn't hear the exhaust of the 20 so obviously Wellons hadn't arrived at the switch. With that in mind, Gilliam headed out towards the main line switch, his idea being to get out to the main line, back down towards the water tank to clear the switch, and let Wellons back his train on around into the branch. Under normal conditions that would have been the correct procedure to follow, provided there was protection from the woods to the main line switch, but there wasn't and that made the difference. Wellons, knowing that he was late and holding up the log train, was running at a lively clip, the empties weaving and lurching with the brakemen hanging on for dear life. The switch was set for the branch so Wellons slowed only enough to insure the cars staying on the track as they curved into the woods branch. As they started in he lay back on the whistle cord to let Gilliam know that he was coming but the normal noise of the hard working 26 drowned out the sound and Gilliam kept coming.

They came together on one of the many curves. In fact, if it hadn't been for the curves there is considerable doubt that they would have run together. The 20 was still working steam when the empties began to climb all over the front end of the 26. Gilliam and his fireman had already taken to the woods when they hit, so they were well clear when the 26 gave up and rolled over on her side. When the shock was transmitted down the string of cars to the engine, Wellons quickly shut off, but not before a goodly number of the log cars were reduced to kindling wood. He made sure that no one was hurt and then walked back to the switch to make the usual call to Dendron.

It was only natural that an explanation was demanded, and given, the blame being put on the mill foreman by Wellons. Causey immediately issued orders that crews bringing loads into the mill yard were to spot their train on designated sidings, pick up their empties and leave just as quickly as possible. Under no condition were they to be detained to do shifting service around the mills.

R. L. Edwards, the commissary manager at Newtown, had been handing up orders off and on since 1905 and prided himself in that during all of that time he had never crossed an or-

der. On this particular day in 1923 L. L. Spain had called in and
Edwards had cleared him to run west to the Surry switch from
over near Central Hill. He was coming in on a section motor
car. A little later Hugh Barrett came up from the south with
No. 8 on a train of empties for Central Hill. He had a clearance
only as far as Newtown and was to be cleared by Edwards for
the rest of the run to Central Hill.

Barrett was a nervous man, always in a hurry, and when he
brought his train to a stop back of the commissary he began to
toot his whistle. When Edwards came out on the platform he
yelled, "Come on, let's get goin' " and continued to toot his
whistle. Edwards became rattled and cleared him, completely
forgetting the motor car. Barrett fed steam to the cylinders
and Edwards started back into the store. Just as he entered
the door he realized what he had done, spun around, dashed
out on the platform and made frantic motions in an effort to
attract the attention of some member of the engine crew, but
Barrett was looking ahead, intent on getting his train rolling.
There were brakemen but they just looked at the frantically
waving Edwards, and waved back. As the speed of the train
continued to increase Edwards realized that there was absolutely nothing that he could do. He stood with his hands over
his ears and his eyes shut tight as if he was trying to shut out
the noise and sight of the impending crash.

They came together just below Newtown, on the first curve,
and both were running full out when they hit. Spain saw No.
8 in time to jump clear and ended up with nothing worse than
scratches and bruises but the motor car was smeared all over
the front of No. 8, being reduced to pocket-size pieces of junk.
It took Edwards some time to get over his fright but he never
repeated the error although he continued to hand up orders until
the branch was pulled up in 1927.

Trains starting out from Dory would call Dendron before
leaving, get clearance as far as Airfield, and when they
reached that point the engineer or fireman would again call in
or would first head into the wye and then call Dendron. However, if a southbound train had to take water at the tank, and
the wait promised to be of some duration, the engineer would
occasionally run on down to the tank against the opposing

train, take water, and then drop back into the wye to wait for the northbound train. Trains headed north seldom stopped for water as they had filled their tanks at Dory, but, if for some reason they did stop, they ran no danger for the tank was south of the wye, in fact, south of the trestle. Both the pump house and the wye were a short distance north of the trestle. To run against a northbound train's time was to take a chance, a dangerous chance, but crews did it repeatedly, and got away with it, at least most of the time they did.

Hugh Barrett, with the 8, had orders to back into the wye on his way to Vicksville to clear the mail train but he made a good run and the engine crew decided that there was plenty of time to drop down to the tank for water. Whurley Faison, with No. 2, had done pretty well himself, and was running a bit ahead of time. Barrett had cleared the lower switch and was headed for the trestle when he saw the mail train approaching. He shut off and let his train drift, figuring that Faison would slow down and let him pull up clear of the switch and back into the clear. Suddenly it dawned on him that Faison wasn't slowing down but was still working steam and no matter what he did, he couldn't possibly get into the clear.

In the meantime, Faison had been stepping right along and, believing that Barrett would be safe in the clear, climbed down and began filling the lubricator while his fireman built his fire. When Faison looked up the two engines were not over 150 feet apart. He let out a yell, slammed shut the throttle, wiped the clock, and went out of the gangway. His fireman looked around the boiler head and didn't bother to yell before he dived for the opposite gangway, but he didn't make it. He shouldn't have taken the time to look. The engines went together with a bang, No. 2 setting down so hard on her springs that she put a dish in the rail under each wheel. At the time the two engines went together, Barrett and his fireman were 40 yards away and still running, but Floyd Hargrave, Faison's fireman, had to be hospitalized after they got him out from under the coal and for a time it was feared that he had permanently lost his voice. Charlie Brittle, the section foreman, had himself quite a time picking up that wreck.

Age was catching up with Charlie, and more and more of the responsibility of maintaining the main line was falling on the shoulders of his assistant, Charlie Kitchen. Kitchen was getting

$1.25 a day for actually doing two jobs, so Brittle, being a fair man, went up to Dendron and had a talk with Rogers. It was agreed that Brittle should retire but how to go about it at the least expense to the company was the problem. Finally it was agreed that Brittle would stay on the active roll but in an inactive status. He would get his regular wage but would pay Kitchen a dollar a day for doing his work. Kitchen's regular pay would be increased to $1.75 a day and he would hold down two jobs, actually, for a total salary of $2.75 a day. Thus was Charlie Brittle retired.

Around about this time, 1924, the company was able to purchase a stand of timber on the Spratley section just northwest of the Dendron town line. To reach it, a switch was put in about half way between Faison Street and the county road which formed the town's northern boundary. The track crossed Main Street and followed along the west side, crossed a branch on a crib trestle, crossed the boundary road and gradually swung north to northwest. It then crossed a second branch on a crib trestle and climbed up to high ground by means of one of the most unbelievably steep grades that anyone has ever seen. It must have been at least 12%; short but straight up. Once on fairly level ground the track swung west across the boundary road again and terminated about a mile further along. Soon after they started cutting the timber in there, additional timber was purchased on the Rose Tract and a line was run from near the second road crossing in a northerly direction for a mile down the east side of the road. This track was in use for only about eight or ten weeks.

A second line was laid off the main line from a point roughly a mile and a half south of the Dendron station and followed the edge of the swamp north of the Blackwater River all the way to where Cypress Swamp joined it, the point being known as Mussel Fork because of the large number of fresh water bivalve mollusks of the Unio Anadonta genera found there. This line also remained in service only a very short while, just long enough to exhaust the standing timber in that part of the Town of Dendron, the entire line being inside the town limits.

Scraping the Barrel

W. L. Gladden, conductor on the mail train, died during the early part of April 1925 while out on his run, somewhere between Dendron and Surry. The train made its scheduled stop at the court house but Gladden didn't put in an appearance. Nothing was thought of it until leaving time and he was still not on the ground. The engineer gave several toots of the whistle after which the brakesman, Willie Bland, set out to find "Cap'm Glad'n". He was seated in his usual seat in the coach, apparently asleep, but it was quickly ascertained that he was dead and a heart attack was later given as the cause. E. T. Atkinson left his post as engineer of the 14 and took over the passenger run.

It was that same spring that a line of track was laid from the Central Hill branch to what was known as "the Peterson's tract", to the northwest of Bacon's Castle. The spur crossed the state road, Route 10, to the east of the village at a point known as Wood Rack. This name had been derived from the fact that for several years a tramway was used to haul cordwood from there to the river and it was customary to rack up, or pile, the wood there to await transportation. It is quite possible that the route of the branch railroad coincided with that of the former tramway for both would have followed the route offering the easiest grades. From the road crossing the branch swung around in a general northwesterly direction between the village and the river, crossed the county road from the village to Hog Island, and ended up in Chippokes Swamp, just east of the creek by that name.

Another branch that was put in around the same time, and ran in the same general direction, was slightly shorter and ran into the W. C. Mitchell tract north-northeast of California Cross Roads, the track passing just to the east of that point. These lines were not in service very long, certainly not over six months.

No. 6 got into trouble over back of Bacon's Castle one morning due to soft track. It had been raining the night before and a little scouring had been noticed, but not enough to worry about. However, when No. 6 came in, shoving the day's supply of empties, it hit what appeared to be a small scour but which proved to be a soft spot in the roadbed. Over she went, landing up against the bank. Gwaltney and his log loader were brought down and set the engine on her feet without any trouble. It is surprising how much wrecking service the log-loading equipment saw.

It was also during 1925 that the line into Birdson's Quarter and Assamoosick Swamp, over to the northwest of Airfield millpond, was taken up and the steel used to lay a branch around the head of Seacock Swamp to Brittle's Millpond. This branch was about three and a half miles long and left the main line about a mile north of Burton's Grove Church, to which point the wye was moved from Airfield. At about the same time a branch about a mile and a half in length was laid from the main line approximately a half mile north of the wye and ran northeast to the head of Seacock Swamp. Both branches came out in 1927 and the steel hauled to Dendron. This light steel had been put down and taken up so often that it was just about worn out.

The 26 got a new boiler in 1925 due to pitting of the plates of the original one, causing several small leaks. The boiler was still in the guarantee period and Baldwin replaced it free of charge, but the company had to meet the cost of removing the old one and installing the new, the two being exactly alike except, it was hoped, for the composition of the steel.

The following year, 1926, the 6 was sold to the Argent Lumber Company of Hardeeville, South Carolina. Although in good condition, it had been retired the previous year as there was no longer a need for it. The next year, 1927, the 18 was retired and subsequently sold to the Gray Pine Products Company who shipped her to Margarettsville, North Carolina. There she was put to work on a logging line some six or seven miles in length and ran with a little saddle-tank that had been purchased from the Fisher Lumber Company at Ivor, Virginia. Due to the short run, the Pine Products people had no trouble with the engine steaming and it is doubtful if they ever knew that they had purchased a lemon. The engine was a little lame when sold to them due to dished valve seats but a bit of careful work with a file soon took care of that trouble.

At about the time the 18 was withdrawn from service, two second hand boxcars were also retired. As a means of cutting tax assessments, 27 miles of woods track was charged off against the lumber company, leaving only the so-called main line from the river to Dory as Railway Company property.

Logging had degenerated to a sort of cleaning up process. Small stands of timber that the company considered it profitable to acquire were purchased, tracks put in, the timber cut and hauled out, and the track removed, all within a week. Logging was also done along the main line, trees that had reached maturity being cut and logs that had been left from previous operations salvaged. Temporary sidings were put in to accommodate the logging equipment where such work was done. The men who knew logging could read the signs and began to look around for other work.

One day Faison managed to wreck the mail train down near Moorings when on his way to the river and although the wreck was bad enough, it could have been a lot worse. On his previous trip the engine had dipped sharply when crossing a culvert, giving them a sharp jolt, but the train made it safely across. On reaching Dendron the bad order culvert was reported and the crew was assured that it would be taken care of immediately. After the usual layover at Dory, Faison started back, giving the culvert no thought. Nothing was said of it at Dendron by anyone, so . . . , but let's let the Rev. Thomas Eugene West, one of the passengers, tell it:

"The faithful little train was doing its best with log cars and red freight cars bumping and jumping down the narrow gauge track which was slightly elevated by a few inches above the ground level. I was proud of her added energy on this particular brisk morning for she seemed to face the world with an extra charming dare of endurance engendered by some potent vitamin as 'Queen of the Tracks'. We had passed Sexton, the hang-out, country grocery store, or rather general all-over-kind of store owned by Noley Morris and E. L. Hart. I had given them my weekly high sign of a hand wave, however this morning we did not stop for a chat, or a glass of buttermilk or to pick up a dozen eggs. On and on the high powered coal engine roared down the little pig tracks towards Elberon. That port-of-call was safely made, mail bags taken off and others put on, then the proud little sighing engine struggled and spun her wheels as she struggled to head out for Surry.

"We were finally under way and I was settling down when, all of a sudden, I realized the bumps were somewhat disturbing and the jumps higher, yet the train continued proudly on when I saw Conductor 'Sam' stand up with an unexplained and most unusual expression on his face. He was bouncing with the train and he said to us in that gentle yet now commanding voice, 'Hold on to something. We are off the track.' But, there was no slackening of the speed. I had the sensation of falling to one side and within a few seconds the sensation became a reality as when I glanced through the opened window I saw that the coach was turning over and that our coupling had broken. We were left there alone with the log and freight and mail cars going gleefully on to Surry.

"Within a few minutes, Mr. Durwood Faison, the engineer, must have missed the extra weight and when looking back discovered what had happened. Stopping the train of some eight or ten lumber and freight cars, he backed up, and with the help of the fireman, whose name I cannot recall, the big rescue work of the conductor and three passengers got under way. Sam, the conductor man, was all right and indeed proved to be a most gallant and brave hero, ever mindful of the condition of his passengers and always considerate of their comfort, trying to allay any growing anxiety especially on behalf of a pious colored 'brother of the cloth and real faith' who held forth the Bible he was reading as we went over. His prayer assured us that God was with us and all would be well. Even so, he walked around and around the overturned car, quoting verses of scripture he seemingly had stored in his memory for just such an emergency.

"I remember that I had previously planned to be calm and composed under all conditions, and this was certainly one of those conditions, so I very quietly said, 'There is no need to be alarmed, no one is hurt', when an elderly woman who was almost sitting in my lap, having been thrown there from the opposite side of the car, said 'Nobody hurt? That's what YOU think. Well, I'm hurt, I'm almost DEAD'. But, fortunately it turned out, as is usual with the fairer sex, only a case of exalted and highly exaggerated imagination.

"When we crawled out of the overturned car, the woman and the colored brother minister through the door, but I more glamorously and pretentiously, through a window, our cool-as-a-cucumber Conductor Sam said that we would be sent to a doctor for examination. I protested, 'For what?' He said, 'For any possible injury or in case of any future development or complaint against the company'. This was all new to me but I liked the excitement of it. About that time I felt something warm on my leg as of a slow running sensation, which turned out to be blood trickling down from a cut on my leg below the knee and which I had not felt before. So on to Dr. W. W. Seward's I went. About a dozen or more community friends had gathered by now on the roadbed. As I remember, the good preacher friend refused to go to the doctor and signed up with the healing of the Lord rather than trusting to earthly remedies and quietly walked away. The good lady and I went to Dr. Seward who tried his best to find something wrong with us but failed on every count, except for my little blood trickle which by this time had ceased. He bound it up and then on to Bacon's Castle I went with a new experience to relate, . . .".

It so happened that Conductor Sam was also slightly hurt in that accident for during the time he was being tossed around inside the overturning car, his elbow was pushed through the glass of a window and received a rather nasty cut. It healed nicely, though, and gave him no trouble afterwards.

Dendron had been notified and the wreck car and crew were sent to the scene of the wreck. In short order the car was set upright on its trucks by means of block and tackle. By the time the train had returned from the river, the line was clear, the offending culvert shored up, and the crowd dispersed. The passenger coach was hauled back to Dendron, shoved into a siding, and another put in service. It is possible that this particular car was the mysterious Barney & Smith combination. It will be noted that both colored and white passengers were being hauled in the car and as a state law required the separation of races, it is only logical to suppose that the car was divided into compartments. E. T. Atkinson made the statement that the Barney & Smith car set out back of the station for some time, its windows broken, until it was finally tipped over on its side and burned.

On October 27, 1927, the Dendron Mills shut down, permanently, and what was considered by some to be a permanent way of life came to a sudden end. Although the older employees knew that the timber supply couldn't last forever, they had hoped that it would outlast them but now that the whine of the saws was no more, it was literally the end of the world for them. They had been raised with the mill whistle as an alarm clock and the smell of pine as the main part of their daily diet. The regular pay day was no more and they were faced with the problem of finding some other means of winning their daily bread. Some owned farms and for them the transition was no great problem but others owned nothing, not even the house in which they lived. It was no wonder that entire families began to move away to Hopewell, to Petersburg, to any place where work was to be found.

It was also the beginning of the end of the town and of the railroad. With the mill closed permanently, Dendron had no reason to exist. The railroad was, after all, purely a lumber road, a part of the lumber company, and the meager amount of farm produce offered could not possibly support it. However, the inevitable was postponed by the huge amount of material to be moved out of Dendron. There was considerable lumber still piled in the storage yards and sheds which would have to be disposed of and after that came the machinery installed in the various mills. All would have to be moved out, by rail, in one form or another. But, for the time being, everything was at a standstill. The mail train continued to make its regular trips, but that was done simply because it was required to do so by law, and to haul the mail. Traffic dropped to practically nothing.

The disposal of the equipment and material didn't begin until the first part of 1928 for the first problem was to compile an accurate inventory and then to find prospective buyers. Many letters were written, advertisements run, and a detailed list of the equipment owned prepared for distribution. On that list was everything from locomotives to spare belting.

Then, as the scrapping of the actual plant began, trains of scrap and lumber began to roll down to the river where the material was loaded on barges and schooners for shipment.

In most cases the mail train was able to handle the traffic, but there were times when special trains of material had to be run. It was evident to everyone, although they hated to admit it, that the railroad would eventually be forced to cease operations. There was a surplus of equipment which filled the Dendron yard to overflowing and that, too, had to be disposed of, in one way or another. It was a colossal task and when it was over some two years later, it was found that some surprising items had put money into the coffers; salvaged cast iron water pipe dug out of the ground, salvaged babbit metal, gasket material, grease, damaged electric motors, second hand lumber reclaimed when the various structures were demolished, scrap iron, and many such items. It proved the old adage that anything could be sold, if you could find someone who wanted it and everything was wanted by somebody. Eventually the company sold everything.

In February 1928 someone ran across an advertisement in the "SOUTHERN LUMBERMAN" in which the George Hemphill Manufacturing Company of Kennett, Missouri, expressed a desire to purchase logging equipment. The company immediately offered to sell them No. 1 for $1,000 or No. 17 for $750. Possibly the sale of one or the other was consummated for eleven months later we find that there was only one donkey on hand. On the other hand, distance and freight rates might have made the purchase inadvisable irrespective of the price at which the equipment was offered, and the donkey was either scrapped or sold elsewhere. It is interesting to note that both locomotives were described as fitted with Pyle-National electric headlights, both front and rear, and that fact was used as a selling point. As has been stated, all of the company's locomotives were so fitted.

There was a rumor current during the early '30's that there was an S.S.&S. donkey stored on a dock at the east end of Water Street in Norfolk, but no one could be found who had seen it. If an engine was ever stored there, the fire that completely destroyed the waterfront during that period also destroyed the engine. We know that four jacks were retired in 1928 and we know that at least one engine of some sort was shipped intact by barge from Scotland Wharf, possibly the one stored on the dock in Norfolk, if there was such an engine. Of the many donkeys, we can say for a certainty that No. 11 and one other was scrapped due to the fact that their bells ended up on the barns of former employees. A bell off one of the engines was installed in the steeple of a local church.

Realizing that bankruptcy of the Railway Company was a certainty if the property wasn't improved and additional business found, the owners began negotiating with New York capitalists to finance extensions and broadening out of the gauge. The negotiations were completed at a meeting held in Roanoke, Virginia, on August 24, 1928. A petition was immediately filed with the Interstate Commerce Commission asking permission to build an extension from Sedley to Franklin, approximately eight miles, and another from Dendron to Hopewell, approximately 25 miles. The entire main line from Franklin to Hopewell and the branch from Dendron to Scotland Wharf would be standard gauge. The estimated cost was $2,000,000, which was to be raised by a re-issue of stock and the sale of bonds.

In the meantime the Seaboard Air Line was endeavoring to get a line into Hopewell from the north but was being vigorously opposed by the Norfolk & Western whose City Point Branch already served the area. As soon as the plans of the narrow gauge became known, both lines forgot their differences long enough to let it be known that they would collectively oppose a third line entering the territory. The S.S.&S. looked to the Virginian Railway as a possible ally but that company persued a strictly "hands off" policy. Left on their own, the backers of the proposed railroad tried repeatedly to overcome the opposition. Each time the petition came up before the Commission, counsel requested, and received, a postponement.

With two such powerful opponents arrayed against it, the company realized that its chances of being granted permission to extend its line were rather remote. The strongest point in favor of the line was that it would provide a belt railroad extending from Richmond to Norfolk and would connect all of the north-south lines with Tidewater Virginia. To appease the N. & W. the company stated that they were not interested in obtaining the business of the nitrogen plant just being opened at Hopewell, but in forest products. They overlooked the fact that everyone knew that forest products, as such, had ceased to exist and that the company's mills at Dendron had been dismantled because of that fact. On the other hand, they were quite frank in stating that unless something could be done immediately, they had no alternative but to take up the road for the narrow gauge had ceased to be profitable. Actually, as a common carrier, it had never been profitable.

While the pot was boiling, a fourth party came forward and tried to purchase the road, contacting Waters in Baltimore first, as president of the company, but was shunted to Rogers in Dendron who, actually, had no authority to do anything but what he did, nothing. The prospects of coming to terms with the S.A.L. and the N. & W. appeared fairly good at that time, or to be exact, there was no reason to suspect that some agreement satisfactory to all three parties could not be reached, so the company ignored the offer.

Although the market for steam logging locomotives was becoming rather restricted, that for log cars was still active. Diesel and gasoline locomotives were replacing steam rapidly. In the letter to Hemphill, dated February 13, 1928, offering to sell them a donkey, ten Kilby Car & Foundry Company log cars were also offered at $75 each. A large number had previously been sold and many more were later sold. In November eight went to the Avondale Lumber Company of Pattillo, South Carolina. In December twenty went to the North State Lumber Company at Withbee, South Carolina, and in January of 1929 five went to the Fisher Lumber Company of Franklin, Virginia. In December of 1928 Gray Pine Products Company asked Rogers if he knew of anyone who would purchase the engine that they had purchased from the company in 1927 as they had cut over their holdings near Margarettsville and were pulling out. Rogers wrote back that he knew of no prospective buyers at that time but he was sure that a purchaser could be found as that type of engine was in great demand. Possibly so, but not by the Surry Lumber Company.

Some unintentional scrapping of machinery took place in September 1928 when the machine shop burned. This was the second time that the shop had gone up in flames. It was thought that the fire was caused by a lighted cigarette dropped by the man who was employed to cut up the mill machinery and boilers for which a buyer had not been found. He made it a practice of using the machine shop as a place to store his equipment and to change his clothes, and it was known that he was the last person in the shop before the fire was discovered. Both the machine shop and the attached blacksmiths' shop were a total loss, due strictly to the fact that the fire mains had been pulled up and sold as junk.

The first fire, back in 1923, had caused the company to separate their shops as a precautionary measure for that fire had destroyed the car shop as well as the machine shop. When rebuilt, the machine and blacksmith's shops had been left attached but the car and engine shops were housed under separate roofs. Prior to the last fire, strictly engine work, such as the reboring of cylinders, was done in the engine shop, but the making of parts was done in the machine shop. After the fire all work was done in the engine shop. The car shop was strictly an erection and woodworking shop where the various cars were repaired, and at times, built.

Maintenance was held to a bare minimum and the condition of the track was allowed to get progressively worse, the engine crew being repeatedly warned to run as slow as possible and still maintain the schedule. The mail train was frequently the only one on the road during the entire day and as long as it managed to get from here to there without breaking rails or spreading the track, everyone was happy. In short, the track was in a terrible condition and getting worse.

One morning the mail train was headed north at its usual leisurely pace when, just north of the Elberon station, the rear truck of the coach, the last car on the train, jumped the track. Faison was feeling no pain that morning, having imbibed just enough to imbue him with a feeling of complete irresponsibility and was propped up on his seat watching the track ahead when the truck left the rails. The engine began to labor a bit more than usual but he paid no attention to it and let her struggle. Back in the coach the conductor hung on, expecting the worse as the derailed truck bounced and jounced over the unevenly spaced, and sometimes missing, ties. Finally, about a mile out of Elberon, the truck dropped through an open cattle guard, the safety chains snapped taut and all forward motion ceased abruptly. For some unknown reason the draft gear held, so there they set with the engine grunting and tugging at the stalled train, her drivers spinning merrily, and Faison still reared back in his seat, staring ahead as though everything was in perfect order and the train still rolling merrily towards Surry.

The sudden drop and stop had a scrambling effect on the contents of the coach, including the conductor, but as soon as he could get clear he headed for the engine, all ready to do battle. The sight that greeted him set him back on his heels; the spinning drivers, the indifferent Whurley Faison. After recovering from his surprise, he demanded to know what was going on, not in those exact words, of course, but didn't he know that he had been dragging a derailed car? "Sure", said Faison as he leisurely closed the throttle and leaned out of the window, "but I wuz goin' t' drag'a plum to Surry, if she would go." Did they fire him? No.

The fact is, there apparently was only one engineer who got himself out and out fired, and that was only after "due provocation". This particular engineer seemed to have had more than his share of wrecks and most of them were directly, or indirectly, caused by fast running. In addition to that, he was a little too full of Life, you might call it, for he took chances unnecessarily. It was he who steered a borrowed Model T Ford down the main street of Central Hill with his feet, waving gaily to everyone in sight. He was like that, and there was no doubt that Jesse Hancock had a heavy hand and liked to step right along when running. Fast running with a donkey was not unusual but the company expected the engineer to at least use reasonable caution, that being an extremely flexible term. Then, too, all of the men knew that to make like an express train with one of those little contraptions was to ask for trouble, to really beg for it. Back in 1920 or '21 Hancock with No. 1 and Harry Gwaltney with No. 11 managed to turn over both engines when coming out of a siding on the top of Bell's Hill and although they blamed it on poor track, it was the consensus of opinion of everyone that it wouldn't have happened if they had been running a little slower.

This time Hancock was told to pick up a boxcar at Newtown with No. 1 and take it over to a stable near Pons. A colored family lived in the car, the man tending the teams, and the car was moved from stable to stable as the need arose and such a need had arisen. Now, there was one really hard and fast rule concerning the operation of a donkey due to the difference in coupler heights and the inability of the engine crew to see ahead when there were loads on the nose of the engine. A donkey was not to be used to shove anything any distance or at any speed faster than a walk, other than log cars. Some front ends had suffered because of that difference in coupler heights and Causey was fussy about that rule. However, when Jesse got ready to pick up the camp car, with its occupants, he thought about the dead end siding at the stable and the trouble it would take to get around behind the car when he got there. Why not? Causey was in Sedley, so he would never know. They left town with the boxcar on the nose of the donkey.

Admittedly the view ahead was obstructed but Jesse should have been able to see such a large obstruction as a tree. When telling of the wreck, there was something about tussling in the cab, which was quickly hushed, but which would certainly have been in character, but both the fireman and the engineer stuck to the story that they simply did not see the tree. That was undoubtedly the unvarnished truth and the first intimation they had of trouble was when they were suddenly shaken up rather violently and found themselves thrashing around in mud and water. Following confusion came facts. A rather violent wind storm had blown down a large tree across the track and the train had run into it, the boxcar going one way and the donkey the other, the donkey turning bottomside up in the ditch beside the track. The colored family was more scared than hurt but their rolling home required rebuilding and refitting. The engine crew was wet and shook, and fairly sure of what was going to happen to them. Jesse and the Surry Lumber Company parted company right then and there although there was a formal investigation when Causey, as assistant superintendent of the railroad, reminded one and all of that no shoving rule. Crews hadn't been exactly conscientious about obeying that particular rule and Causey figured that when he made a rule he expected it to be obeyed right down to the last period. He decided that it was time he impressed that fact on the crews and the best way to do it was to make an example of someone. He did, of Jesse. Perley Edwards, the fireman, worked until the end of the year, 1922, when he left, by suggestion, for greener pastures, and Causey, to show that he understood more than he could come right out and admit, got him a job running a Shay for the Montgomery Lumber Company.

In late January of 1929 the Raleigh Granite Company of Raleigh, North Carolina, wrote to inquire about equipment which might be for sale and Rogers answered that they had a lot of 25-pound rail, a donkey-type locomotive, four consolidations, one mogul, four prairies, a large number of boxcars, and several coaches. No mention was made of having any logging or flatcars although a number were still on hand, nor did he list all of the locomotives.

During March two electric headlights and generators were sold to the Camp Manufacturing Company of Franklin, Virginia who put them in stock as spares. Around the same time the company began dismantling all unoccupied structures and to give notice to the occupants of the company houses. The lumber, windows, doors, and other millwork were carefully disassembled and piled to be sold as salvaged material. Absolutely nothing that could be sold was thrown away. What could not be sold locally was barged from Scotland Wharf to Baltimore. Many of the dwellings were sold to their occupants at a ridiculously low price, which has already been stated.

The Richmond Cedar Works of Richmond, Virginia, with a plant at Camden Mills, Virginia, was in need of additional motive power and contacted Baldwin relative to the cost of broadening out the gauge of the 26. It didn't take them long to conclude that the cost was too great and the matter was dropped. However, the following month, May of 1929, they purchased a skidder from the company and mounted it on two surplus trucks of their own.

The sale of mill machinery, scrap, and railroad equipment continued through the year and the company continued to offer common carrier service. As the condition of the track got progressively worse, more and more care was taken in the operation of the train. The speed hardly exceeded that of a lively trot, the idea being to get over the line without falling through the track, but once on the ground, to do as little damage as possible to both track and equipment. That is possibly the idea on any railroad but not to the extent that it was on the S.S.&S. during those latter days. It was easy enough to get on the ground, too easy, the problem being to stay on the track.

During September the line east from Surry, down through Central Hill, was being pulled up. Enough of the 25-pound rail to lay fifteen miles of track, twelve switches and frogs, and 24 log cars were sold to Coulbourn Brothers at $18 a ton for the iron and $50 each for the cars. All of the material and equipment was shipped out by water.

Coulbourn Brothers and the Surry Lumber Company were never on the friendliest of terms, although that did not prevent the company from taking Coulbourn's money every chance that presented itself. Prior to the closing of the mill, the company had gone through the counties and bought all of the standing timber that they possibly could but in one case Coulbourn Brothers came in and offered more for a certain tract than the company felt that it was worth. Coulbourn then built a logging tramway northwest from just below Elberon, brought in a four-wheel diesel and began cutting timber. The loaded log cars were turned over to the S.S.&S. for transportation to Scotland Wharf. That rankled no end so a new tariff appeared and the freight rate became such that the company ended up with about the same profit that they would have realized if they had been able to purchase the standing timber at their own price. At the same time, Coulbourn complained bitterly that the cost of getting his logs to the river made a profit from the operation practically impossible.

The final blow fell on October 29, 1929, when the stock market crashed for although the results were not immediately felt, the resulting financial freeze eliminated the prospective backing for the construction of the extensions. That, plus the fact that the Seaboard Air Line had finally built a line into Hopewell and the N.&W. promptly swung its full weight, along with the S.A.L., against the S.S.&S., definitely killed any hope that remained of the company being allowed to extend its line. Steps were immediately taken to obtain permission to discontinue service.

Locomotive No. 2, the mail train engine, developed boiler trouble, the kind of trouble that could not be cured by shopping, and the builder was approached in March 1930 relative to the cost of a duplicate of the installed boiler. As was to be expected, the cost of a replacement was excessive. The engine was pulled out of service and eventually cut up for scrap. This left only the four prairies in service, the 20 and 24 being the two generally used while the 22 and 26 were held in reserve, the 22 being used as a source of repair parts. As of the end of 1929 the company had on hand, and in a serviceable condition, 55 boxcars, ten flatcars, five coal cars, three coaches, a combination car, and a baggage car. Again no mention was made of log cars of which there were a few still in the Dendron yard, or the remaining pieces of logging equipment, such as camp cars.

On June 23, 1930, the request for permission to extend the railroad was again brought up for consideration by the Interstate Commerce Commission but this time the attorney for the Railway Company requested that the application be permanently dismissed as they did not feel that the conditions that existed at that time justified the necessary outlay for construction. On these grounds the application was dismissed. The application for the discontinuance of service was still pending before the State Corporation Commission.

Gray Lumber Company of Waverly, Virginia, had a working agreement with the Southern Railway for use of their track south from Waverly to bring logs to their mill. Gray had quite an array of equipment for the run was fairly long and their woods tracks of considerable length. Their motive power consisted of locomotives purchased new and second hand that had just about outlived their usefulness, so during the early part of July 1930 they purchased the 26 and a large quantity of spare parts for $860. They also purchased twelve log cars at the same time. The company was prepared to scrap the 22 and agreed to see that Gray got such additional parts as they desired at a cent a pound for iron and steel parts, and eight cents a pound for brass parts. Four days later, on July 14, Gray purchased two boxcars. Around about the same time they purchased one of the labor coaches, the one that was mounted on freight trucks.

Two weeks later, to the day, permission was granted to discontinue service and on Thursday, July 31, 1930, the last train was run. Almost immediately a gang under R. L. Collier began stripping the sidings around Sedley and on September 2 they began pulling up the main line, slowly working north from Sedley. By this time the passenger equipment had been sold down to two coaches, the baggage car, and the combine. Only one log car remained. Engine 20 was the one used to scrap the road while the 24 was the standby. The freight equipment had been scrapped down to only a handful of flats and boxcars, plus two coal cars. One piece of woods equipment remained, the old baggage car used as a saw flier's car. By November 15, the track was up to Surry and before the month was out the only thing that remained was the trackage up the bluff at the river.

The only pieces of equipment left with wheels under them were the two engines, a passenger car, two coal cars, a log car loaded with weathered lumber, and a push car, all at Scotland Wharf. Also at Scotland Wharf was the body of the baggage car, sitting on blocks. If we must be exact, there was a pump car sitting inside a lumber yard at Surry. The pump car that showed up in 1965 in the mill yard of Moses White at Morgan's Corner, near South Mills, North Carolina, along with six, possibly eight, Surry Lumber Company log cars, was possibly that one. Along the route could be found a passenger car and a boxcar at Surry acting as a lunch room and a coal shed for the school, and two coach bodies at Wakefield used as a roadside restaurant. The body of the pay car was across the street from the N.&W. station at Wakefield being used as a real estate office. Odd pieces of freight equipment were scattered here and there doing duty on farms or as camps. This included one three-compartment camp car that started out as a camp but ended up as fire wood. The S.S.&S. was no more.

During the early part of November 1930 the State Corporation Commission issued a charter to a group of men who had formed the Southampton & Northern Railroad for the purpose of building a standard gauge railroad over the route that the narrow gauge had proposed to build from Franklin to Hopewell. Clement S. Ucker was president, J. A. Pretlow was vice president, Alfred Tyler was treasurer, G. Hibard Massey was consulting engineer, and Claude J. Edwards was general counsel and secretary. The directors were Michael Glennan and G. H. Massey of Norfolk, Barclay Pretlow and J. A. Pretlow of

Franklin, C. S. Ucker and Alfred Tyler of Baltimore, and C. J. Edwards of Franklin. The authorized capital stock was not to exceed 500 shares with no par value and would be the sole voting stock.

The new company seemed doomed from the start for late in November, Ucker died, necessitating a reorganization. J. A. Pretlow became president, Alfred Tyler became vice president as well as treasurer while Edwards and Massey remained at their former posts. The directorate remained the same with John Poe Tyler of Baltimore being brought in.

Almost immediately the entire bond issue of $2,000,000 was taken up by Baltimore bankers and hopes of beginning construction by the first of 1931 ran high but again trouble struck. In late December of 1930 Edward Hambleton, one of the bankers, committed suicide over financial troubles and around the same time another of the bankers, R. L. Montague, died very suddenly, too suddenly. That canceled any financial backing that could be expected from that source. Then Pretlow died. The company quietly folded and nothing more was heard of it.

Today, 1966, practically nothing remains to show that there ever was either a lumber company or a railroad up in that territory. Nature is slowly restocking the cut over land. Some of the towns that existed along the railroad are completly gone, vanished, and even Dendron is a ghost of its former self. On a dark night one wonders if the donkey whistles can still be heard, ghosts of the past, the past that will never live again.

LOCOMOTIVE ROSTER

No.	Builder	Date	Class	Bldr.'s No.	Wheel Arrgt.	Cylinders	Drivers	Notes
1	Tanner & Delaney	12/1883			2-4-0	7"x14"	30"	1
1	Richmond L.&M. Works	1891		2169	0-4-2T	8"x12"	43"	2
2	Baldwin Loco. Works	7/1917	8-14C25	43923	4-4-0	10"x16"	30"	3
3	,,	9/1886	6-10-1/3C-23	8119	4-6-0	9/15"x22"	37"	4
4	,,	5/1892	8-18D70	12675	2-6-0	12"x18"	30"	
5	,,	2/1888	6-10-1/3C-29	9042	0-4-2T	8"x12"	37"	5
6	,,	10/1888	8-18D74	9576	2-6-0	12"x18"	30"	6
7	,,	10/1889	6-10-1/3C-	10399	0-4-2T	8"x12"	37"	7
8	,,	10/1891	10-22E20	12288	2-8-0	14"x18"	30"	
9	,,	9/1891	6-10-1/3C-43	12254	0-4-2T	8"x12"	37"	
10	,,	8/1896	10-22E24	14988	2-8-0	14"x18"	30"	
11	,,	7/1892	6-10-1/3C-59	12805	0-4-2T	8"x12"	37"	
12	,,	5/1898	10-22E30	16011	2-8-0	14"x18"	37"	
13	,,	8/1902	10-22E31	20863	2-8-0	14"x18"	30"	
14	,,	2/1901	10-22E30	20057	2-8-0	14"x18"	37"	
		This number was never used.						
15	Baldwin Loco. Works	11/1902	10-22E31	21236	2-8-0	14"x18"	37"	8
16	,,	8/1902	6-10-1/3C-60	20864	0-4-2T	8"x12"	30"	
17	,,	6/1917	10-22I86	45714	4-6-0	14"x20"	46½"	
18	,,	9/1902	6-10-1/3C-61	20933	0-4-2T	8"x12"	30"	
19	H. K. Porter Company	1880		399	2-6-0	9"x16"	37"	9
20	Baldwin Loco. Works	11/1919	10-18¼D-37	52587	2-6-2	12"x18"	37"	10
		This number was never used.						
22	Baldwin Loco. Works	11/1919	10-18¼D-38	52588	2-6-2	12"x18"	37"	
		This number was never used.						
24	Baldwin Loco. Works	10/1920	10-18¼D-43	53795	2-6-2	12"x18"	37"	
		This number was never used.						
26	Baldwin Loco. Works	10/1920	10-18¼D-44	53796	2-6-2	12"x18"	37"	11

NOTES:

1. Taken over from David Steele in 1886. Named "CORNELIA". Logging tramway locomotive.
2. Built for J. E. and Edward Rogers of Loco, Va. No. 1 on that logging line.
3. Sold by S.S.&S. In service on Rocky Mount & Northern R. R.
4. Vauclain Compound. Built for Altoona, Clearfield & Northern as No. 3. Sold by that road to the Pittsburgh, Johnstown, Ebensburg & Eastern, then to S.S.&S. Later simpled by S.S.&S.
5. Sold to Southern Iron & Equipment Co., Atlanta, Ga., as their Item No. 1789.
6. Sold to Argent Lumber Company.
7. Sold to Planters Box Company, Suffolk, Va., 9/1924.
8. Sold to Southern Iron & Equipment Co., Atlanta, Ga., No. 2283, and by them to International Agricultural Corp.
9. Nothing definite is known of this engine. Sold to Gray Pine Products Company.
10. Built for Milner, Caldwell & Flowers Lumber Co. as No. 2. Sold to Southern Iron & Equipment Co., No. 1024, and by them to the S.S.&S. on 4-23-1917.
11. Sold to the Gray Lumber Company, Waverly, Va., in 1929.

Addendum

When it becomes known that a historical manuscript is, in fact, going to be put out in book form, people who have contributed to the efforts of the author become more concerned and make an added effort to be helpful. Additional information suddenly comes to light and quite frequently that information is of importance to the narrative. Frequently, gaps in the story that could not be filled are plugged and questions of long standing are answered. The compilation of THE COMP'NY is no exception. It is deeply regretted that the information contained in this ADDENDUM was not made available a year ago, but it wasn't. It is of too great an interest and importance to be omitted. I can assure you that this author looks with considerable disfavor on information being tacked onto the end of a story as though it was accidentally omitted or that insufficient research had been done, but after thirty-five years there was no real reason to expect that any new facts would come to light. They did, though, so please read them into their appropriate places in the overall story.

The pay car that was kept at Sedley, and which has been referred to as "Causey's Coach", is the only piece of passenger equipment in anywhere near its original condition. The car was stripped of its trucks and set on a brick foundation across from the Norfolk & Western station at Wakefield. There it did duty as a law office, as a real estate office, as a restaurant, and finally as a community headache when it became vacant and was open to everyone at all times. Finally the town decided to get rid of it but complications arose due to ownership. The car was owned by a non-resident estate and the members of the estate had different ideas about what should be done with the car. After a time the town fathers put their collective feet down and the estate relinquished ownership. There was talk of the public school using it as a lunch room, but that idea fell through due to the cost of moving the car from one location to another and of rehabilitating it. All of the windows had been broken out and it was far from weather-tight. Finally an antique dealer located just out of town was given the car with the provision that he had to move it. He did, and almost immediately found that he had a white elephant on his hands.

Then, around late 1965 Capt. M. H. Ferrell, Jr., of Norfolk, Virginia, agreed to trade marble table tops for it and the antique dealer was more than glad to see the car go. It came to Norfolk and set out back of a commercial establishment, where it still is. Its owner desired to put the car in an operating condition again, including trucks, and to that end contacted the owner of the White Lumber Company at Morgan's Corner, N. C., relative to the procurement of two former Surry Lumber Company logging trucks. To date the car is still without trucks but on the 22nd of April, 1967, Captain Ferrell began to replace warped boarding on the car and uncovered two penciled inscriptions over one of the side doors that tells quite a bit in a rather cryptic manner. The first notation is "T. J. Dillon, Aug. 17, '99, D.&W. Shops". A penciled line was run through that and over top of it is written "H. L. GRUBBS, Sept. 22, '04, Dendron, S. S. & S. Shops".

The first notation tells us that a D.&W. shopped the car in August of 1899, possibly cut the doors in the side of what had been a standard coach for the partition between the baggage and passenger compartments is of a different pattern of sheathing than that used in the other sections of the car. The D.&W. most certainly stands for Danville & Western, a 36-inch gauge road in southwestern Virginia that became a part of the Southern Railway system. The D.&W. came into being on January 14, 1891, through the reorganization of the Danville & New River. That road was opened for service in 1881. On March 1, 1899, the D.&W. absorbed the Danville, Mocksville & Southwestern which it had been operating under lease since 1885. This road had been in service since 1882. Thus, the car in question could have been originally the property of either of the two roads but we know that it did belong to the Danville & Western and that in 1899 something was done to it, possibly its conversion to a combination car.

For a time after gaining control, the Southern Railway operated the two roads as narrow gauge branches, but in 1902 completed the broadening out of the last one of them. That left considerable equipment surplus. The engines were sold to the Southern Iron & Equipment Company but what happened to the large number of passenger and freight cars, we do not know.

We find that in fiscal 1903 the S.S.&S. purchased a second class passenger car and it now seems logical to suppose that this second class coach was the D.&W. combination car for there is that second notation stating that something was done to it, including the replacement of a side door, in 1904. As the records show no other car being procured before or after that time, within a reasonable period before or after, it is reasonable to suppose that the door was damaged in transit or possibly was damaged before shipment, and had to be replaced. We know that it was replaced for there is a very slight difference in the two side doors and the hardware is completely different. It is therefore fairly safe to assume that the pay car came to the S.S.&S. in 1904 from the Danville & Western and was put on the roster as a second class coach.

Locomotive No. 18 is referred to in the text and in the compiled roster of motive power as a mystery. At the time the history was put together nothing was known of the engine prior to the time that she arrived at Wakefield with the 17. Over the years repeated efforts had been made to identify that engine but with absolutely no success. She simply refused to be nailed down.

C. W. Witbeck is the one man who has made a study of the second hand equipment dealers located in the southern states and he has delved rather methodically into the records of the former Southern Iron & Equipment Company of Atlanta, Georgia. It was while he was involved with their records that he unearthed the 0-4-2 Porter saddle-tank that came to the S.S.&S. in 1917 as their No. 17. Now he is delving just as energetically into the records of the Birmingham Rail & Locomotive Company of Birmingham, Alabama, and in so doing has come up with the other second hand engine purchased that year, the elusive 18. Birmingham Rail & Locomotive Company previously disclaimed any knowledge of this engine, it being their policy to answer tersely "No record" without actually checking, but in April of this year, 1967, Mr. Witbeck found that their records show where their Item 605 was sold to the Surry Lumber Company of Wakefield, Virginia, on April 20, 1917.

According to the sketchy information given in the dealer's records, this item consisted of a Baldwin 2-6-0, Construction Number 18395, erected in November 1900. The cylinder size is given as 11x18 inches and the drivers as 37 inches in diameter. Birmingham's records are notorious for their lack of information covering the history of the equipment they procure, but according to the Baldwin construction records, the 18395 was sold to Newell & Bryant as their No. 4, and was shipped to Stony Creek, Virginia. When Newell & Bryant had logged out at that location, they sold the engine to J. L. Fisher of Newsome, Virginia. Newsome and Stony Creek are not too far apart. Fisher sold out to the Pine Lumber Company and in 1912 we find the No. 4 still working out of Newsome.

We do not know when B.R.&L. Co. purchased the engine, nor who from, nor do we know who Baldwin built her for. As has been stated in the text, there is no doubt that she was built for plantation service but was refused upon completion. It can be that Baldwin changed the plates on her when she was finally sold to Newell & Bryant, for Baldwin has been known to do that. When owned by Newell & Bryant and by Fisher, she was habitually referred to as a "plantation engine" and her poor steaming ability was well known. So far as we know, the second hand dealer made no attempt to correct that fault but simply spruced her up a bit and passed her along. So, we find her arriving at Wakefield with a bald smoke box number plate and on arrival at Dendron being assigned road number "18".

During the summer of 1922 the Suffolk Rotary Club visited the Surry Lumber Company, arriving at Sedley over the Virginian on the early morning train. There they were met by Causey who had prepared an itinerary in anticipation of the visit. They were to be conducted on a tour of one of the camps, the mills at Dendron, and shown the wharf facilities at Scotland. Luncheon would be served on the train but the main meal, a late dinner, would be served in the dining-room of Causey's quarters over the company office at Sedley, after which the club would hold its business meeting before returning to Suffolk on the night train.

It so happened that George L. Barton, Jr., Causey's nephew from Suffolk, was visiting him at the time. George was the son of the superintendent of the narrow gauge Suffolk & Carolina and he had learned how to run a locomotive, among other things, during the time he had roamed around the S.&C. yard making friends and absorbing the smell of steam and hot grease.

When it came time for the party to leave Sedley, Causey told George that he would have to drive the engine as far as Indio Siding where a regular engineer would be waiting to take over, there being none available at Sedley at that particular time. That was all right with George for his uncle assured him that they would have a good engine with which to make the trip. He must have said it with his tongue in his cheek for what came up to haul the train was the 17. George took one look at the engine and said to the Negro fireman who had brought her up, "Mr. Causey said that he was going to give us a GOOD engine." The fireman, with a Negro's characteristic sense of humor, never cracked a smile as he replied, "Boss, don' make fun of dat engine. Jes' look at dem two 'lectric headlights dat's jes' been put on her. Boss if you'd jack up dem two headlights an' run a new biler and some new wheels under dem, you'd have de bes' engine on de road!" So, they were stuck with the 17 for the day.

The special was made up of "Causey's coach" and a flatcar on which some crude benches had been erected, but no railing had been provided, it being taken for granted that grown men would exercise the necessary precaution to keep from falling off. The train started out, the engineer was picked up at Indio Siding, a stop was made at Vicksville, and a longer stop was made at Dendron. There was more to be seen there and pictures were to be taken. Causey then left the party in the hands of his nephew and headed for Sedley by auto to prepare for the evening meal. Lunch was served by Causey's personal combination porter-cook who was permanently assigned to his coach, when it was on the road. Exactly what was served we cannot say but it is a sure thing that it was quite a lunch. Causey would see to that. The train then ran on through to Scotland where the party watched the loading of lumber while the train was turned and made ready for the return trip. They were to run straight through to Sedley but by this time the engine crew had begun to grumble about that "good" engine Causey had wished off on them. Incidentally, the crew consisted of only three men, two on the engine and Barton, for a brakesman was not considered necessary.

The trip back to Sedley was rather monotonous for the passengers. They managed to amuse themselves by wandering out onto the "observation car", talking, and just looking at what little there was to see. Up ahead, the engine crew was having increasing trouble for the 17's tubes were now leaking like grandma's teakettle at a meeting of the Friday afternoon sewing circle, as Barton expressed it. The fireman was really fighting to keep up steam. A few miles above Sedley some of the members started amusing themselves by going out on the flatcar and then calling names at others who were standing in the doorway of the coach. It began good-naturedly but gradually got really rough. Barton wanted in the worst way to pull the pin on the observation car and let the name-callers think that they had to walk in, but he remembered that the engine crew was having enough trouble without adding mileage to the run and managed to curb his desire. When he got his charges back to Sedley, he reported to his uncle and included an account of the incident. He said that the only thing that prevented him from cutting off the car and giving the occupants a bad few moments was the behavior of that "good" engine and the crew's uncertainty of its ability to get the train in without having to run a few extra miles. Causey thought about it for a few moments and then said, "Well, if I had been there, I would have done it anyway." Undoubtedly he would have, too, and if the 17 had died before getting home he would have reminded the occupants of that "observation car" that it was their fault.

It was in the Spring of 1960, the early Spring before the leaves were out and the weeds had overrun everything, that a friend and I picked up Sam Atkinson at Dendron and then ran on through to Littleton to pick up Emmett Williams. The idea was to take these two former engineers up over what I thought was the grade of the West Hope Branch from Peters' Bridge on west and north towards West Hope. I had been over the route the previous Fall, following a rarely used fire road that gradually degenerated into a cowpath and finally into something that would be called a path through the woods, but I just wasn't sure that it was the old right-of-way. True, it had all of the earmarks, but I could be wrong. There was a ditch on each side of the slightly raised, weed grown road, and I liked to think that ever so often I could see the imprint of a crosstie, but a strong imagination could be playing me false. Hence, I wanted to be sure.

The two engineers hadn't seen each other since January 1904 when Emmett had quit the company and gone to farming, and there was considerable catching up to be done. While the two men talked of old times, we listened, and while we listened we ran on down to what I thought was Gilliam's Crossing, west of the river bridge, back in the narrow gauge days. There I stopped, pointed out what I thought was the old grade coming up from the river through a shallow cut, how it angled across the road, and how it dived into the woods on the far side. Both engineers were quick to verify the fact that it WAS the old crossing. There was no doubt about it, according to them, so I swung off the secondary road onto the fire road and headed dead west. I knew that it was about four miles through there and that about a quarter of a mile from the far end I would have to swing over onto a newly bulldozed road, of sorts, along which some new, small houses had been built. At that point the old grade, or what I took to be the grade, continued on through the bushes on its way to the Double-Barreled Road Crossing. I had seen that crossing a number of times and had looked east along the grade as it skirted a plowed field and wondered about its route to Peters' Bridge. Now I knew that I was following that route, but I also knew that there were places where considerable washing had taken place over the years, and I just might have a little trouble. How much additional washing had taken place during the previous winter, I didn't know, but it was reasonable to believe that as I had made it once, I could do it again. In addition to that, there was the hard, cold fact that this so-called road was strictly "single track" and if I met anyone, I was in for trouble. Anyone in his right mind would never have started through there in the first place, but who ever claimed that a railroad historian was ever in his right mind? In we went.

Atkinson and Williams were on the back seat, Atkinson on the right side and Williams on the left. All the way to Gilliam's Crossing the two men had kept up a running conversation between themselves and answered questions put by my companion. I had joined in when something particularly interesting had been mentioned but after swinging onto the fire road I was much too busy driving to pay any attention to them. Two fairly bad washes were encountered but we got across them without too much trouble and as the grade improved, I began to make fairly good time, the car swaying and jolting slightly. Suddenly I realized that everyone was particularly quiet. My companion was watching ahead rather anxiously but the conversation in the rear had ceased completely. Remembering the ages of the two men back there, I rather anxiously glanced up in the rear view mirror to make sure that nothing was wrong.

Sam was obviously thoroughly enjoying himself as he picked out landmarks that had not changed too much over the years. In answer to a question he said that the last time he had been through there he was riding the right side of the cab of his jack. I started to ask Emmett when he had last been over the route but what I saw caused me to realize that he was no longer with us, he was back driving his donkey on the way to West Hope, over fifty years before this trip. To break in upon his revery would be pure sacrilege and that I could not bring myself to do. He was sitting up as straight as a ramrod, looking straight ahead with his left arm resting on the arm rest. As he sat he swayed gently with the sway of the car and it took no imagination at all to turn the roar of the exhaust into the steady drum of the exhaust of his donkey. Emmett was reliving one of the happy events of his life.

Not too far ahead was the point where the line had crossed the narrow gauge Southern's Claremont Branch. I remembered it from the previous trip for there had been a clearing in the woods at that place and a small pile of sawdust, the only indication that Man had ever come that way before. As we bore down on the clearing, I felt an impelling urge to blow for the crossing, and feeling a little foolish, I let go with two longs, a short, and another long blast of the horn, holding the last blast until we had passed over what I felt fairly sure was the old A.&D. right-of-way. As I "whistled for the crossing", I watched Emmett's image in the mirror as best I could and I will swear that I saw a sparkle in his eyes. If I live to be the age of Methuselah, I will never regret giving Emmett back that few minutes of a life that he really loved, nor will I ever regret blowing that crossing whistle out in the middle of nowhere. Sam? He just grinned, for that was his way, but I couldn't help but wonder if he, too, hadn't been reliving those long gone days.